D0984687

Counterparts

Lilian R. Furst

Counterparts

The dynamics of Franco–German literary
relationships 1770–1895

Wayne State University Press

Detroit 1977

First published in 1977 by
Methuen & Co Ltd, 11 New Fetter Lane, London EC4P 4EE

© 1977 Lilian R. Furst

Photoset by William Clowes & Sons Ltd
at the Benham Press, Colchester,
and printed at the University Printing House, Cambridge

Published in U.S.A.
by Wayne State University Press,
Detroit, Michigan 48202

ISBN 0-8143-1582-8
LC77-2407

To
Dr S. F.–N.
In loving memory

Il faut du courage pour être romantique,
car il faut hasarder.
Stendhal, *Racine et Shakespeare*

Nach Innen geht der geheimnisvolle Weg.
Novalis, *Blütenstaub*

Contents

Preface

This book originated in a series of lectures I was invited to give at
Westfield College, University of London, in the autumn of 1969. The
lectures formed part of a so-called 'link course' which aimed to show
the nature and extent of the interrelationships between various European literatures. My brief was, simply, to link the Romantic movements of France and Germany. In practice, of course, it was not so simple. My study of European Romanticism had already convinced me
that what was known as *romantisme* in France differed radically in
character and intent from the German *Romantik*. Any attempt at a
straight linkage between the two would therefore result merely in a
catalogue of differences. While the expected parallels had proved
fallacious, others had gradually become apparent to me, more recondite and indirect admittedly, but far more fruitful and illuminating.
The real, organic counterparts seemed, to my mind, to exist between
the German Storm and Stress and French Romanticism, and between
German Romanticism and French Symbolism respectively. This was
the thesis that I proposed in my lectures at Westfield College and that I
am trying to explore in this book.

That is, I realize, a vast topic extending as it does over more than a
century and drawing on the major writers of the period on both sides
of the Rhine. Each of the three sections could well be developed into a
full-length book. But it is not my purpose to be exhaustive; these essays
seek primarily to be suggestive, to outline an underlying structure in
the hope of offering a framework for further and more detailed
analyses of the filiations between French and German literature in the

nineteenth century. The sections may be read independently of each other, although they are connected not only by such recurrent problems as that of the time-lag between France and Germany, but also by the fundamental thesis concerning the dynamics of the Franco–German relationship as well as by the methodology of finding counterparts.

My peripatetic habits in recent years have given rise to some problems in that I seemed nearly always to be separated by an ocean and/or a continent from my own books. The library resources at my disposal have varied greatly, not least in the editions of works from which I have quoted. I have tried in the final checking to standardize my references as far as possible. The translations are my own, and are deliberately literal in order to maintain closeness to the original. For the sake of convenience I have placed them in parentheses immediately after the quotations.

In the four years in which this topic has moved halfway round the world with me I have discussed it with many colleagues and students. From their questions I have received more stimulation than I can ever hope to acknowledge individually. I would single out only the enthusiastic response of my audience at Westfield College and particularly of Professor J. Weightman and Professor C. V. Bock, whose comments first made me aware of the potential of this kind of linkage, and who encouraged me to venture on this synthesis. I owe much gratitude to Professor Lloyd J. Austin of the University of Cambridge for his generous gift of a copy of Edouard Dujardin's article, 'Richard Wagner et la poésie française contemporaine', from the *Revue de Genève* of 1886 which I had been unable to find. For help in tracking down other material I am indebted to the librarians at the University of Manchester, the Baker Library at Dartmouth College and the Widener Library at Harvard University. A special word of thanks should go to Claire Meyer of Inter-Library Loans and Pat Hult of Acquisitions at the University of Oregon for their understanding of an often impatient reader. For frank and constructive criticisms I am very grateful to two of my students, Joel Reader and William Sims.

My acknowledgement to the American Council of Learned Societies is more than just a formality: I am deeply appreciative of the Research Fellowship which gave me the time to finish this book by releasing me from teaching and administrative duties during 1974–5.

Finally, my personal thanks to my father for his good-humoured patience, his wise support through all the vicissitudes of writing this book, and his cheerful tolerance of my domestic short-cuts and short-comings.

Cambridge, Mass.
January 1975

I

Introduction

The word 'counterpart' is derived from the French *contre-partie* meaning the complementary or opposite part. In modern English usage it has a number of specifically technical connotations: in law, for instance, it refers to the opposite part of an indenture, and in music it indicates a part written 'against' or to accompany another. Its more general sense is always that of 'the other half', 'one of two parts which fit', according to *The Oxford English Dictionary*. The precise relationship between the two fitting parts depends, however, on the interpretation of the vital particle 'counter' which came into English from the Latin *contra* via the French *contre*. While 'other' is a neutrally open word, *contra* (and hence 'counter') carries two quite distinct, even conflicting meanings for it can imply either 'against', 'opposite' or, on the other hand, 'in return', 'parallel', 'complementary'. This inherent dualism of the particle accounts for the apparently contradictory synonyms to 'counterpart' given in dictionaries. On the whole nowadays the 'against', which is primary in the Latin *contra*, has been weakened and absorbed into the 'complementary' which has become the dominant element. So in common parlance a 'counterpart' denotes a person or a thing forming a natural complement to another, resembling the other, possessing supplementary qualities and performing similar, corresponding functions. But beneath the married surface there still lurks at least a hint of the original antagonism. Among the analogies to 'counterpart' in *Roget's Thesaurus* both aspects are represented, although the warring relatives – 'contraposition', 'inversion', 'reverse', 'antithesis', 'polarity', 'opposite side' – are far outnumbered by the peaceful co-existers: 'analogue', 'the like', 'match', 'pendant', 'fellow', 'pair', 'mate', 'double', 'family likeness', 'similarity', 'affinity', 'parallelism', 'resemblance', 'correspondence', 'copy', 'facsimile', 'duplicate', 'echo', 'transfer', 'reflection', etc.

With this wealth of implications 'counterparts' is a term singularly apt to comparative literature. Its foremost advantage as a methodological programme lies obviously in its flexibility. It is firmly based on the notion of similarity that is fundamental to all comparisons, but it also embraces the idea of otherness. It thus permits a far more freely ranging kind of comparison than the traditional insistence on likenesses which has sometimes done violence to its objects by forcing them into an excessive closeness. Parallels between writers or movements, however pronounced they may be, are often tempered by differences that can be crucially revealing of the particularity of one or other poet or group. From a comparison of Shakespeare, Racine and Schiller, Blake, Nerval and Novalis, or George Eliot, Flaubert and Tolstoy, we become aware not only of the common factors linking them, but also, and perhaps even more importantly, of the individuality of each one as a writer in the special qualities distinguishing him from his pendants in other literatures or at other periods. By admitting at one and the same time under the cover of a single term the analysis of polarity alongside and within affinity, 'counterparting' as a method in comparative literature can open up possibilities denied to an exclusive attachment to similarities. The study of contrast should be incorporated as a normal component into any delineation of resemblance. Racine is patently the French counterpart to Shakespeare, just as Schiller is arguably a German counterpart to both of them; the collation is highly illuminating for the timbre of each dramatist as for the theatrical climate of their native lands in spite, or rather because, of the essential divergences between them. The balance of opposition and complement innate to the structure of the counterpart can thus be conducive to a fresh and more generous insight.

The idea of seeking counterparts between works, writers or groups has a further valuable asset: it encourages the quest for a genuine coherence in place of the somewhat arbitrary alignments that are a danger to comparative literature. The old belief that a comparison was justified only if an extrinsic connection between two writers could be proven has long been abandoned by most comparatists. With it foreign trade, once the staple of comparative literature, has declined; the former concentration on the reception of an author in another country, on transmissions, and on that trickiest of areas, influences, has given way to newer lines of approach. The two paths most favoured nowadays could be termed the vertical and the horizontal. Each has its attractions as well as its innate pitfalls.

The vertical moves longitudinally over a protracted span of time that can extend from the Biblical or from Classical Antiquity to the present day. Since it may centre on any one of a vast spectrum of features, it can – and frequently does – make original combinations. At its simplest, an archetypal figure often forms the focus of attention; for instance, Don Juan, or Faust, or Christ, or Prometheus. Or there may be a thematic disposition of works dealing with such topics as autumn, the city, alienation, seduction and betrayal, etc. A third alternative is the genre classification: the picaresque, or the novel in letter-form, or autobiography, or the fable, or the sonnet, or tragi-comedy. Of a more complicated kind is the vertical link of a modal or technical character: the categories of satire, the development of chivalric romance, the growth of the novel, or the 'representation of reality in Western literature' which is the subtitle of Erich Auerbach's *Mimesis*, that classic of comparative literature that illustrates the abundant rewards of the vertical cross-section in the hands of a brilliant exponent. On the debit side, because of its very freedom the vertical comparison can all too easily disintegrate into an eccentric array of works strung together with scant regard to sequential succession.

While the vertical comparison normally moves in the medium of time, the horizontal operates primarily in space, latitudinally, by juxtaposing more or less contemporaneous material from various literatures and possibly even from various spheres of artistic expression. Its inner logic is less precarious than that of the vertical comparison because the horizontal comparison almost invariably rests on the acceptance of standard period concepts in its choice of topics: Medieval romance, Renaissance drama, Baroque metaphysical poetry, the thought of the Enlightenment, the Romantic hero, the novel or drama of Naturalism, Symbolist poetry, Expressionist drama, etc. From its indebtedness to period concepts this type of comparison derives a measure of unity, but inevitably it comes up against – and sometimes founders on – the rocks of definition. For period concepts, slippery enough already within one literature, often undergo curious mutations as they cross frontiers or oceans so that their usefulness, even on a purely practical level, is seriously undermined. Hence the problems that bedevil any consistent attempt at periodization within a single literature are mathematically compounded in direct ratio to the number of different linguistic and cultural media that the period concept seeks to enfold. This seems the only explanation for the singular failure of collective efforts by comparatists to arrive at any convincing or even workable temporal divisions of literature. For literature, specially in its variegated international mosaic, cannot be neatly sliced like sausage or cheese. If the vertical comparison runs the risk of disintegration, the horizontal may be paralysed by the inefficacy of the period concept.

The adoption of 'counterparting' as a method is certainly no panacea. It can, however, afford a basis for fruitful comparisons through its blending of elasticity with the postulate of inner cohesiveness. The intrinsic links that are the real business of comparative literature may be sought along vertical or horizontal lines, or indeed diagonally. To return to one of the examples cited earlier: Blake was not a contemporary of Nerval, nor was Novalis, but they are demonstrably counterparts in their use of the symbolic image as the prime carrier of meaning. The relationship between Blake and the Surrealists, in painting as in poetry, offers another counterpart of fascinating potential. In such comparisons period concepts need neither be jettisoned wholesale nor allowed to become a straitjacket. The static periodization that is totally inapposite to comparative literature can be replaced by an awareness of dynamic evolution in the interchange between literatures, from which the salient structural outlines may emerge with greater clarity. The difficulty of the method — and there is no literary ointment without its fly — the difficulty lies in the initial discovery of the inner organic filiation between the elements of the counterpart. Once that is clearly perceived, the interplay of tensions and echoes can be explored at will in all its ramifications.

The notion of 'counterparting' as an approach to the comparative study of literature has arisen pragmatically out of my own work in the field of European Romanticism. Temporal contemporaneity and a shared period label proved a deceptive basis for comparison. In spite of many common features German Romanticism diverges radically in aim, temper and expression from the French movement that bears the same name. The straightforward horizontal comparison is bafflingly unproductive, and indeed downright misleading in Franco–German relationships during the nineteenth century. This holds true not only of Romanticism: the German brand of mid-nineteenth-century Realism is by no means identical to that of France. At every point, be it 1800, 1830, 1850 or 1870, French and German literature present a different aspect and are at a different stage in their development, although the overall direction of that development is strikingly alike. This heightens the temptation to make fallacious equations, and never more so than when one is dealing with two countries as close geographically as France and Germany and both as decisively shaped by the Western heritage from Classical Antiquity, Christianity and Medieval culture. Were the comparison between, say, Chinese and French literature, there is less likelihood of being led astray by an almost subconscious *a priori* expectation of similarity.

Links across the Rhine did, of course, exist in the nineteenth century, and not only in an abundant outer exchange of travellers and ideas. The connections between the two literatures are equally strong, though more subtle than first meets the eye. For this reason the term 'counterpart' with its dualistic charge of 'contraposition' and 'analogy' is especially appropriate. To translate the situation into the concrete visual idiom: the literatures of France and Germany may be likened to two rivers, each moving along its own course, each progressing at varying pace, each with its rapids and stagnant pools. They are flowing in the same direction, on certain stretches far apart, on others closer together; and always there is some subterranean seepage of water from the one to the other. The beds of the two rivers, which help to determine their course, are the native traditions of the two countries; the seepages of water are the foreign exchanges through travellers' reports, translations and contacts of many kinds; while the rapids and pools are the landmarks on the chart of their advance. Carrying the image further, a waterfall on one river may correspond to rapids on the other; they may not necessarily occur on exactly parallel stretches of the river because of the difference in the surrounding terrain, the disposition of hills and vales.

It is with the dynamic flow of these two rivers that the essays in this volume are concerned. This is not an investigation of relations between the two literatures in the narrower sense; such factors as translations, travellers' accounts, all the seepage from the one to the other will be adduced only in so far as they shed light on the trend and pace of the underlying rhythm. The scholarly documentation of interchanges is not my aim. To a large extent the relevant information – on the fate of Goethe, Schiller, Heine, Wagner, etc. in France – has already been gathered, and I draw on it with gratitude. Beneath this outward activity a hidden dialogue was taking place at a deeper level. This it is that I hope to fathom by showing how the literatures on the opposite banks of the Rhine are intertwined in a complex web of counterparts. From the resultant pattern a clearer understanding can be achieved of the structural outline of the Franco–German interrelationship in the nineteenth century.

I have chosen the word 'dynamics' for the subtitle because this is a constantly shifting relationship. On two occasions during the nineteenth century counterparts in the sense of my definition are plainly visible: first between the Storm and Stress and French Romanticism, and then again between the Early German Romantics (*Frühromantiker*) and the French Symbolists. The main substance of this book is devoted to an analysis of the nature and the extent of these two counterparts. In both there is a pronounced basic parallelism, though in each it is also admixed with divergence. The area of affinity is somewhat different in the two cases, residing in a greater similarity of artistic output in the earlier pair than in the later where the community of aesthetic theory prevails. These two counterparts can be called diagonal in that about fifty years – rather more even in the second instance – separate the two elements of the comparison. This recurrent time-lag is no mere coincidence. Its sources are sought in the first essay, which is devoted to a consideration of the circumstances surrounding the emergence of the Romantic movements in France and Germany. Here it is polarity that dominates the counterpart in the great discrepancy between the heritage from the past with which the two literatures entered on the nineteenth century. This background played a significant role in shaping their development during the century, and so in determining the dynamics of their interrelationship.

II

The emergence of the Romantic movements

I

There would seem to be no likelier field in which to find counterparts between French and German literature than in the emergence of their Romantic movements. For the past fifty years or more, ever since the appearance of the first volume of Paul Van Tieghem's *Le Préromantisme. Etudes d'histoire littéraire européenne* (Paris: Rieder, 1924), it has been customary to emphasize the interrelatedness of European literatures from the second half of the eighteenth century onwards into the nineteenth. The evolution of thought and expression away from the Neo-classical patterns towards a Romantic silhouette certainly testifies to the presence of similar forces in various lands. Sentimentality, fascination with the past, attraction to the natural as a way of living and of writing, melancholy, curiosity about the workings of genius and the meaning of originality, the lure of the Gothic and of the picturesque: these are recognized as the familiar features of that rather amorphous transitional phase generally described as Pre-romanticism. A flourishing network of translations, influences and international connections has been traced by Van Tieghem and his disciples: the cult of the nocturnal and the sepulchral in its spread from Gray's *Elegy written in a Country Churchyard*, Young's *Night Thoughts* and Hervey's *Meditations among the Tombs* across the English Channel into virtually every corner of Europe; the almost frenzied sweep of Ossianism into the poetry, painting, drama, music and even garb of the age; the associated dissemination of Scandinavian mythology; the mode for the pastoral stemming from Gessner and his successors; the predilection for the sentimental novel in the manner of Goldsmith and particularly

Richardson; etc. So much so that the later eighteenth century often seems to be regarded as a grand European banquet to which each nation brought its speciality: English gloom, Scottish mists, the German idyll, the French flirtation with the exotic. The community of direction essential to a true counterpart is undoubtedly in evidence here as parallel tendencies develop within the framework of diverse national traditions. In the preface to the first volume of *Le Préromantisme* Van Tieghem indeed advocates the simultaneous study of 'courants internationaux' and 'traditions nationales' (p. 9).

The counterpart with its characteristic blend of affinity and polarity might well be expected to abound under these circumstances. And so it does between England and Germany in the correspondence of the aesthetics of Young's *Conjectures on Original Composition* with the ideas of Lessing and even more so of Herder, in the matching folk collections of Percy's *Reliques* and Herder's *Stimmen der Völker*, in the growing importance of sentiment and sentimentality as well as in the incipient taste for greater simplicity in the poetry of both lands. Between Germany and France, however, the coupling does not work with equal ease in spite of the multiple exchanges and links across the Rhine. It is, sure enough, possible to juxtapose a number of texts that appear to be closely related to each other; but again and again the comparison leads to an increasing awareness of the underlying opposition that outweighs the surface likeness.

For instance, Herder's *Journal meiner Reise im Jahre 1769* brings to mind Rousseau's *Rêveries du promeneur solitaire* (1782).[1] Both are so unconventional in form that neither can be comfortably assigned to any of the acknowledged literary genres; their respective title-words, journal and reverie, could well be switched. Highly flexible and fluid in shape, they progress by a loose association of ideas often prompted by outer incidents so that they encompass a dazzling galaxy of ideas, experiences, speculations and feelings. The focal point in each case is the persona of the writer who appears in the opening sections in a remarkably similar guise as a lone figure taking stock of himself and of his position in the world:

Me voilà donc seul sur la terre, n'ayant plus de frère, de prochain, d'ami, de société que moi-même. Le plus sociable et le plus aimant des humains en a été proscrit par un accord unanime. Ils ont cherché dans les raffinements de leur haine quel tourment pouvait être le plus cruel à mon âme sensible, et ils ont brisé violemment tous les liens qui m'attachaient à eux. J'aurais aimé les hommes en dépit d'eux-mêmes. Ils n'ont pu qu'en cessant de l'être se dérober à mon affection. Les voilà donc étrangers, inconnus, nuls enfin pour moi puisqu'ils l'ont voulu. Mais moi, détaché d'eux et de tout, que suis-je moi-même? Voilà ce qui me reste à chercher.[2]

(Here I am then alone in the world, without brethren, kindred, friend, company other than myself. The most sociable and loving of human beings has been excluded from society by unanimous agreement. In their sophisticated hatred they sought out the harshest torment for my sensitive soul, and they sundered with violence all the ties linking me to them. I would have loved my fellow-men in spite of themselves. Only by ceasing to be men could they withdraw from my affection. So now they are strangers, unknown, nil to me since that is what they wanted. But I, detached from them and from everything, what am I in myself? That is what I must find out.)

Herder is in an equally disillusioned, misanthropic mood:

Ich gefiel mir nicht als Gesellschafter, weder in dem Kreise, da ich war, noch in der Ausschliessung, die ich mir gegeben hatte. Ich gefiel mir nicht als Schullehrer; die Sphäre war für mich zu enge, zu fremde, zu unpassend, und ich für meine Sphäre zu weit, zu fremde, zu beschäftigt. Ich gefiel mir nicht als Bürger, da meine häusliche Lebensart Einschränkungen, wenig wesentliche Nutzarbeiten und eine faule, oft ekle Ruhe hatte. Am wenigsten endlich als Autor, wo ich ein Gerücht erregt hatte, das meinem Stande ebenso nachteilig als meiner Person empfindlich war. Alles also war mir zuwider.[3]

(I did not like myself as a social being, neither in the circle in which I moved nor in the isolation which I had sought. I did not like myself as a school-teacher; it was a sphere too narrow, too alien and too unsuited to me, and I was too broadminded, too alien and too occupied for it. I did not like myself as a bourgeois because my domestic circumstances brought restrictions, petty utilitarian tasks, and an indolent, often loathsome calm. I liked myself least as an author for I had acquired an ill-repute injurious to my standing and hurtful to me personally. In short, I felt revulsion to everything.)

Parallel though these initial self-portraits are, even here the divergence between Herder and Rousseau is already perceptible. Herder's discontent is patently more external and more temporary than

Rousseau's; he rejects his present position and role, and is unhappy too
at the life he has led hitherto, bitterly regretful of the days he has
wasted in becoming 'ein Tintenfass voll gelehrter Schriftstellerei'[4] ('an
inkwell of scholarly scribbling'). But he is still a youngish man, open
to all the new impressions stimulated by his sea-voyage. So after the
preliminary dark self-assessment Herder's *Journal* bubbles with the exciting notions that cross his mind in such profusion and that range from
speculative psychology, arising out of the sailors' superstitions, to
educational reform, a topic that fills much of the *Journal* with detailed
plans of the syllabus and timetable of his ideal school. This interest in
education, another putative link between Herder and Rousseau, is
marginal to the *Rêveries*. This is the last work of an old man deeply
wounded by the injustices which he – rightly or wrongly – feels to
have been inflicted on him. Whether his reactions amount to paranoia
or not, it is clear that Rousseau's problems are primarily of an inner,
existential nature. He counters them by an agonized withdrawal into
himself, proposing to devote 'mes derniers jours à m'étudier moi-
même'[5] ('my last days to the study of myself'). In these conversations
with himself Rousseau often expresses his emotion in lyrical terms,
while Herder, for all the vividness of his exclamatory rhetoric, remains
more dryly intellectual. This contrast in style is just one facet of the dif-.
ference between Herder's *Journal* and Rousseau's *Rêveries*. These are
counterparts where the element of contraposition is stronger than that
of kinship. With his hopes for the future betterment of education and
of society in general, Herder is an optimistic precursor of the Storm
and Stress, whereas Rousseau turns his back in pessimistic disgust on a
civilization that strikes him as corrupt and inhuman. In his
constructiveness Herder foreshadows the approaching renewal of German culture and literature; Rousseau in his negativity forebodes
Romantic solipsism.

   Perhaps Rousseau's *Rêveries* would find a nearer match in Goethe's
Werther (1774). In their fundamental lyricism, their musical structure as prose-poems, as well as in their subject-matter, they are closely
related. Both centre on the exposition of a mind in a state of stress. Like
the *promeneur solitaire*, Werther is acutely aware of the gulf between
himself and society from which he has cut adrift and which he experiences, in his final attempt at re-integration, as a hostile force. The
two outsiders, feeling themselves rejected, retreat from the world of
men, thereby compounding their isolation. They retreat physically and
emotionally: physically into the depths of nature, and emotionally into

the depths of their own ego. Both tend to idealize nature, hoping to find in it the sympathetic understanding lacking in men. In the famous fifth section of the *Rêveries* Rousseau gives an ecstatic description of the isle of Saint-Pierre in the Lake of Bienne, where he derives an inner calm from his absorption into the beauty of his milieu. The protracted, relaxed sentences reflect his drift into a dream-world:

> En sortant d'une longue et douce rêverie, en me voyant entouré de verdure, de fleurs, d'oiseaux, et laissant errer mes yeux au loin sur les romanesques rivages qui bordaient une vaste étendue d'eau claire et cristalline, j'assimilais à mes fictions tous ces aimables objets et me trouvant enfin ramené par degrés à moi-même et à ce qui m'entourait, je ne pouvais marquer le point de séparation des fictions aux réalités; tant tout concourait également à me rendre chère la vie recueillie et solitaire que je menais dans ce beau séjour.[6]

> (Coming out of a long and happy reverie, seeing myself surrounded by greenery, flowers, birds, and letting my eyes wander afar to the picturesque shores of a huge expanse of shining, crystalline water, I would gather all those lovable objects into my dreams, and returning gradually to myself and to my surroundings I could not fix the point of delineation between dreams and realities; so potently did everything combine to endear to me this secluded and solitary life that I was leading in this beautiful haven.)

Nature has an equally consoling effect on Werther, at least at the beginning when he rejoices in the haven he has found, writing with a rare humour in his first letter to his friend on 4 May:

> Übrigens befinde ich mich hier gar wohl. Die Einsamkeit ist meinem Herzen köstlicher Balsam in dieser paradiesischen Gegend, und diese Jahreszeit der Jugend wärmt mit aller Fülle mein oft schauderndes Herz. Jeder Baum, jede Hecke ist ein Strauss von Blüten, man möchte zum Maienkäfer werden, um in dem Meer von Wohlgerüchen herumschweben und alle seine Nahrung darin finden zu können.[7]

> (And I am feeling fine here. The solitude in this heavenly part of the country is a welcome balsam to my heart, and this season of youth warms my often shuddering heart with its abundant gifts. Every tree, every hedge is a bouquet of blossom; I wish I were a ladybird and could float in this sea of scents and draw all my sustenance from it.)

But later even nature fails Werther: on 30 November he refers to the cold damp wind and dark oppressive clouds, adding significantly, 'ich hatte keine Lust, zu essen'[8] ('I had no desire to eat'); and this is before his disturbing encounter that day with the madman whose total alienation from nature is epitomized in his search for flowers for his beloved in mid-winter. The mad peasant symbolizes in grim foreboding the transgression beyond the point of no return on the journey into the self. This is a point that the *promeneur solitaire*, in contrast to Werther, never crosses. He cultivates 'l'habitude de rentrer en moi-même'[9] ('the habit of turning inwards on myself'), but his pursuit of flowers denotes the objective interest of the botanist; he never wholly loses touch with reality, nor indeed a measure of rational control.

   The structure of the two works reinforces the interplay of similarity and difference between them. Both are episodic in organization, the episodes in *Werther* being welded into an architectonic entity as the story of Werther's life, while those of the *Rêveries* draw their organic unity from the voice of the *promeneur solitaire* himself. The *Rêveries* stop abruptly at a more or less arbitrary point in the middle of the tenth section. Recording as they do the self-exploration of a troubled soul, to which there is no logical ending, and consisting of a string of episodes, they could just as well have stopped sooner or gone on further. Their potential continuity is as much a result of their inner content as of their outer form. In contrast to the expansive stasis of the *Rêveries*, *Werther* is relentless in its progression. Besides its poetic pattern, it has also the outer movement of a narrative in a plot that advances with ever heightening tension to its conclusion. Perhaps the terms 'progression' and 'advance' are inappropriate to Werther's development which is in effect an increasing regression into himself, into his private world. He goes very much further than the *promeneur solitaire*, almost as far as the mad peasant. Although Werther's difficulties are of the same ilk as those of his French counterpart, they become so intense as finally to destroy him. The *promeneur solitaire* could find an objective correlative – not to say, corrective – in his botanizing, and thereby achieve some degree of balance, however tenuous. Werther, on the other hand, is unable to attain the same release in his art, unable and, towards the end, unwilling to contrive any way of living with his temperament. Compared to the wildness of Werther's youthfully uncompromising Storm and Stress personality, the *promeneur solitaire* appears quite moderate, tempered by a heritage of social demeanour that clings to him as if in spite of himself. The parallel between the *Rêveries* and *Werther* must therefore be qualified by the polarity of tone, structure and degree.

The same gradual discovery of divergence recurs in the comparison of *Werther* and *La Nouvelle Héloïse* (1761), two major examples of the sentimental epistolary novel in the eighteenth century. At first sight they seem to have much in common, thematically as well as formally. The conflict between sensibility and sense is worked out in the triangular situation that places Julie between Saint-Preux and M. de Wolmar in the same way as Lotte stands between Werther and Albert. The extent and nature of Lotte's love for Werther is a moot question, nor is it of any relevance since the spotlight always falls on Werther himself. In Rousseau's novel it is Julie who forms the pivotal point, as is indicated by its full title *Julie ou La Nouvelle Héloïse*. This disparity is of some importance. *Werther* is the story of an individual, an exceptional individual who breaks out of the social confines even if it is at the cost of self-destruction. Undoubtedly it is more a chronicle of malady than a story of love. The unhappy love for Lotte is the occasion rather than the ultimate cause of Werther's suicide; he is destroyed not by his failure to win Lotte, but by his own character, his temperamental inability to accept things as they are and to come to terms with them. Given his passionate commitment to an all-or-nothing alternative, his fate has the stamp of inevitability.

La Nouvelle Héloïse, by contrast, is fundamentally a book of love; its title alludes, of course, to the archetypal love tale of Heloise and Abelard, while its subtitle is *Lettres de deux Amans* (*Letters of two Lovers*). The nature of the obstacle confronting the lovers is social, not temperamental. From Saint-Preux's first letter to Julie onwards his social inferiority to her is in the forefront, automatically disbarring him from serious consideration as a suitor. His subordinate position is cruelly rammed home by Julie's father in the letter he writes to Saint-Preux on discovering their relationship. It opens with the phrase 'S'il peut rester dans l'âme d'un suborneur quelque sentiment d'honneur et d'humanité ...' ('If any sense of honour and of humanity can dwell in the soul of a subordinate ...'), and closes with: 'ne croyez pas que j'ignore comment se venge l'honneur d'un Gentilhomme, offensé par un homme qui ne l'est pas'[10] ('do not think that I do not know how to avenge the honour of a Gentleman, offended by a man who is not one'). That capital letter for 'Gentleman', together with the arrogant tone, underline the cardinal role of class distinctions in *La Nouvelle Héloïse*. Even in the idealistic household of M. de Wolmar[11] social levels separating masters and servants are still meticulously observed. Saint-Preux is therefore *a priori* ruled out as a potential husband for Julie by an outer circumstance. Unlike Werther, who lives in growing isolation, Saint-Preux is capable of a positive human relationship in his attachment to Milord Edouard. Again unlike Werther, he does accept compromise, first in renouncing and leaving Julie, and once more in returning to live in the Wolmar home as tutor to her children. That this is no easy road for him is shown by the outbreaks of passion he suffers, as in the scene by the lake that ends the fourth part of the novel. But however much they may lament their plight, Saint-Preux and Julie both exercise self-control because they subscribe to the rational concept of virtue fostered by the society in which they live. Werther, on the other hand, tempestuously asserts the paramount rights of the individual's feelings as he opts out of society to go his own way.

This basic dichotomy of ethos between *Werther* and *La Nouvelle Héloïse* is reiterated in structural and stylistic divergences. The French novel is spread over many years and comprises a considerable number of characters and a fair amount of intrigue. Such a broadly generous view of the situation is necessitated by its essentially social approach to its theme; the fabric of society, far from being a mere backcloth, is a leading actor in the drama. *Werther* can be as intensely concentrated in time, place and action as it is because its exclusive focus is on one individual. It already maps the Romantic dilemma to its utmost limits, whereas *La Nouvelle Héloïse* remains deeply embedded in the moral imperatives of the eighteenth century. Stylistically too, the two works progress along inverse paths: *La Nouvelle Héloïse* from turbulence to a transfigured serenity, *Werther* from a relative calm to an ever more intense agitation. So in spite of the parallels of situation and genre, the counterpart between these two novels bespeaks more of antithesis than of parity.

A further multiplication of such attempts at match-making between France and Germany in the later half of the eighteenth century is of little avail. It is no coincidence that all the French examples so far have been drawn from the works of Rousseau, who stood effectively outside, and ahead of, the dominant trends of French literature of his day. There were signs of Pre-romanticism in France, although even this has recently been questioned by such critics as Jean Fabre in *Lumières et romantisme* (Paris: Klincksieck, 1963) and Roland Mortier in *Clartés et ombres du siècle des lumières* (Geneva: Droz, 1969). They argue convincingly against the very existence of a French Pre-romanticism on the grounds that the ideals of the Enlightenment persisted far longer in

France than elsewhere. To be sure, the Enlightenment achieved such distinction in France that it hardly admits comparison with its sketchier and briefer manifestation in Germany. The relative quality and duration of their respective Enlightenments was to prove a determining factor of some consequence and of lasting effect, for Germany obviously had less to lose and more to gain than France by rushing forward into Pre-romantic innovations. For this reason Germany so excelled in its Storm and Stress movement which can be called the climax of European Pre-romanticism. The ebullience of the Storm and Stress had no equivalent whatsoever in later eighteenth-century France, which had nothing to correspond to the freshness of Goethe's early lyric poetry or to the vigour of Storm and Stress drama.

That statement stands in need of some modification. Although no equivalent to the Storm and Stress exists in late eighteenth-century France, counterparts may be cited across the Rhine: in the poetry of Lamartine and Musset, in the plays of Hugo and Alexandre Dumas, and in the filiation between *Werther* and *René* and its successors. That correlationship will be examined in some detail in the next essay. For the present suffice it to point out that these French works appeared some thirty to fifty years later than their German analogues. This time-lag, which runs right through the nineteenth century in the diagonalism of the Franco–German interconnection, first becomes manifest in the later eighteenth century when the two literatures do not dovetail neatly into each other, as our examples have revealed. Where an approximation does occur, it tends to be across that strange temporal gap.

This is the case with Lessing's *Hamburgische Dramaturgie* (1768) and Mme de Staël's *De la Littérature* (1800). In approach, manner and style they are poles apart, yet they share certain deep concerns which bring them closer together than might seem possible from their outer heterogeneity. In genesis and method they are utterly contrary. The *Hamburgische Dramaturgie*, a loosely structured series of articles, originated as a theatrical journal kept by Lessing on his appointment as a consultant to the newly founded National Theatre in Hamburg. The first few sections, through their comments on the performances as well as the plays, aroused such anger among the actors that Lessing shifted the emphasis on to the literary problems raised by the plays in the repertoire. The reviewing of the often mediocre plays being performed soon fell into abeyance as Lessing came to concentrate on such vital topics as the guiding principles of domestic tragedy and historical

drama, the role of the three unities and the function of tragedy. The
Hamburgische Dramaturgie thus grew pragmatically in extent and in
stature from its modest practical beginnings into one of the major
documents of European dramatic theory. Starting always from the
analysis of a particular piece, Lessing proceeded by the deductive
method to a probing inquiry into fundamental issues. His judgements
are backed by his wide Classical learning which enabled him to refer to
the primary sources. Through his reinterpretation of Aristotle, Lessing
not only attacked the misguidedness of French Neo-classical theory,
but also justified the practices of Shakespeare, the supreme genius.
Historically this rehabilitation of Shakespeare was a crucial turning-
point for German drama. What is more, Lessing's arguments carried
the weight of his close-knit reasoning, his scholarship and his
authoritative style.

De la Littérature may seem remote indeed from the *Hamburgische
Dramaturgie* in that it presents a theoretical system in an inductive,
speculative manner. Its full title, *De la Littérature considérée dans ses rapports avec les institutions sociales* (*Concerning Literature considered in relation
to social institutions*), gives some indication of its theme and scope,
although the work transcends the limits even of its own generous
boundaries in its survey of world literature in relation to social conditions from ancient Greece to eighteenth-century France. In undertaking this encyclopedic enterprise Mme de Staël already had certain
ideas, not to say prejudices, fixed in her mind. Foremost among them
was the belief in the perfectibility of the human species, reiterated at
frequent intervals throughout her deliberations. This led to the patently
fallacious assumption that 'later' invariably meant 'better', and hence to
some ludicrous misjudgements, specially of ancient Greek literature.
Hardly less bizarre are two of the other underlying notions of *De la
Littérature*: the conviction that the literature of the North, being more
melancholy and thus (?) more closely allied to philosophy, is prefer-
able and superior to that of the South; and the dogma that the cultural
and literary achievements of any given period are in direct proportion
to the participation of its women! These idiosyncratic suppositions lend
a peculiar piquancy to Mme de Staël's history of Western literature, as
do the flamboyant shots of her lively style, reputed to reflect her
brilliant improvizations at the previous day's dinner-table.

It is hard to imagine two works apparently further apart than the
staid *Hamburgische Dramaturgie* and the quirky *De la Littérature*. But
beneath their surface incompatibility they do correspond to each other
in the parity of their historical position within the literary development

of Germany and France. Both Lessing and Mme de Staël were motivated by a disturbing awareness of the 'dégradation actuelle'[12] ('present low state') of their respective literatures, and both were in search of the best means of improvement. Each in his own land was among the first to sense the staleness of mid-eighteenth-century writing and the need for that creative renewal that was eventually to be accomplished in the Romantic movement. Moreover, both expected the new stimulus from England, though Lessing is much more specific in his championship of Shakespeare than Mme de Staël with her grandiose but vague praise of the bards in the misty, mysterious North. Both also implied new standards in literary criticism in their admission of the emotional effect of art, in their insistence on the appreciation of beauties rather than the counting of so-called faults, in their questioning of the absolute validity of the three unities in drama, and in their conviction that genius towers above any rules. Both children of the eighteenth century, they were naturally still relatively cautious in their advocacy of innovation. Though no longer willing to countenance a mechanical conformity to dogmatic codes, they recoiled as yet from the outright rebellion that was to come later. Even in his most passionate polemic towards the end of the *Hamburgische Dramaturgie*, Lessing frowns on any unseemly 'Gährung des Geschmacks'[13] ('ferment of taste') in the same way as Mme de Staël pleads for 'un genre intermédiaire entre la nature de convention des poètes français et les défauts de goût des écrivains du nord'[14] ('a manner intermediate between the conventionalism of the French poets and the defects in taste of the Northern writers'). Lessing and Mme de Staël are thus two moderates, carefully – perhaps precariously – poised astride the Enlightenment and nascent Romanticism. Both attempted a reassessment of their native literatures, eschewing the over-trodden and misleading paths to point to new and more promising avenues. In the place they hold and the function they fulfil within their own literatures the *Hamburgische Dramaturgie* and *De la Littérature* form a counterpart to each other.[15] The thirty odd years dividing them are an early instance of the time-lag that casts its metaphoric shadow over Franco-German relationships from Pre-romanticism onwards.

II

That time-lag is most striking and most perplexing in the emergence of the Romantic movements. Of its realness there can be no doubt. The first German Romantic group, the *Frühromantik*, gathered round the brothers Schlegel in Berlin and later in Jena in the closing years of the eighteenth century. Its journal, *Das Athenäum,* launched in 1798, was during its short life-span the prime vehicle of German Romantic theory. The major creative works of the *Frühromantik* were published about the turn of the century: Wackenroder's *Herzensergiessungen eines kunstliebenden Klosterbruders* and Tieck's *Volksmärchen* in 1797, Friedrich Schlegel's *Lucinde* in 1799, Novalis's *Hymnen an die Nacht* in 1800 and his *Heinrich von Ofterdingen* in 1802. With the premature death of its two most gifted poets, Wackenroder and Novalis, the *Frühromantik* to all intents and purposes came to an end. A decade or so later the second wave of German Romanticism, known as the *Hochromantik*, found expression in the writings of Chamisso, Uhland, E. T. A. Hoffmann, Arnim and Brentano, whose collection of folk-songs, *Des Knaben Wunderhorn*, appeared in 1805–8. By the 1820s Romanticism was clearly past its peak in Germany; its early metaphysical tendencies were superseded not only by the immediate political preoccupations of the activist *Jungdeutschland* writers, but also by an increasing consciousness of the demands of the real world on the part of the later Romantics, notably Hoffmann whose tales, for all their fantasy, acknowledge darkly the claims of the here and now. At the time when Romanticism was on the wane in Germany, it was in the ascendant across the Rhine. The publication of Lamartine's *Méditations poetiques* in 1820 and the triumph of Hugo's *Hernani* in the theatre in 1830 are the milestones of its breakthrough in France. This time-lag is repeated twice more in the century in the correspondence between the Storm and Stress and French Romanticism, and between the *Frühromantik* and French Symbolism. These later instances of a diagonal relationship are the direct outcome of the retardation in the emergence of the French Romantic movement in relation to the German *Romantik*. Because of its far-ranging importance the time-lag must be examined in some detail at this juncture in order to ascertain its sources before later observing its effects.

The time-lag is the concrete result of the antithetical forces governing the emergence of the Romantic movements in France and Germany. The blend of analogy and opposition implicit in the notion of a counterpart is at its most complex here. In accounting for the time-lag it is perhaps tempting to emphasize the differences, just as many previous critics have tended to underscore the similarities. Even at the risk of repeating the obvious, it is essential at this point explicitly to reiterate the intrinsic cohesiveness of Romanticism at its deepest level. Its infiltration marked a decisive watershed in the history of European literature. In place of the admiration for the Classical ideal traditional since the Renaissance and the affirmation of rationalism, it was henceforth the imaginative and emotive powers of the individual genius that were glorified as the pivot of the universe. So a floating subjectivity, owing allegiance only to itself, supplanted the former pursuit of definitive standards. The old ethical and artistic order was virtually reversed in the radical re-orientation that Romanticism implied. There is no need to elaborate on its ramifications, nor surely to belabour the truism that the eruption of Romanticism, explosive though it was in impact, was the product of a lengthy evolution maturing throughout the second half of the eighteenth century. In no consideration of a specific area, such as the movement's emergence, must its total import − the depth, significance and basic consistency of the changes it wrought − ever be lost from sight. However great the national variations in pace, scope or character, the assertion of Romanticism denoted a momentous revolution, one of the cardinal upheavals in the annals of Western culture on a par with the establishment of Christianity, the advent of the Renaissance, and possibly the enunciation of Marxism.

In its gradual growth and sudden blossoming the emergence of Romanticism may well be likened to the development of a plant. And just as the same seeds sown in different soils and nurtured with differing amounts of light and of water will germinate and grow at uneven rates and maybe produce somewhat variegated crops, so too the Romantic movements. To continue the horticultural image, the ground in which the seeds of Romanticism were planted in the France and Germany of the eighteenth century could hardly have been more unlike. The weather during the sprouting period was also quite different on the two banks of the Rhine. It is this discrepancy not just of literary background but of social and political conditions too that is at the root of the time-lag between the two countries.

Paradoxically, the slowness of France stemmed from her opulence; conversely, the poverty of Germany acted as a spur to rapid advance. France was unquestionably the rich man of Europe with its splendid court, its brilliant *salons*, and its prestigious theatres. In spite of the difficulties that were before long to lead to the Revolution, on the surface and in its national consciousness the country was whole and wealthy. Moreover it had a justified pride in its past achievements, in its dazzling recent literary heritage of Racine, Molière, Corneille and La Fontaine.

Since the Renaissance France had been the acknowledged fountainhead of European culture, her language the *lingua franca* of the educated. Germany, on the other hand, was plainly the poor relation. Looking back from the vantage point of the present, after the abundant creative harvest of the Storm and Stress, Romanticism, and the nineteenth and twentieth centuries, it is hard to imagine Germany's destitution at that period. Even to refer to 'Germany' is misleading because the land was fragmented into umpteen small states, many ruled by princes as notoriously despotic as those that are the object of barely veiled attacks in Lessing's *Emilia Galotti* (1772) and Schiller's *Kabale und Liebe* (1784). The area was economically impoverished too for it had never fully recovered from the aftermath of the Thirty Years' War when it was devastated by the battling armies and ravaged by bands of marauders. The consequent shifting of trade from the overland to the sea routes was severely to Germany's detriment. As a result of its fragmentation, the country had no capital so that it lacked the single focal point that France found in Paris. Leipzig, which was sometimes called 'little Paris', had some theatrical and intellectual life – it was in Leipzig that Lessing abandoned the study of theology and the young Goethe that of law in favour of literature – but as a European cultural centre it could hardly compete with its namesake. The political, social and economic disunity of Germany militated strongly against any sense of national identity. Nor could the Germans find a rallying-point in their literature since they could not appeal to an immediate native tradition such as existed in France. The great German monuments of the Middle Ages – in painting as in literature – had fallen into oblivion; their re-discovery was to be one of the achievements of the Romantic poets. By the first half of the eighteenth century the Germans had as yet had no poet of the stature of Shakespeare, Racine, Dante or Cervantes. The brilliance of seventeenth-century France made the Germans all the more acutely conscious of their own backwardness. At no period was the contrast between the two countries and the two cultures as crass as at the beginning of the developments that were eventually to lead to the Romantic movements. Yet in the long run France's wealth was a deterrent to innovation, whereas Germany's initial underdevelopment proved an advantage. Lack of traditions meant an absence of conventions that could – and did in France – have a clogging effect. The bareness of their own literary cupboard made the Germans avid to stock it quickly so as to catch up with their neighbours. After a period of comparative inertia they were eager for a fresh start, and therefore receptive to new ideas.

However, the steps suggested by Johann Christoph Gottsched were far from auspicious. As a brief and ill-conceived attempt to establish a direct counterpart to French seventeenth-century literature in Germany they hold special interest in the present context. In the naïve belief that the art of writing – and writing well at that! – could be acquired by diligent application, Gottsched exhorted the Germans to study and translate the masterpieces of the French theatre so as to learn how to write equally fine plays. He showed greater ingenuity in implementing his schemes than sagacity in concocting them. His *Versuch einer kritischen Dichtkunst für die Deutschen* (*Attempt at an Ars Poetica for the Germans*) of 1730 is a textbook intended to teach the Germans the rules of poetry. Armed with a reprint and translation of Horace's *Ars Poetica* as a preface, and supported by frequent appeals to, and quotations from Boileau, Gottsched tritely and dogmatically re-stated all the standard Neo-classical formulae (the indispensability of the rules, the importance of good taste, the primacy of imitation, the need for learning, morality, reason, etc.) in the conviction that he was providing the recipe for good works of art.

Practising what he preached, Gottsched was at the same time translating Racine's *Iphigénie* as a preliminary exercise to the writing of tragedies of his own devising. In the postscript to his version he ardently recommended such schooling in the skills of tragedy, but his own efforts hardly testify to its efficacy. His rendering of Iphigenia's great speech (Act II, scene iii) is worth quoting for the light it sheds on Gottsched's ineptitude not only as a translator, but as a spokesman for Neo-classicism in Germany.

Mais de lui-même ici que faut-il que je pense?
Cet amant, pour me voir brûler d'impatience,
Que les Grecs de ces bords ne pouvoient arracher,
Qu'un père de si loin m'ordonne de chercher,
S'empresse-t-il assez pour jouir d'une vue
Qu'avec tant de transports je croyais attendue?
Pour moi, depuis deux jours qu'approchant de ces lieux,
Leur aspect souhaité se découvre à nos yeux,
Je l'attendois partout; et d'un regard timide
Sans cesse parcourant les chemins d'Aulide,
Mon coeur pour le chercher voloit loin devant moi.
Et je demande Achille à tout ce que je voi.
Je viens, j'arrive enfin sans qu'il m'ait prévenue.

Je n'ai percé qu'à peine une foule inconnue;
Lui seul ne paroit point. Le triste Agamemnon
Semble craindre à mes yeux de prononcer son nom.
Que fait-il? Qui pourra m'expliquer ce mystère?
Trouverai-je l'amant glacé comme le père?
Et les soins de la guerre auroient-ils en un jour
Éteint dans tous les coeurs la tendresse et l'amour?

Allein wie kömmt es wohl, dass dieser junge Held
Der mich so heftig liebt, sich noch nicht eingestellt?
Er schien vor Ungeduld mich hier zu sehen, zu brennen,
Die Griechen konnten ihn nicht von dem Heere trennen.
Drum rief mein Vater mich auf sein Begehr und Wort,
Aus solcher Ferne her, an diesen fremden Port.
Und itzo, da ich längst in Aulis angekommen,
Hat er sich noch zur Zeit die Mühe nicht genommen,
Mein Angesicht zu sehn? So lange bin ich hier,
Warum verfügt er sich nicht freudenvoll zu mir?
Und warum eilt er nicht, mir einen Blick zu schenken?
Was soll ich immermehr von solcher Säumnis denken?
Seit ich zween Tage her die Reise vor mich nahm,
Und diesem Lagerplatz allmählich näher kam,
Hab ich ihn überall mit schamhaft-blöden Blicken,
Gesucht und ausgespürt. Ich eilte voll Entzücken
Durch meiner Augen Strahl den schnellen Rossen vor:
Bis auch Weg und Bahn vor ihrer Kraft verlohr.
Ich fragte jedermann, wen ich nur angetroffen;
Und endlich lang ich an, eh, wider mein Verhoffen,
Er mir entgegen eilt! Mein eifriges Gesicht
Sieht hier zwar Zelt und Heer, doch den Achilles nicht.
Selbst Agamemnon scheint sich traurig zu entbrechen,
Und seinen Namen mir mit Fleiss nicht auszusprechen.
Wie kömmt das? Wer erklärt mir diese Heimlichkeit?
Ist meinem Liebsten auch sein Vorsatz wieder leid?
Hat wo die Kriegeslust das Zärtlichseyn und Lieben
In beyder Brust erstickt, aus beider Geist vertrieben?[16]

With this as the salesman's sample, Neo-classicism was bound to be a
dismal failure in Germany. Gottsched's translation is utterly devoid of
the delicate balance of the French, the instinctive progression through a
rising crescendo of climaxes. The economy of Racine's pregnant

reticence is replaced in Gottsched's rendering by a shallow expansiveness that weakens the emotional tension into mere verbiage. The bathos is compounded by the long-winded, heavy-footed verse in a jagged metre unsuited to German. With unconscious irony Gottsched pronounced the truest verdict on his own activity when he described himself, in the preface to the second edition of his *Kritische Dichtkunst*, as an industrious bee gathering material 'auf fremden Fluren, mit vieler Mühe'[17] ('in foreign parts, at great pains')! The material that this bee gathered was by no means honey to the Germans. The fiasco of Gottsched's abortive attempt to bring French drama onto the German stage effectively discredited the dogma of Neo-classicism in Germany. Far from stimulating the Germans to imitate the French, Gottsched's endeavours provoked a salutary opposition and thereby indirectly fostered a readiness for new initiatives.

These came from Lessing. If Gottsched had unwittingly undermined the prestige of Neo-classicism through his efforts, Lessing deliberately and convincingly questioned the authority of the rules in drama in his *Hamburgische Dramaturgie*. Even more important is his constructive contribution in his recommendation of a path more congenial to the Germans than that indicated by Gottsched. For Lessing recognized 'dass wir mehr in den Geschmack der Engländer, als der Franzosen einschlagen; . . .; dass das Grosse, das Schreckliche, das Melancholische besser auf uns wirkt als das Artige, das Zärtliche, das Verliebte'[18] ('that we incline rather to English than to French taste; . . .; that the great, the terrible, the melancholy appeals to us more than the pretty, the gentle and the amorous'). These observations on German taste, together with Lessing's rejection of the need for rules, led him to his advocacy of the English theatre and, above all, of Shakespeare, whom he extolled as a natural genius without any of those reservations concerning his alleged infringement of the rules of drama that Voltaire and his contemporaries in France still felt constrained to make. Lessing's critical writings, as well as the practical example he offered in such plays as *Miss Sara Sampson* (1755), *Minna von Barnhelm* (1767), *Emilia Galotti* (1772) and *Nathan der Weise* (1779), are landmarks in the history of German literature; they denote the ultimate emancipation from the French Neo-classical ideal which Gottsched had sought to import.

This is one of the crucial points of bifurcation between French and German literature. Through Lessing's insight and courage, the Germans escaped the yoke of the effete Neo-classicism under which the French continued to labour for some thirty years or more. So the

emergence of the Romantic movement in France is in effect the saga of
its struggle against the lasting dominance of the old ways. In Germany,
by contrast, where Neo-classicism had never gained a firm foothold, its
traces were rapidly dispelled. The road to a new freedom was early and
clearly signalized by Lessing. Herder, with his fervent enthusiasms,
particularly his adulation of Shakespeare, careered along that road at
full gallop, launching the notions of genius, spontaneity, natural force-
ful expression and dynamic feeling as the popular currency of the
Storm and Stress. After this preparation by Lessing, Herder and the
Storm and Stress, the birth of the Romantic movement was easier in
Germany than in France. Thus it came about that, ironically, Germany's poverty in the mid-eighteenth century, the dearth of an immediate native tradition and the failure of its Neo-classicism all made
the Germans more willing to experiment and more inclined to
welcome the innovations of the emergent Romantic movement. With
the Storm and Stress of the 1770s Germany pulled suddenly and unexpectedly ahead of her neighbours across the Rhine. 'Les Allemands sont
comme les éclaireurs de l'armée de l'esprit humain;' Mme de Staël
shrewdly observed in De L'Allemagne; 'ils essayent des routes nouvelles,
ils tentent des moyens inconnus'[19] ('The Germans are like the scouts in
the army of the human spirit; they explore new routes, they try unknown means').

As is so often the case in De L'Allemagne, Mme de Staël's comment
was no mere neutral exposition. She used her findings on Germany as a
barb with which to goad the French whom she implicitly accused here
of a timid hesitancy. She was indeed right, for this was the time when
France's illustrious past became a handicap, not to say, a millstone.
While Germany, like a youngster carrying only a light backpack,
could race forward unencumbered, France was a dignified *grande dame*
with a substantial baggage of finery which she was understandably
loath to abandon. The Neo-classical canon which had taken firm root
in France in the pattern elaborated by Boileau, was associated in the
minds of the French with the great artistic glory of its *grand siècle*. It is
hardly surprising that they cherished a deep loyalty to such an heritage
and were most reluctant to depart from it. The prevalence of conservative attitudes in the eighteenth century is well illustrated by the activities of the linguistic purists who were resolved to protect the
language, especially the literary *style noble*, from any decline by fixing
it in the traditional moulds. The same considerations determined the
approach to literature; the *status quo* had to be maintained, although

the glitter of the seventeenth century had become decidedly tarnished
by the mid-eighteenth. The lyric poetry, all too often page after page
of unimaginative description, was of a soulless aridity, while the plays
were at best a shadow, and at times almost a mockery, of the
overwhelming dramas of the previous century. The exponents of
French Enlightenment included men as far-sighted as Voltaire and
Diderot, whose speculative ventures took them far ahead of their times.
But they were in the last resort ambivalent in their attitude, tending to
make a prudent retreat, as if startled by their own adventurous sallies,
and finally settling for only limited and carefully circumscribed advances. Voltaire, for example, in his *Dictionnaire philosophique*, admitted
a certain measure of 'enthousiasme' – provided it was an 'enthousiasme
raisonnable'! Always the spectre of reason reared its head. It is well to
recall that the foundations of Neo-classicism lay in the revered
rationalism of Descartes. Here again there is a striking antithesis to Germany where essentially irrationalist lines of thought had predominated
since Böhme, Spener and Francke.

French caution and attachment to the traditions of the past were
nowhere more pronounced than in regard to literary practices. This is
vividly illustrated in La Harpe's *Lycée, ou Cours de littérature ancienne et
moderne*. Reading it, one might hazard the guess that it had appeared in
the 1670s or 1680s; its actual date of publication is, unbelievably, 1799.
In two weighty volumes, each of a thousand folio pages closely
covered in minute print, La Harpe gives a sweeping survey of the
literature and thought of three periods: Ancient Greece and Rome, the
age of Louis XIV, and the eighteenth century. His overall view of the
cultural evolution of Europe is highly tendentious for he sees it as large
stretches of lowland between two great pinnacles of achievement. He
writes first in praise of 'ces beaux siècles de la Grèce et de Rome, qui
ont été ceux de la gloire et des prodigues de l'esprit humain'[20] ('those
fine centuries of Greece and Rome which gave us the glories and the
prodigal gifts of the human mind'). After those days of splendour came
decadence 'jusqu'au temps où le génie vit renaître de beaux jours sous
les Médicis, et répandit ensuite sous Louis XIV cette éclatante lumière
qui a rempli le monde'[21] ('until the time when genius again produced
fine days under the Medicis, and then under Louis XIV spread that
resplendent light which filled the world'). The message is clear: only
French Neo-classicism is comparable in stature to the Ancients, indeed
even outstrips them in the plays of Racine and Corneille. As for the
eighteenth century, it is in every respect a sorry contrast to that of

Louis XIV, to which La Harpe looks back with such nostalgia from
'ces jours d'une dégradation entière et inouïe de la nature humaine'[22]
('these days of a total and unprecedented decadence of human
nature'). The counter-Revolutionary political bias, already hinted in
these words, becomes obvious in the title of the preface to the third section of the *Lycée*, that devoted to the eighteenth century: 'De la guerre
déclarée par les Tyrans révolutionnaires à la Raison, à la morale, aux
Lettres et aux Arts' ('Of the war declared by the revolutionary Tyrants
on Reason, Morality, Literature and the Arts'). In this war La Harpe
sees himself as the defender of the true values, i.e. those of Aristotle and
of Boileau, the twin pillars of his *Lycée*, to whose judgements he frequently refers. The aesthetic system that La Harpe formulates is,
however, less a tribute to his idols than a travesty of them. For he posits
as the indispensable prerequisites of art the absolute validity of the
rules, the unassailable dominion of good taste and the necessity for
a wholehearted rationalism. Constantly on the look-out for any
transgressions against these categorical imperatives, La Harpe has a
deep distrust of genius, except in Boileau's usage of the term as tantamount to aptitude. This rigidity lands La Harpe in certain difficulties;
for instance in his attempt to accommodate Dante and Milton on the
grounds that they were well versed in the Ancients, 'et s'ils se sont faits
un nom avec des ouvrages monstrueux, c'est parce qu'il y a dans ces
monstres quelques belles parties exécutées selon les principes'[23] ('and if
they made a name for themselves with monstrous works, it is because
these monsters contain some beautiful parts written in accordance with
the rules').

La Harpe's *Lycée* reveals just how ossified the old system had become. Yet it still survived, and what is more, it still had its staunch supporters, for many Frenchmen undoubtedly longed for a pronounced
code of law and a definitive order after the convulsions of the Revolution. It is surely a telling comment on the climate of opinion in France
in the closing years of the eighteenth century that Jean-Marie
Chassaignon's *Cataractes de l'imagination, déluge de la scribomanie, vomisse-
ment littéraire, hémorrhagie encyclopédique, monstre des monstres*, an attack on
Boileau, Corneille and Voltaire as eccentric as its title, was immediately
suppressed on its appearance in 1779, although it was published under a
fictitious imprint. Whereas La Harpe's *Lycée*, the mouthpiece of
authoritarianism, enjoyed considerable esteem among the powerful
literary Establishment. The opposition of the traditionalist *Académie
française* is not to be underestimated either, nor even that of such in-

fluential actors as Talma and Mlle Mars who not only clung to the old
style of declamation, but went so far as to refuse to utter 'broken' Alex-
andrines, let alone language they considered insufficiently lofty. The
steady stream of pamphlets against, and satires on Romanticism never
really abated in France, and many were exceedingly vitriolic. It was
this die-hard reactionarism with which the Romantic movement had to
contend in France in a long and hard combat. If the access of Romanticism into Germany was along an open highway, its entry into France
was up a stony track.

Though La Harpe's *Lycée* is an extreme example, strong devotion to
the past continued to persist in France throughout the Romantic
period. This trait is often overlooked when the French Romantics are
represented simply as iconoclasts whose revolutionary ardour was
directed against anything that savoured of the old regime. It is true that
the once sacred rules were infringed with joy, and that Musset loudly
proclaimed: 'il faut déraisonner'[24] ('we must be unreasonable'), as if in
refutation of Boileau's earlier exhortation to love reason. But this overt
rejection of the accepted system was only one aspect of the French
Romantics' equivocal attitude to their native heritage. Alongside, indeed within the opposition to the Neo-classical creed there lingered a
nostalgia for the past, and even traces of a perhaps subconscious
adherence to it. Hugo, Vigny and Lamartine had in 1821–2 been mem-
bers of the conservative *Société des Bonnes Lettres*, founded to buttress
the old doctrines by counteracting liberalism; and Hugo had contributed to the *Conservateur littéraire*, a journal known for its open admiration of Boileau and Racine. Vestiges of the past seem to haunt the
Romantics long after they had allegedly broken with it. The love of
antithesis in the grandiloquent flow of much Romantic lyric poetry,
however personal its theme, strangely echoes the symmetry of the old
oratorical Alexandrine. Even in drama, where the Romantic revolution seemed at its most virulent, the position is surprisingly ambiguous.
Though Shakespeare was the prime model, it is often forgotten how
slowly and grudgingly he was admitted into France. As late as 1809
Lemercier's *Christophe Colomb*, which bore the subtitle 'a
Shakespearean comedy', was driven off the stage in a tumult of scandal.
Since drama was the Bastille of the *ancien régime* in literature, the
struggle was hardest and longest in this field. For there were noticeable
differences in the rate with which new ideas and new modes infiltrated
into the various genres: first into prose in the works of Rousseau and
Bernardin de Saint-Pierre, no doubt because prose was the genre least

bound by the Neo-classical canon; then into lyric poetry, and last into
drama where the rules had been at their most exacting. In many
respects Romantic drama still bears the marks of its tardy and painful
emergence. Far greater attention was paid to dramatic technique in
Romantic theory in France than in Germany. What is more, much of
it, like the actual practice, is predominantly negative in character, inspired by an urge to rebel against what had hitherto been obligatory.
French Romantic drama is *against* the strict observation of the unities,
against the segregation of tragedy and comedy, *against* anonymous
settings, *against* high-flown verse, *against* the avoidance of violent action on stage. The adoption of Shakespeare as a model is motivated, in
part at least, by the fact that he represents all that was anathema to the
French seventeenth-century theatre: mingling of the tragic and the
comic, of verse and prose, disregard for the unities, vigour of speech
and action. The progressiveness of the French Romantics is somewhat
deceptive; they continued to look backwards as much as forwards.
There is no need to espy their Classicism in every resonance of the past,
in every use of a word such as *char*, as Pierre Moreau does in *Le
Classicisme des romantiques* (Paris: Plon, 1932). Nevertheless the evidence
strongly suggests that the French Romantics never wholly succeeded in
escaping the shadow of their native Classical tradition.

III

Apart from this fixation on the grandeur of the seventeenth century, a
variety of other factors, some apparently quite remote from the literary
scene, played an important part in the emergence of the Romantic
movement in France, and specifically in delaying its breakthrough.

Foremost among them is the impact of the Revolution. That a
cataclysm of such magnitude was bound to leave its mark on the
literature of the day is self-evident. What is less straightforward is the
scope and even the tenor of that influence. Since the *ancien régime* in
literature had been so closely linked to that in government in its
associations with the court, it is plausible to assume that the overthrow
of the absolute monarchy would topple Neo-classicism too. Its
authority was certainly undermined in the widespread reassessment of
values implicit in the Revolution. One of the popular slogans of the
day, *A société nouvelle, littérature nouvelle* (For a new society, a new
literature), seems to hold the promise of a renewal. But that promise

was not fulfilled, at least not for a while. For the idealistic Revolution in the name of *liberté, fraternité* and *égalité* was very quickly debased into the bloodiness of the Reign of Terror. This was hardly conducive to the propagation of new ideas for no one was sufficiently foolish to risk his head for the sake of a literary opinion – and heads were lost for less. So any initiatives that might have been encouraged at the dawn of the Revolution came to an abrupt and premature end. Napoleon's subsequent instatement as Emperor was tantamount to a return to absolute monarchy, and it brought in its wake a revival of Neo-classicism, as we shall see. Equally damaging to the emergent Romantic movement was the aftermath of the Revolution in the Napoleonic Wars and the continued disruption of France well into the nineteenth century. The rapidity of the changes during this period of French history is matched only by the long duration of instability as one form of government succeeded another in a whole series of upheavals. The kingdom of the *ancien régime* was overthrown by the 1789 Revolution that created the Republic; with the meteoric rise of Napoleon, the Republic was turned into the Empire, established in 1804. In 1814 Napoleon was ousted by the Restoration of the monarchy under Louis XVIII; apart from the brief interlude of the Hundred Days of Napoleon's Empire in 1815, the monarchical Restoration lasted until the Revolution of 1830 when Louis-Philippe replaced Charles X, who had succeeded Louis XVIII in 1824. In practical, human terms this meant that within the space of barely forty years Frenchmen were asked to swear allegiance to a king, a republic, an emperor, a king, an emperor again, a king again, another king, and yet another king. Even between the actual changes of regime, the utmost precariousness prevailed in the incessant strife between those in favour of 'progress' and those who wanted 'restoration' of some kind. The first thirty or more years of the nineteenth century in France were overshadowed by the mental and emotional reckoning that had to be made with the past and the present alike.

During this protracted unrest political and social problems loomed so much in the forefront of men's minds as to detract attention from the patently less pressing artistic questions. 'Les Français', Mme de Staël laments on the opening page of *De L'Allemagne*, 'depuis vingt années, sont tellement préoccupés par les événements politiques, que toutes leurs études en littérature ont été suspendues'[25] ('For the past twenty years the French have been so engrossed in political happenings that literary activity has been in a state of suspension'). The twenty years to which she refers are those between about 1790 and 1810 when there was indeed a striking hiatus in the publication of new works in France. It is not merely that the Revolution and its sequel diverted men from the arts; it also offered in the political arena an exciting alternative that attracted the most active and inventive talents. The political explosion was of such vehemence that it commandeered all the intellectual gunpowder. So, contrary to expectation, the Revolution, after a few perfunctory sweeps with the new broom, was largely detrimental to literary development in France at the turn of the century, just when the Romantic movement was crystallizing into shape in Germany.

Literary discussion in early nineteenth-century France became, and long remained, to a considerable extent ancillary or even subsidiary to political debate. The emergent Romantic movement was sucked into the political maelstrom too. 'Derrière leurs doctrines de philosophie, d'histoire ou de littérature, c'est encore la lutte politique qui continuera'[26] ('behind their philosophical, historical or literary doctrines, it was the political struggle that continued'), Moreau has rightly pointed out. The fighting was as fierce as it was complicated. It is daunting to pursue it in René Bray's *Chronologie du romantisme* (Paris: Boivin, 1932), a year by year, month by month, day by day, blow by blow account of the proceedings. The imbroglio was intensified by switches of opinion, and hence of political alignment. Victor Hugo, for instance, who had in the early 1820s been a member of the conservative *Société des Bonnes Lettres*, moved from the Right to the Left wing after the middle of the decade. Nor were political and literary views split along clear-cut lines. In politics there were Liberals and Royalists, and in literature Classicists and Romantics, so that four possible permutations could, and did, jostle together: Classicist Liberals, Romantic Liberals, Classicist Royalists, and Romantic Royalists. The presence of no fewer than four warring factions led to a grotesque confusion as well as to a plethora of journals. The divisions were by no means such as might be expected, for generally the opponents of the Restoration were against Romanticism; in other words, those who were liberal and progressive in politics were pro-Classical and reactionary in the arts, and vice versa. Thus the staid *Académie française*, the notorious adversary of the Romantics, had grown out of the Revolutionary *Institut*. There seems to be more than a little truth in the perspicacious comment, attributed to Benjamin Constant, that the progressives sought a certain air of respectability in upholding the literary conventions while overthrowing the political system. However ambivalent the effects of the Revolution, and however perplexing the consequent situation in

France, one thing stands out with clarity: this political complication was of paramount importance to the emergence of the Romantic movement, and it undoubtedly acted as a potent retardent.

So did Napoleon when he extended his empire into the realm of literature. In his youth Napoleon, like most of his contemporaries, admired the fashionable sentimental literature of the day: he read *Clarissa Harlowe* at the age of eighteen, took with him on his Egyptian campaign a copy of Ossian which he is reported to have kept at his bedside throughout the voyage, and claimed to have read *Werther* seven times – he certainly made some acute observations on Werther's suicide when he met Goethe in October 1808. But once he came to power, his personal literary tastes gave way to public calculations. Literature was judged by the criterion of its direct political and social usefulness to his reign. Quickly grasping the possibilities for manipulating public opinion, he deliberately furthered some types of writing and proscribed others. Much though he liked Ossian, he disapproved of the Romantics' strong individualism, their tendency to non-conformism and their undisciplined indulgence in feeling, all of which struck him as inimical to the manly tone of his Empire. Far more appropriate to his ambitions was the French Classical theatre with its preference for political themes, its grandiose issues and its large-scale heroes. He himself attended theatrical performances with surprising frequency for a man of his background and preoccupations. His choice of plays, almost exclusively from the Neo-classical repertoire, reveals his ulterior motives in his cultivation of the theatre. He was especially attracted to Corneille, whom he praised for his understanding of historico-political problems. Among the plays of Corneille his favourite was *Cinna*, which he saw no less than twelve times and knew almost by heart, esteeming no doubt its wealth of constitutional allusions felicitous to his own regime.[27] Napoleon thus inaugurated a revival of Neo-classicism as part of his studied policy to arouse and sustain French nationalism; this was at the expense of literary cosmopolitanism, which he actively discouraged. One of Napoleon's *Prix décennaux*, for example, was awarded to La Harpe's *Lycée*, while Mme de Staël's *De l'Allemagne* was banned from publication in France because its commendation of German culture seemed to imply criticism of France. In art and architecture too, in the paintings of David and in the design of the Madeleine and the Palais Bourbon, the tendency to revert to the Classical style reached a new peak during the Empire.

It is a measure of Napoleon's success in directing literary taste that

Benjamin Constant had such deep misgivings about the appearance of his translation of Schiller's *Wallenstein* in 1809. By present standards Constant's *Wallstein* seems innocuous to the point of insipidity, so drastically has the translator truncated and emasculated Schiller's mighty trilogy. In Constant's version it is reduced in length from over 7,500 lines in German to 900 in French, the number of characters is ruthlessly cut, and the whole of the preliminary *Wallensteins Lager* omitted. Besides these abbreviations, other more radical changes are made: the three unities are meticulously observed, *récit* replaces action on the stage, and the rhetorical Alexandrine with its stock-in-trade vocabulary is used to render Schiller's vigorous, natural dialogue. The result deserves Constant's description of it on the title-page: 'tragédie en cinq actes et en vers' ('verse tragedy in five acts'), the standard formula of the French Neo-classical theatre, for it is wholly assimilated to that pattern. Yet in spite of its conformity to the habitual rules and conventions, its German origin would have sufficed to make it suspect to the Napoleonic censorship. For this reason, in order to defend himself against possible accusations of treason to France, Constant decided to preface his *Wallstein* with *Quelques réflexions sur le théâtre allemand*. This preface is a masterpiece of tightrope acrobatics. In contrasting the dramatic methods of the Germans with those of the French, Constant shows a wide knowledge and a sensitive appreciation of the German theatre. This does not, however, inhibit his categoric declaration: 'Je suis loin de recommander l'introduction de ces moyens dans nos tragédies. L'imitation des tragiques allemands me semblerait très dangereuse pour les tragiques français'[28] ('Far be it from me to recommend the introduction of these methods in our tragedies. The imitation of German tragedy would strike me as highly dangerous for French tragedy'). In the concluding paragraph of the preface he is again at pains to stress that 'la tragédie française est, selon moi, plus parfaite que celle des autres peuples'[29] ('French tragedy is, to my mind, more perfect than that of other nations'), although in many respects this article of faith has been belied by his shrewd observations on the merits of the German theatre.[30] *Wallstein* is of symptomatic importance in that it reveals which way the wind was blowing in France in the opening years of the nineteenth century. The earlier interest in foreign literature, which had reached its highest pitch in the 1790s, declined sharply during the First Empire, a period of reaction in literature as well as in government. The demands of loyalty to the indigenous tradition in the cause of French nationalism once again buttressed the old literary regime. So the glories of the past, re-instated in supremacy, served to impede the advent of the new.

Constant's *Wallstein*, with its cautiously added preface, draws attention to another factor that complicated and retarded the emergence of the Romantic movement in France. It can best be described as a mistaken kind of patriotism that bred a profound distrust of foreign importations. Many of the stimuli for the evolution of Romanticism came into France from England and Germany; the great wave of interest in Shakespeare, Scott and Byron, Goethe and Schiller in the early years of the nineteenth century is well known and well documented. So much so indeed that one of the satirical definitions of Romanticism put forward by Musset in the *Lettres de Dupuis et Cotonet* was: 'l'imitation des poésies allemande, anglaise et espagnole'[31] ('the imitation of German, English and Spanish poetry'). But this curiosity about foreign literatures was coupled with a xenophobia that grew in intensity during the Napoleonic Wars. England and Germany came to be regarded as foes not only on the battlefield, but also on the literary front. However fascinating foreign writers might be, they were suspect in French eyes as a potential threat to the French tradition, to the cultural hegemony that France still maintained throughout Europe. The sway of the French language and of French manners was in fact widespread at that time; French was the language of polite society almost everywhere, the language of the Berlin Academy, the Austrian Diplomatic Service, the Russian court under Catherine the Great and that of Prussia under Frederick; it was also the language written by Leibniz and even by Gibbon, whose first work, published in London in 1761, was an *Essai sur l'étude de la littérature*. Together with the language the influence of French civilization spread through the prestige of French architecture, jewellery, porcelain, furniture, tapestries, clothes and cookery. So the French genuinely envisaged themselves as the cultural leaders of Europe, and reacted with indignation to any foreign challenge to their preponderance. They seemed to imagine that Goethe was ganging up with Shakespeare in a sinister plot against the *gloire* of France and all it represented. This xenophobia spiced the conflict surrounding the emergence of the Romantic movement with an element of eccentricity. A good example of it comes in the incident reported by Stendhal in *Racine et Shakespeare*: at the performance of a Shakespeare play in Paris in 1822 shouts came from the audience, 'A bas Shakespeare! c'est un aide de camp du duc de Wellington!'[32] ('Down with Shakespeare! he is an adjutant to the Duke of Wellington!'). The cause of Romanticism became in France 'une querelle nationale' ('a national contest'), as the journal *Débats* put it in January 1816, enmeshed in the susceptibilities of national pride and honour.

Most of these problems that bedevilled and retarded the emergence of the Romantic movement in France have no immediate counterpart in the formation of the *Frühromantik* in Germany. Because Germany's past was so different from that of France, the pressures of the present and the ambitions for the future were also quite other. On the Eastern bank of the Rhine there was no *grand siècle* to look back to, no theatrical conventions, no sacred system of rules to wield their tyranny. Nor was there any single leader of the standing of Napoleon to impose his own tastes in literature or to harness it into the service of the state. Since there was no unified Germany, patriotism was a relatively marginal sentiment among the *Frühromantiker*. Their interest in the Middle Ages and their re-discovery of the German art of the past were more an expression of their nostalgia for Utopia than an outcome of nationalistic fervour. It was only later, in the wake of the Napoleonic Wars, that national consciousness grew into a major force with the second generation of German Romantics and even more so with their successors of the *Jungdeutschland* group. The *Frühromantiker* tended rather towards cosmopolitanism in their idealistic aspirations; their concern was with all spheres of human endeavour and with the whole universe, not just with literature or with Germany. In this too they contrast with the French Romantics, whose attention was firmly riveted on their own literature. The German Romantics could allow themselves to be more open to the world for they were never subjected to the suspicion of treason in their own land, as were the French; they stood within the native tradition of irrationalism, and had immediate local antecedents in the Storm and Stress of the 1770s.

The German Romantics are again distinct from the French in their essentially apolitical stance. This was partly a matter of inclination, partly of outer pressures. There was, of course, no equivalent in Germany to the shattering Revolution in France; on the contrary, the aim of most of the German rulers was frankly a state of somnolence. Terrified by the excesses perpetrated across the Rhine in the name of liberty, they cherished conservatism and sobriety to the point of stuffiness, and on occasion, reactionary repressiveness. Since the enlightened notions of the *philosophes* had precipitated such disastrous consequences in France, the Germans concluded that it was dangerous for poets and philosophers to engage in political thought. So men of letters were strongly discouraged from active participation in this field; with the restrictions imposed by many of the despotic German princes after the French Revolution, few areas remained safe for free expression; aesthetics and metaphysics were the notable exceptions, for they were considered too remote from daily life to have any dangerous potential. The *Frühromantiker* of the turn of the century therefore showed less practical interest in the political issues of the day than either the previous generation, the Storm and Stress, or the succeeding one, the *Hochromantik* and *Jungdeutschland*. Political thinking *per se* may not have been alien to them, but they did shun the hurly-burly of the arena, maintaining a lofty detachment from the immediate social and political problems of the time.[33] Their fundamental impulses led them away from the present and from the outer surface of the world towards the exploration of the transcendental. This inner remoteness is reflected in their political thought too. Friedrich Schlegel's aphorisms about the state and the social order, like those of Novalis in *Blütenstaub*, are primarily concerned with the definition of the *ideal*, not the critique of the extant. The *Frühromantik*'s most substantial contribution to political thought, Novalis's *Die Christenheit oder Europa*, well exemplifies that process of sublimation so characteristic of German Romanticism. Its Utopianism is such that it deserves the scathing description: a 'fairy-tale solution for the problems of the post-Revolutionary age in Europe'.[34] Virtually writing the present off, Novalis looks back with nostalgia in the opening sentence to those 'schöne glänzende Zeiten, wo Europa ein christliches Land war, wo *eine* Christenheit diesen menschlich gestalteten Weltteil bewohnte; *ein* grosses gemeinschaftliches Interesse verband die entlegensten Provinzen dieses weiten geistlichen Reichs'[35] ('those beautiful, resplendent times, when Europe was one Christian land, when *one* Christianity inhabited this humanly oriented part of the world; *one* great common interest united the remotest provinces of this far-flung spiritual empire'). And again in the closing paragraph all hope for the future is invested in the eventual restoration of that dream-like state, 'die heilige Zeit des ewigen Friedens, wo das neue Jerusalem die Hauptstadt der Welt sein wird'[36] ('the holy age of eternal peace, when the new Jerusalem will be the capital of the world'). How far removed this faith in the return of a Golden Age is as a political credo from the pressing strife of the moment that preoccupied the French Romantics.

The comparison of the political and social circumstances that conditioned the emergence of the Romantic movements in France and

Germany thus yields a picture of contrasts. In France the dominant influences were retardent: the persistence of the prestigious Neo-classical tradition, and its reinforcement under Napoleon; the hyperactivity of political life that overshadowed the arts in sheer excitement, almost inevitably involving writers in its entanglements; the rationalistic track preferred of French philosophy; the limitation of free expression at various phases by overt or clandestine censorship; and finally, the xenophobia that made the French hesitant to follow a foreign lead. Conversely, in Germany the stagnation of the political scene, the habitual inclination towards irrationalism in thought, the lack of a firmly established Neo-classicism, and the powerful spurt to innovation given by the Storm and Stress: all these impelled the Romantic movement onwards. In these divergences between the two countries in the late eighteenth and early nineteenth centuries lie the sources of the time-lag separating the emergence of the *Frühromantik* from that of *romantisme*. And once that time-lag had set in, it continued through the next hundred years.

IV

The divergences that I have just summarized had results beyond the creation of the time-lag. They affected the actual manner in which the two Romantic movements made their appearance, and ultimately also their character.

In France, taking its cue no doubt from the contemporary political struggles, the emergence of the Romantic movement was very much of a battle, a battle against certain things and for others. Who was fighting for what is not, however, always clear; issues and sides changed with bewildering speed. From about 1810 on and throughout the 1820s violent controversies raged in Paris, culminating in the notorious and rather ludicrous confrontation at the first performance of *Hernani* in 1830. The theatre offered the most convenient arena for the final showdown, but most of the real warfare was waged in the series of campaigns that filled the host of journals active at this period: *Le Conservateur littéraire, La Muse française, Débats, Le Courier français, La Revue de Paris, Le Miroir, Le Mercure du XIXième siècle, La Pandore, La Jeunesse française, Le Constitutionnel, Les Tablettes universelles, La Minerve française, Annales de la littérature et des arts, Le Lycée français, Le Diable boiteux, Le Globe, La Revue française*, etc. Several of these were short-lived, some killed by the repressive press laws following the murder of the Duc de Berry in 1820, but many were quickly reactivated under another name, with a slightly altered set of collaborators and updated slogans. Alongside the journals, and sometimes associated with them, were the societies and *salons*, such as the *Société des Bonnes Lettres, L'Athénée*, Nodier's *L'Arsenal* and Hugo's *Cénacle*. Like the journals, they were rallying-points for partisans of particular doctrines, forums for the discussion of ideas and centres for the formulation of policies. Opinions were so impassioned, exchanges so sharp that in March 1817 *Débats* referred to the schism tearing Paris into opposing camps as a civil war. The extraordinary acrimony of these literary quarrels can be understood only in the wider context, that is in relation to the political divisions, and as a reflection of fears about the loss of national supremacy.

The battle was eventually resolved by two events, one well-known, the other less so but in fact of greater ultimate importance. In 1827 Hugo's *Cénacle* came into being. This was more than just another in the long line of literary *salons*; here for the first time, following Hugo's own political conversion from the Right to the Left wing, the Liberal Romantics of the Left joined forces with the Royalist Romantics of the Right in a common front against the die-hard traditionalists. Through this armistice on the political and religious hostilities among its supporters, the cause of Romanticism gained immeasurably in strength. A further impetus was given in the winter of 1827–8 by the visit of a group of English actors performing Shakespeare plays. The decisive blow came, however, with the publication in 1828 of Sainte-Beuve's *Tableau historique et critique de la poésie française et du théâtre français au seizième siècle, suivi des oeuvres choisies de Pierre de Ronsard*. It may well seem far-fetched to ascribe to a critical work on sixteenth-century literature a momentous part in the breakthrough of the Romantic movement. Yet this is just what happened. Sainte-Beuve's survey of sixteenth-century French literature was the crucial manifesto that gave the French Romantics a respectable ancestry in their native land. Until then they had been suspect as traitors to the indigenous tradition who were trying, under the nefarious influence of foreign models, to bring into France modes alien or even inimical to time-honoured French custom. It was Sainte-Beuve's achievement to show that worthy precedents for the so-called innovations of the Romantics existed in the practices of French poets of the sixteenth century. His *Tableau historique et critique de la poésie française et du théâtre français au seizième siècle* is clearly written with an eye to contemporary polemics, as he confesses in the preface: 'je n'ai perdu aucune occasion de rattacher ces études du XVIe siècle aux questions littéraires et poétiques qui s'agitent dans le nôtre'[37] ('I have missed no opportunity to link these studies of the sixteenth century to the literary and poetic questions astir in our time'). In discussing the work of Baïf, for instance, he points to the 'analogies frappantes'[38] ('striking analogies') with Chénier. He argues most convincingly that the *alexandrin primitif* with its movable caesura, its rich rhymes and its free *enjambement*, the verse form 'que la jeune école de poésie affectionne et cultive'[39] ('which the newest school of poetry favours and cultivates'), is identical to that used by Du Bellay, Ronsard, d'Aubigné, etc. He even tries to prove, though with rather less success than in the case of the Alexandrine, that the theatrical practices of the sixteenth century, notably in regard to the unity of time, were close to those advocated by August Wilhelm Schlegel, Visconti and Manzoni.[40] Sainte-Beuve thus draws a constant parallel between the sixteenth and the early nineteenth centuries in France, between the endeavours of the *Pléïade* and those of the *Cénacle*, between the poetic styles of Ronsard and Hugo. In his Conclusion he maintains unequivocally that 'l'école nouvelle en France a continué l'école du XVIe siècle'[41] ('the new school in France is a continuation of the sixteenth century school'); granted that Chénier and his successors had broken out of the 'moule étroit et symmétrique' ('narrow and symmetrical mould') formulated by Boileau, but in so doing they had found 'dans nos origines quelque chose de national à quoi se rattacher'[42] ('in our past a national element on which to build'). Sainte-Beuve's contentions ushered in a radical change in the Romantics' image in France. Suddenly they appeared in a totally new light: no longer as the enemies of France, but as the guardians of a native heritage even more venerably ancient than that of the Neo-classical seventeenth century. By siting the Romantics within the frontiers of the French domain, Sainte-Beuve not only forged a link with the past, but at the same time salved national pride.

While this organic link with their antecedents was a panacea for many of the ills besetting the emergent Romantic movement in France, it was, on the contrary, the source of a certain malaise in Germany. The antithesis is not, however, as outright as may at first appear because there is, beneath the surface contrast, a curious resemblance between the German Romantics' attitude to their past and that of the French, different though that heritage was in the two instances. Like the French, the *Frühromantiker* came to feel overshadowed by their predecessors for whom they developed a love-hate relationship similar to the ambivalent bearing of the French *vis-à-vis* the *grand siècle*. The predicament of the German Romantics was intensified by the fact that they had to live alongside their *grand siècle*, so to speak. For German literature evolved with a startling, almost uncomfortable rapidity, soaring from its nadir in the earlier part of the eighteenth century to its zenith before the end of that century. Between Gottsched's ill-conceived attempts at reform and the dazzling fireworks of the Storm and Stress that astonished and captivated the whole of Europe, less than forty years elapsed. From Lessing onwards, through Klopstock, Wieland, Winckelmann, Hamann, Herder, and culminating in the works of Goethe and Schiller, Germany's cultural progress was a rocketing ascension, so that by the 1770s she had moved from the tail-end into the vanguard of European literature. The climax of Pre-romanticism, the Storm and Stress, also represents the first distinct wave of the European Romantic movement. The Storm and Stress prefigured Romanticism in many cardinal aspects of theory and practice: the assertion of the rights of the individual, and specifically of the individual of genius whose creative power was extolled as partaking of the divine; the primacy of instinct and feeling; the release of the imagination from all constraints; the notion of organic growth and development, which led on to the interest in the past and to the new attitude to nature as a single living cosmos; the poet's freedom to express himself in any form at will; the delineation of the prototype of the Romantic hero in such works as *Urfaust, Werther* and *Die Räuber*. This formidable list suggests that the Storm and Stress pre-empted many points of the *Frühromantik* programme, though it would be a mistake to assume that the two movements were identical. There were vital differences too which will be discussed later. However, the achievements of the Storm and Stress undoubtedly took some of the wind out of the sails of the Romantic revolution in Germany. Whereas the emergent Romantic movement in France had to do battle on account of its apparently excessive and shocking novelty, in Germany it attracted too little attention as a second, rather more pallid manifestation of notions already partially familiar from the outburst of the Storm and Stress.

Nor was this the only difficulty facing the emergent Romantic movement in Germany. The *Frühromantiker* were literally a side-show for another important reason: it was Goethe and Schiller who held the centre of the German literary stage unchallenged in the final decade of the eighteenth and the first years of the nineteenth century. With their development towards poetic maturity they had outgrown their early Storm and Stress phase. Goethe's visit to Italy in 1786-8 revealed to him the art of the Classical land, as he called it. He not only experimented with hexameters and pentameters and treated Classical themes in his poetry; he also came increasingly to prize tranquillity, gradual evolution and organic harmony as the basic laws of human existence and of art. In this middle period of his life, the time of his friendship with Schiller until the latter's death in 1805, Goethe wrote some of his finest works. He vied with Schiller in the creation of Germany's greatest ballads, while Schiller himself was engaged on the dramas that are the pride of the German theatre. One might with justification argue that these years at the turn of the century are the true German counterpart to France's *grand siècle* of two centuries earlier.

It is in this sense that the *Frühromantiker* had to live with their past, as I put it before. For the poets of the younger generation the situation was fraught with extraordinary tensions. They began with an admiration for Goethe so fervid as to amount to adulation. In the *Athenäum* (no. 216) Friedrich Schlegel cited Goethe's *Wilhelm Meister*, together with the French Revolution and Fichte's *Wissenschaftslehre*, as one of the outstanding events of the age. In his critical writings in the 1790s Friedrich Schlegel repeatedly returned in fascination to the subject of Goethe's commanding greatness, ranking him with Dante, Cervantes and Shakespeare as one of the incarnations of the spirit of poetry. His universality and harmony are singled out in the essay 'Versuch über den verschiedenen Stil in Goethes früheren und späteren Werken' ('Essay on the varying styles in Goethe's earlier and later works') in the *Gespräch über die Poesie*, while the appreciation 'Über Goethes *Meister*' emphasizes the purity and sublimity of *Wilhelm Meisters Lehrjahre*, which appeared in 1796 and was to be of paramount importance for the Romantics' conception of the novel. Novalis was reputed to know *Wilhelm Meisters Lehrjahre* almost by heart; like Friedrich Schlegel, he envisaged Goethe as the true regent of the poetic spirit on earth. Tieck went even further by quite simply exalting him as a God. To August Wilhelm Schlegel he was a Proteus, adept at every genre, the supreme example of a progressive, universal poet. His brother, Friedrich, summed up the *Frühromantiker*'s paean on Goethe in the phrase: 'ein göttlicher Dichter und ein vollendeter Künstler'[43] ('a divine poet and a complete artist'). In their eyes he seemed to fulfil all the demands they made of the artist; here, before them, was the ideal to which they aspired.

The strain inherent in such a position is obvious. The *Frühromantiker* could scarcely hope to compete with the pre-eminence of the German *Klassiker*. Goethe was *the* German poet and sage of the period, and his presence in the small town of Weimar made it *the* cultural centre of Germany, to which all foreign visitors flocked. Beside the lustre of Goethe's stardom, the Romantics were a slight and hardly noticed constellation; no wonder they felt literarily and psychologically overshadowed. Beyond their own circles their fame was relatively slow to spread. For instance, Novalis, the major creative poet of the *Frühromantik*, was unknown outside Germany until Carlyle's biography of 1829, which, incidentally, presented him as a thinker rather than as a poet; it was through Carlyle also that he eventually came on to the poetic horizon in France. Of more immediate relevance to the emergence of the Romantic movement than these questions of subsequent reputation is the effect that Goethe had on the German Romantics' consciousness of themselves and of their role in German literary history. For German literature had already achieved its decisive regeneration in the Storm and Stress, and with Goethe and Schiller had attained unprecedented distinction. Of this the *Frühromantiker* were painfully aware with the result that they felt like epigones or eccentric outsiders. The predicament facing them was in some ways not unlike that of the French Romantics. While the French were in competition with the glories of the past, the Germans had to contend with the splendour of the present – an equally awkward proposition. The emergence of the Romantic movements in both countries therefore contains a strong element of defiance, a defiance that was in both cases directed against the Classical establishment, although this denoted something different in Germany than in France.

In the form that this defiance assumed there is again both similarity and contrast. The similarity resides in the ambivalent attitude towards the overshadowing greatness. It is more pronounced in France where the Romantics' virulent rejection of the Neo-classical system is counterbalanced by a deep-seated attachment to the native tradition. There is a parallel to this in Germany where the Romantics' attitude to Goethe 'ran the whole gamut of human emotions, from veneration to detestation, within a few years', as Wolfgang Leppmann[44] has put it. The disenchantment was mutual. As he grew older, Goethe showed his lack of sympathy for Romanticism, which ran counter to some of his most cherished convictions. He is reputed to have poked fun at Tieck's *Franz Sternbalds Wanderungen*, written in imitation of *Wilhelm Meister*, by coining the term *sternbaldisieren* to describe vague effusions. His personal dealings with Friedrich Schlegel were never felicitous, and Schlegel, after his later conversion to Catholicism, responded with unconcealed disapproval of what he pleased to call Goethe's 'paganism'. Goethe's aphorism contrasting 'healthy' Classicism with 'diseased' Romanticism has, of course, become notorious. Whatever its ulterior implications, it leaves no doubt as to the disfavour with which Goethe viewed Romanticism.

Goethe's own fall from grace in the eyes of the *Frühromantiker* is conspicuous in 1799 already in Novalis's fragment 'Über *Wilhelm Meister*'. Though still appreciative of its form and style, Novalis condemns *Wilhelm Meister* in vituperative terms as pretentious, prosaic, unpoetic, indeed anti-poetic. Branding it a *Candide* against poetry, he suggests it might be sub-titled 'die Wallfahrt nach dem Adelsdiplom'[45] ('the pilgrimage for a title of nobility') since Wilhelm, after his youthful flirtations with the theatre, falls back into that bourgeois society which the Romantics scorned. Goethe's novel aroused their anger to such a pitch because its basic tendency contravened their aspirations. Hence Novalis's *Heinrich von Ofterdingen* was consciously conceived as an anti-*Wilhelm Meister*, a corrective to the fallacious trend of Goethe's work. Like *Wilhelm Meister,* it is a *Bildungsroman*, tracing a young man's growth to maturity as he gradually finds his rightful path in life. But Heinrich's path leads in a diametrically opposite direction to that of Wilhelm. At the beginning of both novels the hero leaves the security of his childhood home. In the belief that he has a theatrical vocation (*Wilhelm Meisters theatralische Sendung* was the title of the first version), Wilhelm runs away to join a troupe of actors. After sundry adventures and encounters with enigmatic figures, he comes to recognize the erroneousness of his youthful venture into the theatre, which he then sees as only one stage in his quest for himself; eventually he becomes a useful member of the community in his capacity as a barber-surgeon. Novalis's Heinrich, by contrast, moves further and further away from the common life of ordinary men. He is the born poet whose journey through the world is an initiation into its mysteries in preparation for his elevation into the higher realms of art, symbolized by the blue flower of which he dreams at the outset. The antithesis between the two novels is surely evident even from so cursory an outline: *Wilhelm Meister* advocates the individual's responsible integration into society and his acceptance of his duty to contribute to the common weal, whereas *Heinrich von Ofterdingen* glorifies the poet's apartness in the unqualified triumph of the imaginative over the real. This contrast between Novalis's work, the epitome of the *Frühromantik*, and Goethe's novel, the embodiment of his mature thought, clearly illustrates the gulf separating the Romantics from their illustrious senior. The tension was more than a mere question of personal antagonisms: a genuine ideological opposition exists between German Classicism and Romanticism, in spite of certain lines of continuity.

Overshadowed by Goethe, virtually disbarred from an outlet in political activity and little heeded by their contemporaries, the *Frühromantiker* were in a position forlorn enough to have daunted lesser spirits. Two possible avenues could lead out of their frustration: withdrawal or self-assertion. From their rare capacity to combine these apparently contrary alternatives stems the idiosyncratic character of the *Frühromantik*. The withdrawal from the common round of reality had both negative and positive motives: negative in the rejection of Philistinism, stuffiness and timidity; positive in the cult of harmony on the personal and metaphysical plane. The *Frühromantiker* envisaged themselves as a guild of artists, of chosen spirits united in a collective individualism, a web of friendships that grew out of each one's respect for the personality of the other, and that blended happily into a communal ivory-tower. Acutely conscious of the damaging effects of the dualism which the eighteenth century had inherited from Cartesianism, the German Romantics deliberately sought a re-unification of the spiritual and the material at every level. Harmony was to be restored between man and God, man and nature, man and his fellow-men by means of a sympathetic, loving understanding, a kind of intuitive empathy. Hence the *Frühromantiker* believed in a personal relationship to God, who was accessible through fervent feeling rather than through theological dogma. Similarly, they saw the whole of external nature as an extension of man: 'Gehören Tiere, Pflanzen und Steine, Gestirne und Lüfte nicht auch zur Menschheit?'[46] ('Do animals, plants and stones, stars and breezes not also belong with man?'), Novalis scribbled in the margin to one of Friedrich Schlegel's aphorisms, expressing in theoretical terms a conviction that clearly inspires all his poetry. To the *Frühromantiker* the attainment of such an ideal state of harmony was one of the primary aims of Romanticism. Novalis actually used the term *romantisieren* as synonymous to *kombinieren*, and in antithesis to *polarisieren*. The togetherness among themselves was taken with the greatest seriousness. The theologian Schleiermacher wrote a *Versuch einer Theorie des geselligen Betragens* (*Attempt at a Theory of Social Behaviour*), while Friedrich Schlegel, in *Lucinde* as well as in some of his aphorisms, expounded his concept of marriage as the companionship of kindred souls, and pleaded for the emancipation of women and their inclusion in the guild. *Synexistenz, Symphilosophieren,* and *Sympoesie,* all exploiting the Greek particle *syn* to denote unity, were fashionable occupations. This cohesive loyalty found its most cogent expression in Tieck's efforts to complete Wackenroder's *Phantasien über die Kunst* and to piece together the second half of *Heinrich von Ofterdingen* from Novalis's notes after his friends' early deaths; it also sent the *Frühromantiker* on frog-catching expeditions at dawn to help Ritter, a scientist member of the fraternity.

Their withdrawal into the ivory-tower of a Utopian harmony forms a striking contrast to the practical belligerency and internecine strife typical of the French Romantics. The existence of only two main periodicals in Germany, the *Athenäum,* the organ of the *Frühromantik,* and the *Zeitung für Einsiedler,* that of the *Hochromantik,* underlines the difference to France with its multitude of feuding journals; even their very titles, *Atheneum* and *Journal for Hermits,* are indicative of their calm aloofness. The dissimilarity in character between the Romantic movements in France and Germany in this respect can be traced back directly to the divergent political, social and literary circumstances surrounding their emergence. This holds true in regard to self-assertiveness too. As revolutionaries the Romantics had perforce to assert themselves, but the object, direction and degree of that assertiveness was strongly at variance in the two Romantic movements.

The chief concern of the French poets and critics of the early nineteenth century was the reconciliation of the new modes and styles with the traditional heritage of French literature. Political, religious and philosophical issues were drawn into these artistic problems, particularly in so far as they infringed on the central dilemma of tradition versus innovation. The prefaces and articles that expound French Romantic theory turn constantly on specific, largely technical questions: whether the three unities must be observed in drama; how much freedom is permissible in the handling of the Alexandrine verse form; whether the tragic and the comic, the sublime and the grotesque, prose and poetry should be mingled at will; the appropriateness of certain types of language for drama or for lyric poetry etc. These matters stood in the forefront of the polemics. By the opening decades of the nineteenth century the inevitability of change in the arts as in government had come to be accepted; the contention centred less on the intrinsic desirability of change, than on the best way to implement it with the least possible disruption, let alone damage to the glory of France. In literature, as in politics, the focus was on the here and now, the realities of the effective choices facing the creative artist.

None of these concrete topics so prominent in the French controversies interested the German Romantics. Such things as verse form, technique, means of expression were of scant importance to them since the Storm and Stress had already firmly instituted the principle of absolute freedom. Their strongest inclination was towards the *Roman* and the *Märchen*, the narrative modes hardly heeded by the French. But it was the metaphysical and transcendental aspects of art that really fascinated them: the perception of the ineffable through the artist's imagination, the mediation of that perception in symbolic images, the artist's quasi-divine role in that process as perceiver and mediator, the interconnection of all the arts as expressions of the absolute. 'Wir sind auf einer Mission: zur Bildung der Erde sind wir berufen' ('We are engaged on a mission: it is our vocation to transform the world'), Novalis proclaimed in *Blütenstaub* (no. 32). No phrase could summarize with equal vividness the all-embracing aim of the *Frühromantiker*: to transform the world. Theirs was not just an artistic movement in search of new styles, but an attempt at a fundamental existential re-valuation of truly Titanic proportions. For this reason their programme is of such an expansive comprehensiveness, including the arts, science, religion, philosophy and government in its reconstructionist system. And their quest is coloured by a pervasive mysticism that has its source in the perpetual appeal to the infinite (*das Unendliche*) that is their ultimate destination. Such pursuits were utterly alien to the French Romantics whose self-assertion assumed a more definite form in response to the immediate demands of the moment. Of these particular artistic reforms introduced by *romantisme* in France the Germans in turn had no need since they had already been accomplished by the Storm and Stress.

It almost seemed as if a combination of circumstances were conspiring to drive the *Frühromantiker* further into the extreme transcendentalism which they espoused. Firstly, this was the sole area where they were free to indulge in daring speculation with impunity; it thus acted as a vent for that restless urge forwards that was denied to them by the repressive climate of the small German states. In a sense therefore, the German Romantics' radical plans for the transformation of the whole world appear as a substitute for, and indeed a counterpart to, the political Revolution in France. Their contemporaneity with German Classicism also undoubtedly fostered their transcendentalism as a means of self-assertion. Unable as they were to offer a serious challenge to Goethe's sovereignty over the present, they invested their hopes in the future. Theirs was 'eine progressive Universalpoesie' ('a progressive universal poetry'), as Friedrich Schlegel defined it in the *Athenäum* (no. 116), where he stressed that: 'Die romantische Dichtart ist noch im Werden; ja das ist ihr eigentliches Wesen, dass sie ewig nur werden, nie vollendet sein kann' ('Romantic poetry is still in the process of becoming; therein indeed lies its very essence, that it is eternally evolving, never perfected'). Here the favourite Romantic notion of organic growth is used as a sort of defence of Romantic poetry. For that is what Friedrich Schlegel's contention in fact amounted to: an apologia for the shortcomings in the works of the *Frühromantiker* on the grounds that they marked only one, preliminary stage in the limitless advance to the future. The finite perfection that German literature had achieved in the *Klassik* of Goethe and Schiller would eventually be far outstripped by the infinite progressiveness of Romantic poetry which would reach out in eternal yearning until it attained the poeticization of the entire universe under the inspired leadership of the prophet-poet.

In their longing to poeticize the world the *Frühromantiker* proposed a speculative, metaphysical programme incomparably more extravagant than the relatively moderate concrete literary reforms advocated by the French. In spite of the sound and fury attendant on its birth, French Romanticism was in effect more modest in scope and objective than German Romanticism. This is the paradox inherent in the emergence of the two Romantic movements: that it was the seemingly quieter one that proved in the long run more deeply revolutionary than its rumbustious cousin. The overshadowing presence of Goethe, the forestalling impact of the Storm and Stress, and the closure of political expression drove the German Romantics onwards to adumbrate an aesthetic far ahead of their time. Just as the forces of retardation predominated in France, so a forward thrusting momentum emanated from the unique set of pressures operative in Germany. This is at the root of the time-lag, as well as of the differences in character, separating the emergence of the Romantic movements in the two countries. And it was this also that led to those later diagonal relationships in the nineteenth century, making French Romanticism the counterpart to the Storm and Stress, and French Symbolism that of the *Frühromantik*.

III

The Storm and Stress and French Romanticism

I

It was Goethe who first noted the affinity of the French Romanticism of the 1820s to the Storm and Stress. Eckermann's *Gespräche mit Goethe*, particularly in the years 1825–30, are studded with references to French literature. Goethe was widely read in the newer as well as in the Classical authors: the names of Diderot, Voltaire, Béranger, Chateaubriand, Hugo, Delille, Lamartine, Vigny and Mérimée all recur with some frequency. And even in relation to the most recent writing Goethe's judgements were extremely astute; as early as 4 January 1827, for instance, he was full of praise for the vivid pictures in Hugo's lyric poetry, whereas he directed the severest criticism at *Notre-Dame de Paris* (27 June 1831). According to Eckermann's testimony (6 March 1830), Goethe was also reading *Le Globe* and *Le Temps* 'seit mehreren Monaten mit dem grössten Eifer' ('for the past few months with the greatest avidity'). The combination of this good acquaintance with French literature together with his detachment as a foreign observer – not to mention his shrewdness and sagacity – gave Goethe an uncanny insight into the true direction and underlying implications of contemporary developments in France. From his vantage-point in Weimar, he was able to place the immediate surface controversies of Paris in their true perspective and to interpret their long-term significance. On 21 January 1827 Eckermann records the following comment:

'Die Franzosen', sagte er, 'machen sich heraus, und es ist der Mühe wert, dass man sich nach ihnen umsieht. Ich bin mit Fleiss darüber her, mir von dem Stande der neuesten französischen Literatur einen

Begriff zu machen und, wenn es glückt, mich auch darüber auszusprechen. Es ist mir höchst interessant zu sehen, dass diejenigen
Elemente bei ihnen erst anfangen zu wirken, die bei uns längst
durchgegangen sind.'

('The French', he said, 'are coming on and it is worth taking the
trouble to find out about them. I am assiduously trying to gain insight
into the most recent French literature and, if all goes well, to express
my views. It fascinates me to note that certain elements, which have
long since passed through and into our literature, are only just beginning to come into effect in theirs.')

That last rather cryptic sentence was amplified more than three years
later in the important conversation of 6 March 1830 when, Eckermann
reports, Goethe spoke

über den Zustand der neuesten französischen Literatur, die ihn sehr
interessiert. 'Was die Franzosen', sagte er, 'bei ihrer jetztigen
literarischen Richtung für etwas Neues halten, ist im Grunde weiter
nichts als der Widerschein desjenigen, was die deutsche Literatur seit
fünfzig Jahren gewollt und geworden.'

(about the state of the most recent French literature in which he is
very interested. 'What the French', he said, 'now regard as a new
tendency in their literature is basically nothing other than a reflection of what German literature has sought and attained in the last
fifty years.')

Working back fifty years from the time of Goethe's comment takes us
straight to the Storm and Stress movement of his own youth. That
Goethe was in fact referring to the Storm and Stress is clearly confirmed by the sentence immediately following the above quotation: 'Der
Keim der historischen Stücke, die bei ihnen jetzt etwas Neues sind, fin-
det sich schon seit einem halben Jahrhundert in meinem *Götz*' ('The
seed of the historical plays, which are now a novelty for them, was
already contained fifty years ago in my *Götz*'). Incidentally, Goethe
goes on specifically to deny any deliberate intent on the part of the
Germans to exert influence on the French. What he does suggest,
however, is that the innovations of the French protagonists of Romanticism in the 1820s were a counterpart to those of the *Stürmer und
Dränger* in Germany in the 1770s and early 1780s. That is the proposition to be investigated here.

The complexity of the *Sturm und Drang* is already hinted in its name – surely as strange a name as any ever given to a literary movement. Unfortunately, the subtle overtones of the German are not fully conveyed in either the accepted English equivalent, Storm and Stress, or in the customary French connotation, *assaut et élan*. The first part can be adequately translated without much difficulty: 'Storm' and *assaut* bring to mind the same aggressive momentum, the same rebelliousness as *Sturm*. The real problem arises over the rendering of the word *Drang*, partly no doubt because it shimmers with a variety of implied meanings in German, not all of which can be contained in any single English or French term. For *Drang* is connected with both *dringen* and *drängen*, intransitive and transitive forms, which have come to acquire not only a different sense, but also a different aura. *Dringen* means literally 'to press forward', 'to thrust'; as the noun derived from this verb, *Drang* is associated with urgency, hurry, violence, impetus, impulse, urge forwards. *Drängen*, on the other hand, in addition to its simple meaning of 'to press someone forward', has come to denote 'to urge', 'to hurry', 'to harass', 'to oppress', as in the common usage *unter Drang*, denoting 'under pressure'. Indeed, German dictionaries give at least three distinct meanings for *Drang*: firstly the physical 'crowd' or 'throng'; secondly, *das Bedrängende* ('the oppressive'), i.e. 'pressure', 'distress', 'misery'; and thirdly, *das zu etwas Drängende* ('that which impels to something'), i.e. 'impulsion', 'impulse', 'zeal', 'passionate ardour', 'craving', 'longing'. In the German phrase *Sturm und Drang, Drang* can therefore be interpreted either as complementary to *Sturm* or in contrast to it, either as a passionate impulse forwards or as a sign of distress. In translation, this highly appropriate equivocalness is almost inevitably lost. Certainly the French *élan*, with its idea of an upward movement, of enthusiasm and buoyancy, while not unapt, does omit any reference to the darker sides of the *Sturm und Drang*. The English 'Stress' seems rather closer to *Drang*, although it tends, in antithesis to *élan*, to lay too much emphasis on the notions of 'strain', 'tension', 'constraint', 'compulsion', an aspect that has come much to the fore recently in references to the 'stresses and strains' of modern life, and more specifically 'stress diseases'. If *élan* is too positive a rendering of *Drang*, 'stress' is too negative. Neither has quite the tantalizing ambivalence of *Sturm und Drang*. As a final ironic comment on the name, it is worth recalling that it was taken from a play by Klinger, who surely envisaged no such subtleties for he had originally intended to call his drama *Wirrwarr* (*Confusion*)!

Enigmatic though the phrase *Sturm und Drang* may be, it is in fact a wholly apposite name for the movement that encompasses Goethe's *Urfaust*, *Götz von Berlichingen*, *Werther*, his Strasbourg lyric poetry, the early plays of Schiller, the works of Lenz, the essays of Herder, as well as a host of lesser writings. It is a bewildering assortment that defies comprehension unless the fundamental dualism of the *Sturm und Drang* is clearly posited. In this context the ambiguity of the German word *Drang* is of paramount importance. For there is something schizophrenic in the *Sturm und Drang*, in the movement as a whole and in its individual manifestations. The aggressive momentum, the forward thrust implicit in *Sturm* and in one sense of *Drang* seems to be in contradiction to the withdrawal under outer and inner pressures that is strongly inferred in the second half of the German phrase. Or, to translate the problem into concrete terms, the dynamic energy of Götz von Berlichingen, Karl Moor and all the supermen in the plays of Klinger, Wagner and Leisewitz is the diametric opposite to the yielding melancholy of Werther and of Lenz's 'Waldbruder' ('sylvan brother'). On the one side stand the strident, extrovert heroes and on the other the passive, introvert anti-heroes. And both faces are equally typical of the *Sturm und Drang*.

Nowhere are these conflicting elements more plainly apparent or more closely interrelated than in the *Urfaust* fragment which dates from the early 1770s. Faust's later self-diagnosis of the two souls within himself ('Zwei Seelen wohnen, ach! in meiner Brust')[1] is already amply substantiated in the opening monologue of the play. In an emotional revulsion against the hollow sham of the life he has been leading, his dominant drive is towards rebellion. He thirsts for mysterious knowledge, instinctive insight into the innermost workings of the universe in place of the dry, sterile academic learning, in the value of which he no longer believes. Yet even as he expresses this craving, he sinks back into a mood of despair in which death seems the only solution. In its tempo and language too the elegaic apostrophe to the moon acts as a foil to the vehement outbursts with which the play's opening monologue begins. But Faust's despondency soon gives way to another wave of anger, heralded by the cry of sheer pain that breaks his reverie when a renewed awareness of his prison-like cell intrudes on his flight of fancy. The decomposing staleness that is the ambience of his study is objectified in the 'Tiergeripp und Totenbein'[2] ('skeletons of animals and of men'), symbols of death that offset the seeds ('Samen')[3] of living nature, for which he yearns. Through the recurrent pattern of contrasting images in this monologue, even more than through Faust's actual words, his dilemma is gradually uncovered in all its intensity. He cannot bear the living death of his existence, and yet he is not fully able to escape its shackles either. At one moment he gathers his strength in the hope of somehow breaking out of the vicious circle; at the next he relapses into dejection. The chasm between reality and aspiration appears unbridgeable. The more acutely Faust comes to realize the nature of his problem, the more conscious he feels of his tragic impotence. So he swings with uncompromising extremism and in rapid succession between the longing to savour life to the full and the temptation to end it abruptly in suicide, between a heightened confidence in his own personality and an abject self-doubt.

This polarity of rebelliousness and despair is the characteristic structure of the *Sturm und Drang*. In no other single figure are the two aspects – really the two facets of *Drang* – as tightly interwoven or as delicately balanced as in Faust. More commonly, the one or the other is uppermost: rebelliousness in Götz, Karl Moor, Ferdinand (in Schiller's *Kabale und Liebe*), Wild, the hero of Klinger's play *Sturm und Drang*, Simsone Grisaldo, the title figure again of another drama by Klinger, Guido, one of the brothers in *Julius von Tarent* by Leisewitz, not to mention Prometheus, Caesar and Mohamed, figures compellingly attractive to the young Goethe because of their unconventional greatness. In contrast to these activists are the men (or more frequently, youths) of feeling: first and foremost Werther, then Herz (whose name means 'heart') of Lenz's *Der Waldbruder*, Robert Hot in *Der Engländer* also by Lenz, Julius, the other brother in *Julius von Tarent*. The popularity at this time of the motif of the warring brothers (in *Die Räuber*, Klinger's *Die Zwillinge*, as well as *Julius von Tarent*) is a variant on the interest in the two sides within one and the same personality. For although either extrovert rebelliousness or introverted melancholy tends to predominate in these larger-than-life characters, often there are also traces of the complementary opposite, as with the male and female principle in the human being. Götz and Karl Moor have their moments of softness, of reflection, just as Werther and Herz occasionally rise up against their fate. This very alternation of mood is the special hallmark of the *Sturm und Drang*, together with the heightened tone, the passionate force of the language, and the depth of emotional involvement.

It is this fundamental timbre and colouring, as much as any specific themes or techniques, which French Romanticism has in common with the *Sturm und Drang*. Goethe chose the word 'Gährung' ('ferment') to describe the condition of French literature in a conversation recorded by Eckermann on 11 June 1825. Five years later, on 14 March 1830, he used a related image when he said of French literature: 'Ich vergleiche die jetzige literarische Epoche dem Zustande eines heftigen Fiebers' ('I compare the present period of literature to a state of violent fever'). He may in this later comment have had in mind his association of the Romantic with the diseased; more likely, however, in the light of his explicit *rapprochement* of contemporary French literature with that of Germany some fifty years earlier, he was referring to the parallelism of emotional temperature between the *Sturm und Drang* and French Romanticism. For the French Romantics have the same intensity as the *Stürmer und Dränger*, and with them too this almost excessive energy may burst forth in a grandiose urge to reconstruct the world, or it may eat inwards in a surfeit of despondency. There is here the same dichotomy between rebellion and despair, and again as in the *Sturm und Drang*, the two at times coalesce, although no single creation of French Romanticism embodies both sides as completely as Faust – which may, incidentally, account in part for the immense appeal of *Faust* to the French. The core, and indeed the ideal, of both movements is one of extravagance. Whatever the differences between them – and various differences do exist, as we shall see – in essence Goethe's intuitive judgement is borne out by detailed analysis: what is known as Romanticism in France is the counterpart of the *Sturm und Drang* in Germany in its temper, in many of its techniques and in its historical function.

II

The mainspring of the *Sturm und Drang* and of French Romanticism alike is the urge towards a creative renewal; both represent an upsurge after a period of relative quiescence. Neither is primarily a revolt against any specific restriction, although outbursts against various particular grievances do occur, and it is easy to take – in fact, to mistake – one of these issues as the centre of the whole movement. For instance, in France the form of the Alexandrine, the exact division of the verse-line, was the subject of much heated discussion, while in Germany arguments in favour of 'natural', in contrast to 'correct', language exercised a good many minds and covered a fair amount of paper. Both these matters were obviously important to the respective protagonists and to the movements concerned. But just as Coleridge's *Rime of the*

Ancient Mariner can hardly be summed up as a poem about a bird, so the *Sturm und Drang* and French Romanticism cannot be defined in terms of a revolt against this or that. The antagonism provoked by the so-called rules of literature was more a symptom of a total syndrome, more an expression of discontent than its ultimate source. In any case, these rules had never carried much authority in Germany, nor were they helped by the dismal failure of Gottsched's efforts. In France too, by the late eighteenth century already, they were, in practice, heeded with far less devotion than the fervent lip-service paid to them might suggest. There is considerable truth in Lessing's pertinent criticism of the French in the *Hamburgische Dramaturgie*,[4] particularly in his objection that they were indulging in all sorts of compromises in the observance of the rules by stretching the unities of time and place far beyond their original limits and having recourse to a variety of other subterfuges. The rules were laxly applied, yet they did still exist as established rules, and this in itself provoked the *Stürmer und Dränger* and the French Romantics to strong protests. But had the rules by then commanded even less respect, had the French Alexandrine enjoyed greater flexibility and German poetic language greater naturalness, they would no doubt have found other causes for dissent, other arenas to explode their pent-up anger.

For theirs was less a specific revolt than a general rebelliousness, in so far as a revolt is directed against some particular abuse, whereas rebelliousness is rather a state of mind, the readiness to erupt volcanically at any one of a number of points and often at apparently slight provocation. And the violence of that eruption may well seem out of proportion to the spark that triggers it off unless it is seen as just one, perhaps even incidental, manifestation of a much larger phenomenon. Some of the controversies of the *Stürmer und Dränger* and of the French Romantics, such as those regarding the position of the caesura in the Alexandrine and the necessity or otherwise of syntactical correctness, may appear exaggerated and tedious, mere molehills inflated into mountains. So they are, if taken at their face value, and not in their true perspective, as pretexts for that latent rebelliousness that could, and did, break out with extraordinary vehemence in relation to unexpected topics, just as strangely as those peculiar enthusiasms (e.g. for Ossian) which are an equally integral part of the picture. The targets of attack, though not picked arbitrarily, are in effect Aunt Sallies on which the rebellious vented their anger. But the real roots of that anger lay far deeper in the mortifying sense of restriction from which both the *Stürmer und Dränger* and the French Romantics suffered.

Their final objective was not so much flexibility of verse-form or
naturalness of language as simply freedom in every direction: personal,
social, political and religious as well as literary. Theirs was the desire to
create a new world, and in this sense Faust, with his grandiose longing
to explore and grasp the universe, is the epitome of their secret aspirations. So the specific, negative protest is subsidiary to a wider positive
programme. In the *Préface de Cromwell*, for instance, Hugo is concerned
with the present state of French drama within the context of his view
of world history; the new type of drama is introduced as the natural
complement to the new world. Stendhal uses the same approach in
Racine et Shakespeare when he argues for radical reform on the grounds
that the plays of 1670 are no more appropriate to 1823 than its clothes
or wigs. From the writings of Hamann and Herder the aim of radical
reorganization emerges even more clearly, and it is plain that for them
the literary revolution was accessory to a fundamental change in man
and his world. The rebelliousness characteristic of the *Stürmer und
Dränger* and of the French Romantics is therefore so multifarious and so
obdurate because it springs less from any well-defined grievances than
from a general and deep sense of dissatisfaction with the world in
which they lived.

It is perhaps easier to understand this discontent in mid-eighteenth-
century Germany than in post-revolutionary France. The circumstances
were very different in the two countries, and yet the ultimate effects
were curiously alike.

Any young man of intelligence and imagination brought up in mid-
eighteenth-century Germany was bound to be irked, angered and impeded by the reigning social order, particularly if he had been born
into the middle class, as were most of the *Stürmer und Dränger*. The
political splintering into umpteen small sovereign states, so important a
factor in the emergence of the Romantic movement, was equally
decisive for the climate of the *Sturm und Drang*. For it meant that the
subjects of each state were dependent on the personal whims of an absolute ruler, whose aim was often to imitate the court of Versailles – at
his subjects' expense, both literally and morally. Corruption,
favouritism and pettiness were rife in an ossified social structure, keenly
conscious of class distinctions, and intensifying them by a system of
private education for the high-born. Economic conditions too were often wretched for all but the wealthy, partly as a lingering result of the
Thirty Years' War when the country had been sucked dry, and partly
because industrial and commercial methods had hardly evolved ap-

preciably since the Middle Ages. One of the least remunerative professions was that of man of letters: even Goethe lost money with his private printing of *Götz von Berlichingen*, as did Schiller with his *Räuber*, and all the *Stürmer und Dränger* were forced to seek means of support other than by the pen. But this would surely have mattered less to them than the lack of encouragement – and patronage – from the courts which were still oriented towards France, and consequently neglected native artistic efforts. The theatre suffered most from this fashion for all things French, as the *Stürmer und Dränger* soon discovered to their cost and grief. All in all, as any reader of W. H. Bruford's *Germany in the Eighteenth Century* (Cambridge: Cambridge University Press, 1935) will conclude for himself, there was ample cause for becoming an 'angry young man' in the Germany of this period. Against this social background, as Roy Pascal has suggested, 'all the circumstances of life seemed to conspire to intensify that temperamental restlessness that is common to the Stürmer und Dränger'.[5] Sensitive young men were bound both to feel the stress of confinement, and to turn their energies into a storm of protest against corruption, class distinctions, inane conventions and sterile stereotypes of every kind. And this rebelliousness, prompted originally by the narrowness of their milieu, quickly grew for many into a way of life whose motto was simply: freedom. The dangers of this stance are plainly evident in some of the wilder plays as well as in the frenzied careers of several of the *Stürmer und Dränger*. Yet even when rebelliousness and the call for freedom deteriorated into chaos and libertinage, they are explicable as a desperate break-out from the prison of mid-eighteenth-century Germany.

In France that break-out had occurred, at least in theory, in the Revolution of 1789 which proclaimed the era of *liberté, fraternité* and *égalité*. But the triumph of these ideals was in fact as hollow as the outcome of the symbolic storming of the Bastille, which resulted in the release of five common criminals and two madmen, and not in the anticipated mass freeing of repressed idealists. The irony is curiously appropriate to the Revolution as a whole. While it would be wrong to belittle either the reforms within France consequent to the Revolution or its long-term effect throughout Europe, it would be equally mistaken naïvely to envisage 1789 as the dawn of a new epoch of freedom. The Revolution rapidly degenerated into the Reign of Terror, and before long France was in the authoritarian grip of the Emperor Napoleon. Far from heralding an age of free experimentation, the Revolution seems paradoxically to have led to a rule sterner than the *ancien régime* because it was so much better organized. Napoleon's police state is notorious; nor was there much greater liberty under the Restoration. In 1820, for instance, after the murder of the Duc de Berry, in a wave of panic-stricken repression, the freedom of the press, together with certain individual liberties, were suspended. A new electoral law, which introduced the double vote and reserved the final ballot for the highest taxpayers, reinforced the caution of a system that had fixed the minimum age of an elector at thirty, and of a deputy at forty. In short, the Revolution had by no means made a clean sweep of the old political and social attitudes nor of the artistic institutions; in somewhat altered forms, the monarchy, the Academy, the *Comédie française* all survived into the nineteenth century. As Musset so trenchantly summarized it, a king had perished in the Revolution, but not the monarchy itself. The new society had not become a reality, any more than had the new literature.

This failure of the 1789 Revolution, in spite of its noisy upheavals, really to achieve a radical and immediate social re-structuring of France inevitably produced a tremendous sense of disappointment in the succeeding generation. 'The single propelling force of the age was, to use modern terminology, the trauma of revolution',[6] J. L. Talmon has astutely commented on the period 1815–48. That trauma sprang from the incompleteness of the 1789 Revolution, and it bred 'a Revolutionary tradition and myth, and a deep-seated, passionate conviction that the Revolution had not really come to an end. It had only been overpowered for a while.'[7] Hence the constantly renewed revolutionary momentum of the France of the first half of the nineteenth century, characterized by innumerable plots, conspiracies, coups and revolts, only one of which, the 1830 July Revolution, managed to effect a change of regime. Perhaps it is no accident that this single successful revolt coincided with the final, symbolic breakthrough of Romanticism in the French theatre. For the protagonists of French Romanticism in the 1820s were among those who laboured most acutely under this 'trauma of revolution'.

A brilliant sketch of the young Romantics' problems *vis-à-vis* the past, the present and the future is given by Musset in the second chapter of the novel that bears the significant title *La Confession d'un enfant du siècle* (*The Confessions of a Child of the Century*) with its hinted allusion to the *mal du siècle*. Octave, 'the child of the century', is of the 'génération ardente, pâle, nerveuse'[8] that grew up during the Napoleonic Wars. With the fall of Napoleon, the giant who had shaken the very foundations of the world, the past was shattered, the future still a void, and the present a frightening chaos that Musset personifies in the figure of an 'ange du crépuscule qui n'est ni la nuit ni le jour; ils le trouvèrent assis sur un sac de chaux plein d'ossements, serré dans le manteau des égoistes, et grelottant d'un froid terrible. L'angoisse de la mort leur entra dans l'âme à la vue de ce spectre moitié momie et moitié foetus'[9] ('angel of twilight, neither night nor day; she was found sitting on a sack of lime full of bones, wrapped in the egotists' coat, and shivering in the terrible cold. A deathly anguish fills the soul at the sight of this ghost, half mummy and half foetus'). Only a poet as imaginative as Musset could conjure up so unforgettable an image of his contemporaries' dilemma. The youth of his day was dogged by a sense of emptiness; although former institutions had been revived after the fall of Napoleon, faith in them had evaporated. 'Tout ce qui était n'est plus; tout ce qui sera n'est pas encore. Ne cherchez pas ailleurs le secret de nos maux'[10] ('All that had been no longer existed; all that is to be does not yet exist. Do not seek elsewhere the source of our ills'): that is Octave's conclusion to his summary of his generation's problems.

The young French Romantics of the 1820s were thus facing a somewhat different historical constellation to that in which their counterparts in mid-eighteenth-century Germany were placed. Perhaps their situation was even less enviable than that of the *Stürmer und Dränger* for France had had its political Revolution, and it had not ushered in a Utopia. With their expectations of *liberté, fraternité* and *égalité* unfulfilled, indeed their hopes cheated, they were as unable to accept the *status quo* as the Germans of the 1770s. Different though the background circumstances were, the result was the same in both cases: a sense of acute frustration and profound discontent that burst out as a vehement rebelliousness in an attempt to find a meaningful salvation. And it was the bond of their common rebellion that forged the *Stürmer und Dränger* into allies, as it did the French Romantics. The sound and fury of this rebelliousness seems at times disproportionate to the object under attack because the explosive force of what was in effect an existential revolution was in both movements an occasion precipitated, in a kind of *pars pro toto*, on to one small segment of the whole complex. So the impassioned pleas of the *Stürmer und Dränger* and of the French Romantics for a fresh, more natural form of expression, their rebellion against the conventions of literary language, were really expressive and symbolic of their thirst for a new way of life.

This rebelliousness erupted most fiercely in the fields of aesthetics and of drama in both the *Sturm und Drang* and French Romanticism. Here there is a clear parallelism between the two movements. The reasons for this choice of arena are easy enough to surmise. To begin with, drama was traditionally the most elevated and prestigious literary form so that triumph in the theatre was tantamount to the victory of the new school. But if drama was the most important genre to conquer, it was also the most difficult. The theatre, which had been the strongest bastion of Neo-classical authoritarianism in seventeenth- and eighteenth-century France, remained even in the early nineteenth century the last fortress of scholasticism, as Emile Deschamps called it in the preface to his *Etudes françaises et étrangères* (1828). In the polemics of the 1820s the *Comédie française* was frequently compared to the Bastille, an emblem of the old regime, whose capture alone could denote the total breakthrough of Romanticism in France. Writing in *Le Globe* on 11 June 1825, Cyprien Desmarais refers to drama as 'le véritable champ de bataille' ('the real battlefield') between the Classicists and the Romantics. This explains why the rebelliousness of the French Romantics centres on the drama, and in aesthetics on dramatic criticism in an attempt to enunciate and justify their innovations to their audience. In Germany too the emphasis was on drama, though for somewhat different reasons. The theatre had become the focal point of the German endeavours to create a national literature. Gottsched's importation of foreign, Neo-classical plays had, by its very erroneousness, acted as a catalyst to German initiative. Lessing's efforts to establish a German national theatre in Hamburg, as well as his own plays, formed important starting-points. But the courts continued to favour the French theatre, and there was also still a dearth of native German plays. The mastery of the German stage by characteristically German drama thus became as much of a necessity – and of a symbol – for the assertion of the *Sturm und Drang* as it was for French Romanticism.

In both cases, a revolution in poetics prepared for, and accompanied, the decisive offensive in drama. The guiding lines of this revolution in poetics in Germany of the 1770s and the France of the 1820s are remarkably alike. The recurrent *leitmotif* is the cry for freedom. The German *Sturm und Drang* and French *romantisme* were envisaged by their respective protagonists as movements of liberation. The ideal of freedom was thus hoisted as a flag to be waved on every occasion. Hamann already posited in one of his aphorisms: 'Die Freiheit ist das Maximum und Minimum aller unserer Naturkräfte'[11] ('Freedom is the summit and the threshold of all our natural powers'), thereby framing the whole of the *Sturm und Drang* in the concept of freedom. The poet's absolute freedom to express himself at will is the fundamental doctrine of the *Sturm und Drang*, explicit or implicit in every facet of its aesthetics. It inspires Goethe's essay *Zum Shakespeares Tag* of 1771 and Herder's rhapsody on Shakespeare in *Von deutscher Art und Kunst* (1773), both of which extol Shakespeare as the prototype of the dramatist who created masterpieces not according to any set rules, but in divine freedom. For Stendhal and the French Romantics too Shakespeare was a cipher for freedom: in his *Racine et Shakespeare* (1823) Stendhal used the example of Shakespeare as a stick with which to beat the Neo-classical routine in drama. 'La routine' was also the foe in the eyes of Duvergier de Hauranne, while the Jerusalem of the Romantics' aspirations, 'c'est la liberté'.[12] But by far the most ardent apostle of freedom was the youthful Hugo who repeatedly pleaded for 'la liberté de l'art contre le despotisme des systèmes, des codes et des règles'[13] ('the freedom of art as opposed to the tyranny of systems, laws and rules'), and who defined Romanticism quite simply as 'le *libéralisme* en littérature'.[14] His demand 'que la poésie ait la même devise que la politique: TOLÉRANCE ET LIBERTÉ'[15] ('that poetry should have the same motto as political life: TOLERANCE AND FREEDOM') would have been heartily endorsed by the *Stürmer und Dränger* who were fighting for the same freedoms of the individual.

Beside this cardinal unanimity of aim, the Storm and Stress and the French Romantics are alike also in the means they propounded to achieve that freedom. The key words here are 'genius' and 'nature', and again the parallelism is extraordinarily close. The creative genius, as exemplified by Shakespeare, soars above all the old rules in a God-like freedom; unfettered by outer shackles of any kind, he lives and creates solely according to the prompting of his instincts. This insistence on the rights and powers of genius is common to the *Sturm und Drang* and to French Romanticism; the term 'Genie', so prominent in the writings of Hamann, Herder, Goethe and Lenz, finds an echo in the 'génie' of Hugo, Mme de Staël, Constant and Vigny. The examples of its occurrence are much too frequent to cite in detail. And in so far as genius is to have any external mentor, it must be 'nature' in the sense of naturalness. On this point the French Romantics held views virtually identical to those of the *Stürmer und Dränger*. For Hamann true poetry could reside only in a natural manner of expression, while the cry 'Natur! Natur!' rings out from Goethe's and Herder's critical essays as the supreme term of praise for any artist. Both Hugo in the *Préface de*

Cromwell and Vigny in the *Lettre à Lord xxx* put forward the same ideal: 'Le poète, insistons sur ce point, ne doit donc prendre conseil que de la nature, de la vérité et de l'inspiration, qui est aussi une vérité et une nature'[16] ('The poet, let me emphasize this point, must seek guidance only from nature, truth and inspiration, which is also truth and nature'), Hugo wrote; or more briefly, as a battle-cry: 'La nature donc! La nature et la vérité'[17] ('Nature then! nature and truth'). Similarly Vigny, like Constant in his *Réflexions sur la tragédie*, asserted that the art of the future must be based on truth to nature.

This stress on naturalness among the *Stürmer und Dränger* and the French Romantics is obviously a reaction against the rule-ridden Neo-classical theatre. The arguments against the three unities advanced by Hugo and by Duvergier de Hauranne (in a series of articles in *Le Globe* of 1825–6) are strongly reminiscent in content and tone of Gerstenberg and even of Lessing. The parallel extends beyond the merely negative aspects of rebellion. For the aesthetics of the *Stürmer und Dränger* and of the French Romantics really amount to a demand for an art-form that is at once spontaneous and realistic. The revolution in poetics in Germany in the 1770s and in France in the 1820s, starting from a scorn for the stale *status quo*, reached out far beyond its age to lay the foundations of the great creative renewal of European literature in the nineteenth century. In this respect, i.e. in the historical perspective, the French critics of the 1820s fulfilled the same function of liberating catalysts as their German counterparts in the 1770s.

This fundamental coincidence of ideals between two groups separated by the Rhine as well as by fifty years is all the more striking when the differences in presentation are taken into account. In Germany the revolution in poetics happened almost casually, so to speak; the crucial statements of doctrine are carelessly scattered in letters, journals, asides and fragmentary essays. Indeed, the very word 'statement' seems too formal for the enthusiastic ejaculations characteristic of the *Sturm und Drang*. For, as Pascal has pointed out, 'the Stürmer und Dränger not only freed themselves from the artistic conventions of polite society, but also from every dogmatic approach to aesthetics. Abstract and general definitions were in their view the very antithesis of the energetic, dynamic nature of beauty.'[18] Herder alone attempted a somewhat more systematic exposition of his views, yet he too soon veered into the subjective irrationalism that is the crux of the *Sturm und Drang*. So it is the intrinsic 'fire and urgency'[19] of these notions that is their salient quality; they are grandiose and enticing, but at the same time strangely elusive, largely because their essence lies in that very state of intoxicated enthusiasm in which they surge forth.

In comparison with the Germans of the 1770s, the French of the 1820s are rather more systematic. They too write in an aura of enthusiasm, though with a militancy more pronounced than is usually found with the *Stürmer und Dränger*. For the French always remain aware of their fight against their Neo-classical tradition. The vocabulary is often patently aggressive as in Hugo's exhortation: 'Aux armes, prose et vers! formez vos bataillons', which echoes the *Marseillaise* and underlines the parallel between the political and literary Revolutions, as does his famous claim:

Je fis souffler un vent révolutionnaire.
Je mis un bonnet rouge au vieux dictionnaire.[20]

(I made a revolutionary wind blow.
I put the red cap of liberty on to the old dictionary.)

Because of their conscious opposition to an established system, the French Romantics were more programmatic in their approach than the *Stürmer und Dränger* ever needed to be. In their many journals and prefaces the French produced more or less coherent manifestoes such as hardly exist in the Germany of the 1770s where the literary circumstances were so different. While the Germans were scattering seeds in a fallow field, the French Romantics were to a large extent formulating a counter-system to displace that of Neo-classicism; the word *romantique* was used in the 1820s 'pour désigner toute composition contraire au système suivi en France depuis Louis XIV'[21] ('to denote any work contrary to the system established in France since Louis XIV').

This divergence of aim may also account for the relative rationalism and concreteness of French Romantic theory as compared to the grander but vaguer German aspirations. For the French had to convert their opponents, and to do this they had to grapple with specific literary, and more particularly, theatrical problems. A good example of their approach is found in *Racine et Shakespeare*, in which Stendhal engages in discussion with an adherent to Classicism and endeavours to win him over to the Romantic viewpoint by means of reasoned arguments in favour of a greater freedom in drama. Even Hugo's *Préface de Cromwell*, that declaration of artistic independence in France, seems mild and orderly beside, say, Herder's panegyric of Shakespeare, not to mention the aphorisms of Hamann, which proclaim irrational subjectivism as much in their manner as in their matter. Yet these differences, that arise from and reflect the dissimilarity of the literary background to the *Sturm und Drang* in Germany and to *romantisme* in France, are of minor importance in the total picture. They illustrate the way in which the expression of ideas is conditioned by milieu without, however, detracting from the basic parallelism in the poetics of the Storm and Stress and French Romanticism. When Duvergier de Hauranne, writing in *Le Globe* of 24 March 1825, summarized the essence of the new school as 'vie, activité, mouvement en avant' ('life, activity, forward-thrusting movement'), he gave a definition that is as applicable to the *Sturm und Drang* as to *romantisme*.

III

This turmoil of life, activity and forward-thrusting movement found its main outlet in drama. A major affinity exists between the Storm and Stress and French Romanticism in that drama was central to both (in contrast to its peripheral role in German – and English – Romanticism). Drama was the primary forum of protest in the Germany of the 1770s and early 1780s as in the France of the late 1820s and early 1830s. In the content, direction and form of that protest there are multiple resemblances between the two movements as well as certain divergences, which together amount to a striking instance of a counterpart relationship.

The most obvious point of contact is in the character of the main figures, many of whom are, like their creators, young men for one reason or another at loggerheads with the society of their age. Their revolt stems from their idealism so that even when they are thrown into the role of bandits and law-breakers, they maintain a kind of inner virtue, a nobility of intent that justifies the criminal means they are at times forced to adopt in order to achieve their righteous ends. These young men then are portrayed as fighters for freedom, for natural justice, for the rights of man, especially the rights of the heart, against the moral corruption, the misguided laws and the twisted conventions of society. Frequently they have in some mysterious way been wronged by society so that they appear as outcasts, victims of a malignant fate, which they are determined to avenge. For these heroes of the drama, in contrast to their brothers in the novel, as we shall see, have the extrovert energy to rebel against the situation in which they are imprisoned. Their awareness of their absolute goodness, on a level above the accepted social criteria, inspires their fight even to the point of self-sacrifice; though the plays often end with the technical defeat, even the death of the hero, no doubt is left either of his moral victory or of the worthiness of his cause. From the superman's single-handed crusade against the conspiracy in which he is trapped there emerges loud and clear the message of these plays: a plea for individual freedom and for a radical revision of social standards and ethical values.

The prototype of these heroes is Goethe's Götz von Berlichingen, who was based on a Franconian knight of the early sixteenth century, the time of the Peasants' Revolt in Germany. At the beginning of the play Götz has already withdrawn from the court in anger at its intrigues, its duplicity and its greed; at his own castle he cherishes forthrightness, humanity and purity. In a series of contrasting scenes that lead up to the main action, Goethe vividly sets off the atmosphere, values and speech and the court against those of Götz's domain at Jaxthausen. In the eyes of the court Götz is a troublesome, dangerous fellow, an enemy of the established system, suspect because he refuses blindly to play its game. 'Er hat eine hohe unbändige Seele' ('He has a lofty, untamed soul'), Adelheid, one of the court ladies, rightly says of him (Act II, scene vi). It is the combination of loftiness and impetuosity that causes Götz to come to grief. Without going into the details of the plot, suffice it to say that Götz is persuaded to assume the leadership of the peasants in their revolt. He decides to do so because of his ardent sympathy for the ideals for which he believes them to be fighting. Yet he takes this momentous step with some reluctance since he thereby becomes technically a traitor, breaking his vow of allegiance to the Emperor. That the peasants in turn betray their promises to Götz by savage looting and marauding is an ironical comment on his predicament and on human nature, but it does not invalidate Götz's struggle nor diminish the nobility of his character. On the contrary, Götz stands out as a bastion of uprightness caught between the baseness of the hypocritical court on the one side and the scarcely lesser wickedness of the self-seeking peasants on the other. His tragedy lies perhaps in the fact that he is, as his loyal friend, Sickingen, realizes 'zu ehrlich' ('too honest' – Act IV, scene iii), too true to his inner convictions and too unwilling to compromise. Such loftiness is a provocation to his depraved age, which must needs destroy him in self-protection. To the very end, however, Götz remains not only faithful to his ideals, but also convinced of his fundamental innocence in spite of all appearances.

In reply to the indictment of rebellion against the Emperor, he vehemently protests 'Das ist nicht wahr. Ich bin kein Rebell' ('That is not true. I am not a rebel' – Act IV, scene ii), for he sees himself as a reforming champion of liberty, upholding the rights of the repressed, and not as a destructive rabble-rouser, the role assigned to him. His sister pleads for his life on these same grounds: 'er ist unschuldig, so strafbar er scheint' ('he is innocent, however guilty he may seem' – Act V, scene x). When Götz dies with the word 'Freiheit' ('freedom') on his lips, and his sister adds the comment 'Edler Mann! Edler Mann! Wehe dem Jahrhundert, das dich von sich stiess!' ('Noble being! noble being! woe to the age that rejected you!' – Act V, scene xiv), the play's theme and message are abundantly clear.

Many of the heroes in the drama of the *Sturm und Drang* and of French Romanticism are brothers to Götz, although none equals him in stature. Götz towers over them in many senses: physically and morally, as a dramatic creation, and also as a model. This is not the place, nor is it my intention, to investigate the influence of *Götz von Berlichingen* on Goethe's contemporaries and successors at home and abroad. That the play did make a tremendous impact, particularly on his fellow *Stürmer und Dränger*, is beyond doubt. It was translated into French for inclusion in Friedel and Bonneville's *Nouveau théâtre allemand* (1782–5) and on several later occasions, but it was apparently less enthusiastically received than *Werther* or *Faust*, or indeed Schiller's *Die Räuber*, which enjoyed staggering success and popularity.[22] These problems of the transmission of concepts and styles are, however, marginal to the central concern of this study, namely the question of the affinity between the *Sturm und Drang* and French Romanticism. And that affinity is very obvious in the dramatic hero. His fight for the rights of the individual in the impassioned plea for freedom, his rebellion against society and his criticism of its false standards: these are the features common to Götz, to Schiller's Karl Moor (in *Die Räuber*) and Ferdinand (in *Kabale und Liebe*), to the hero of Klinger's *Sturm und Drang* who bears the self-explanatory name of Wild, to Simsone Grisaldo in the play of that name also by Klinger, to Hugo's Hernani and Ruy Blas, Musset's Lorenzo and to Alexandre Dumas's Antony.

Karl Moor's very first words in *Die Räuber*, 'Mir ekelt vor diesem tintenklecksenden Säkulum, wenn ich in meinem Plutarch lese von grossen Menschen' ('I am disgusted by this ink-stained century when I read about great men in Plutarch' – Act I, scene ii), set the tone of his bitter onslaught on his own age, coupled with an idealization of greatness typical of the Storm and Stress. Karl's repeated outbursts against the society of his day spring partly from the injustices that have been inflicted on him through the machinations of his evil brother, and partly from an innate nobility very similar to that of Götz. He too becomes leader of a band of robbers in an attempt to redress the inequality between men. 'Mein Geist dürstet nach Taten, mein Atem nach Freiheit' ('my spirit thirsts for deeds, my soul for freedom' – Act I, scene ii), he exclaims. Indeed, his whole figure and person are of the larger-than-life dimension of the so-called *Kraftmensch* (mighty man) favoured by the Storm and Stress and epitomized in Goethe's Prometheus, whose greatness rivals even that of the Gods, to whom he addresses his defiant self-assertion:

> Hier sitz' ich, forme Menschen
> Nach meinem Bilde,
> Ein Geschlecht, das mir gleich sei,
> Zu leiden, zu weinen,
> Zu geniessen und zu freuen sich
> Und dein nicht zu achten,
> Wie ich!

> (Here I sit, shaping human beings
> According to my image, '
> A race that will be like me,
> In suffering, in tears,
> In joys and pleasures,
> And in defiance of you,
> Like me!)

Prometheus, as the dual symbol of rebellious independence and of a free re-structuring of the world according to one's own ideals, is the prototype of all the Storm and Stress champions of liberty: from Götz and Karl Moor to Klinger's Wild who has left the corrupt Old World to join the army of liberation in America, and even to the love-lorn Ferdinand in *Kabale und Liebe* who demands freedom of choice in consonance with his heart's natural instincts and who dies rather than accept the perverted code of the 'insect souls' at his father's court. Their disgust at the reigning social order acts as a catalyst to their natural nobility that bursts forth in a frenzy of reforming zeal. More sinned against than sinning in spite of their violent fire-spitting, the rebels of the *Sturm und Drang* drama channel their thwarted idealism into a social criticism as searing as their own sense of justice.

In most of the essentials the heroes of the French Romantic theatre are close relatives of the Storm and Stress *Kraftmensch*. Hernani, who defines himself as 'une force qui va' ('a dynamic force' – Act III, scene iv), who has been dispossessed of his rightful inheritance, has become a bandit like Karl Moor; yet his actions are eloquent testimony to his chivalric code of honour, even to the surrender of his life in response to Ruy Gomez's horn in fulfilment of his earlier promise. Although he is technically an outlaw with a price on his head and is called a 'rebelle' no fewer than eight times in the course of the play, his virtue is never in question. His rumbustious energy and violent temperament match those of his counterparts in the Storm and Stress, as does a certain menacing sense of ill-fatedness. For in his final downfall at the hands of Ruy Gomez after his honourable reinstatement by the Emperor and his marriage to Doña Sol there is an underlying irony reminiscent of the betrayal of Götz by the peasants after his release from prison by Sickingen. The death of both could be attributed to an over-developed sense of lofty duty which results in a certain atrophy of the selfish instinct of self-preservation.

While the rebelliousness of Hernani easily matches that of the Storm and Stress heroes, the accompanying element of social criticism is rather less to the fore. By and large this is true of most French Romantic drama in contrast to the majority of the plays of the *Sturm und Drang*, in which overt attacks on the social system are so prominent. It may well be that some of the most vexing issues of the Germany of the 1770s had been, at least partially, resolved in the reforms in France following the Revolution. So there is no immediate counterpart to such dramas as Wagner's *Die Kindermörderin* and *Die Soldaten* by Lenz, both of which deal with the theme of seduction, betrayal and dishonour, nor to the class tensions on which pivot *Kabale und Liebe*, Lenz's *Der Hofmeister* and *Die Soldaten*. All these plays testify to the impact of the bourgeois drama which Lessing had imported from England with *Miss Sara Sampson* and which had introduced the problems of the middle classes on to the German stage at a time when French drama still centred primarily on the court. Curiously enough, neither the Revolution nor the Romantics' advocacy of freedom and naturalness altered the situation to any marked degree. French Romantic drama operates on a far higher social level than that of the Storm and Stress, continuing to move predominantly among kings and nobles, as Neo-classical drama had done. This means that such social criticism as does occur tends to come from those outside the established order. Hernani, himself a noble and as proud as any of his lineage, subscribes to the code of his class; on the other hand, Ruy Blas, the servant, and even more Antony, the socially unplaced, do voice social criticism as part of their rebellion. Ruy Blas indeed rebels doubly: first, when he is elevated by his master's intrigues and by the Queen's love to the rank of first minister he lets forth an indignant tirade (Act III, scene ii) against the Spanish aristocracy who are bleeding the country to death for their own profit and pleasure; and then he rebels in another, more personal manner when he reveals his true identity and standing in the penultimate scene of the play: 'Je m'appelle Ruy Blas, et je suis un laquais!' ('My name is Ruy Blas, and I am a lackey!' – Act V, scene iii). This second rebellion leads virtually to the collapse of Don Salluste's plot for he had reckoned on being able to use his servant without any reaction, let alone outspoken revolt, on the latter's part. Contrary to what was expected of his class, the bearing of Ruy Blas is, within his own sphere, as much that of the defiant, independent man of action as that of Götz. His sacrificial death by his own hand to save the Queen's honour is in the best tradition of the hero noble and virtuous beneath his blustering rebellion.

Alexandre Dumas's Antony, on the other hand, takes the more dubious action of killing his mistress in order to preserve her reputation! This strange denouement is presented as the only possible solution to a plot that is in any case so improbable as to verge on melodrama. The action is largely motivated by the character of Antony himself. From his first appearance, bespattered with the blood he has shed in stopping Adèle's runaway horses, thereby saving her life, he is obviously a man of violent deeds; and sure enough, he soon inflicts further injuries on himself so as to be allowed to stay in Adèle's house, while later (in Act III, scene vii) he breaks into her room at an inn from a balcony, having carefully rigged the whole set-up. This peculiar behaviour is attributed to Antony's background, or rather, his lack of background; for he is, as he himself reveals, a foundling, 'sans nom' (Act II, scene iii) and therefore without the social standing that would have admitted him as a suitable husband for Adèle. In spite of his wealth, his good education, his aristocratic aura and his noble heart, he is condemned to remain on the fringe of society. Consequently he is 'au-dessus des préjugés' ('above the pre-conceived notions' – Act III, scene iv) and arrogates to himself the right to act as he pleases. Whereas

Adèle, integrated as she is into the social fabric, feels bound to convention: concerned from the beginning about appearances 'aux yeux du monde' ('in the eyes of the world' – Act I, scene iv), she makes her attitude clear to Antony when she tells him: 'Le monde a ses lois, la société ses exigences; qu'elles soient des devoirs ou des préjugés, les hommes les ont faites telles, et, eussé-je le désir de m'y soustraire, il faudrait encore que je les acceptasse' ('the world has its laws and society its demands; be they duties or prejudices, men have made them so, and even if I wished to except myself from them, I should still have to accept them' – Act II, scene v). The stiltedness of those rather unusual past subjunctive tenses underlines the artificiality of her stance. These are the same arguments about the role of conventions as in the plays of the *Sturm und Drang*; and for all her moralizing, Adèle in practice submits to convention no more than does Marie in *Die Soldaten* or Evchen in *Die Kindermörderin* or Faust's Gretchen. Although social criticism is less abundant and virulent in the plays of French *romantisme* than in those of the Storm and Stress, it is by no means absent, and its lines of attack are often the same as across the Rhine. Above all, the development of personal rebellion into social criticism is as evident in the heroes of the French Romàntic theatre as in those of the *Sturm und Drang*; the difference lies in a greater emphasis on the personal in France and on the social in Germany.

The parallelism between the drama of the Storm and Stress and of French Romanticism extends beyond similarities of content. The rebelliousness that is at the heart of both movements explodes most startlingly in the form of the dramas. Here the affinity is deep and close. In the first place, the *Stürmer und Dränger* and the French Romantics alike eschewed the traditional division of plays into tragedy or comedy. They generally gave their plays the neutral label *Schauspiel* (play) and *drame* respectively, and they also had the courage to practise the mingling of the genres which they preached. Although most of the plays are tragic in tendency, they are not of an unrelieved blackness; a lighter note is introduced, for instance, with the celebration of the peasant wedding in *Götz von Berlichingen* (Act II, scene x), with the phantasies of La Feu in *Sturm und Drang*, the comedy of errors in Act IV of *Ruy Blas* and the king's caustic reply in *Hernani* (Act I, scene ii) as he emerges from his closet hiding-place:

Hernani

Que faisiez-vous là?

Don Carlos
Moi? Mais, à ce qu'il paraît,
Je ne chevauchais pas à travers la forêt.

(What were you doing there?
            Me? Well, it is plain
That I was not riding through the forest.)

This ironic note is sustained when Don Carlos complains a few lines later that in the closet

Mais j'entendais très mal et j'étouffais très bien.
Et puis, je chiffonnais ma veste à la française.

(But I heard very badly and I suffocated very well.
And besides, I was crumpling my fine tunic.)

If comic touches enter into serious situations, the reverse is even more often the rule. The purported comedies of Musset, such as *Les Caprices de Marianne* and *On ne badine pas avec l'amour*, have a dark undertone which intermittently breaks out on to the surface; the tragic potential is never lost from sight. It becomes dominant in Lenz's *Die Soldaten*, which was originally intended as a comico-serious portrayal of garrison life.

This blend of the tragic and the comic is only one example of the innovations introduced into drama by the *Stürmer und Dränger* and the French Romantics. In part at least this dramatic renewal sprang from a revolt against previously accepted dramatic conventions which included the separation of the tragic and the comic. These conventions had ossified into a dogma in France, and Gottsched had tried hard to establish their authority in Germany too. So the young generations of the 1770s on the Eastern bank of the Rhine and of the 1820s on the Western bank were provoked to an iconoclastic opposition. But another factor was also crucial in shaping the drama of the Storm and Stress and of French Romanticism: the impact of Shakespeare in both countries. This was in many ways so important that it will have to be examined in greater detail later. For the present suffice it to say that Shakespeare was the divinity whom the dramatists of the *Sturm und Drang* and of French Romanticism worshipped and on whom they modelled their dramatic practices. In Shakespeare they hailed the embodiment of their own creed: a genius creating masterpieces freely and naturally at the prompting of his innermost instincts. The emulation of Shakespeare combined with the rebellion against the past to determine the form of their dramas. The mingling of the tragic and the comic, for instance, had its source in the ribaldry of the grave-diggers in *Hamlet* and in the drunken porter in *Macbeth*, scenes that filled the Neo-classicists with real horror because they infringed on the consistently elevated tone considered indispensable to tragedy. Similarly, the emancipation from all rules and specifically from the notorious three unities was a sloughing of restrictions, inspired by the need for freedom and backed by the example of Shakespeare.

The abandonment of the unities in most of the plays of the Storm and Stress and of French Romanticism meant more than the lengthening of the duration of the action and the multiplication of location, although this in itself was striking, indeed shocking, particularly in France. To allow five days to elapse between Acts I and II, three months between Acts III and IV, to site Act III in a different town, and what is more, to make no bones about it, as in *Antony*: this was tantamount to an act of treason against the French tradition! Yet compared to *Götz von Berlichingen* it is very moderate; critics tireless in counting the number of scenes in *Götz* arrive at figures that range from the mid-fifties into the sixties depending on their choice of the first or the revised, more sedate version. Nor is *Götz* an isolated example of such agitated, incessant movement in a staccato series of short scenes. This dramatic form, which reflects the temperamental restlessness of the *Stürmer und Dränger*, occurs in many of their plays, notably in the first three acts of Wagner's *Die Kindermörderin* and throughout Klinger's *Otto* and *Sturm und Drang*, which well deserves its original title *Wirrwarr* (*Confusion*). Herein lies one of the great dangers of that freedom so vociferously claimed by the *Stürmer und Dränger* and the French Romantics: that it can, and often did, result in an undisciplined turbulence close to melodrama and even to farce. The constant storming about, the ranting, the violence, the mysteries and surprises certainly produce a theatre much livelier and more full-blooded than its Neo-classical predecessor, but the pitfalls attendant on this manner are not always successfully avoided. Certainly the lesser dramatists frequently fall victim to excesses that evoke unintentional laughter from the audience, while the better constructed plays too are not devoid of a melodramatic streak. The arrival of Don César down the chimney in Act IV of *Ruy Blas*, the concealment of Don Carlos in a closet in Act I of *Hernani* and of Hernani in a hidden recess behind a picture in Act III, the disguises and revelations in both plays, the exaggerations of character and situation in *Die Räuber*, the violence of Klinger's *Die Zwillinge* and *Simsone Grisaldo*, not to mention the eccentricities of *Antony* and of *Sturm und Drang*: all these are cogent reminders of the undercurrent of melodrama in the Germany of the Storm and Stress and the France of the Romantic period. The numerous plays of Kotzebue and of Pixérécourt enjoyed tremendous popularity in their respective countries. In their parallel exploitation of freedom the dramas of the Storm and Stress and of French Romanticism once more show the full extent of the affinity between the two movements.

The ideal of naturalness, also inherent in both, leads to further similarities between their plays. Truth to nature takes the form of particularity of milieu, *couleur locale*, as it was known in France, and of the aspiration to more natural language. Here too the opposition to the traditional norms of formal drama merges into the new orientation towards the Shakespearean pattern. This is well illustrated in the inclusion of popular crowd scenes in *Götz von Berlichingen* and in Hugo's *Cromwell*, a play as impossible to stage as the first version of *Götz*. Often in the drama of the Storm and Stress it is these popular scenes that are the vehicle of local colour as, for instance, in the portrayal of garrison life in *Die Soldaten* and in the seduction in the inn-cum-brothel at the opening of *Die Kindermörderin*. The same realistic effect is sought in the French Romantic theatre by stage settings and descriptions of costumes and movements as detailed as those in the Naturalistic drama of the late nineteenth and early twentieth centuries. Such precise instructions are necessitated by the preference, again shared by the Storm and Stress and French Romanticism, for either the Renaissance or the modern period, in contrast to the vaguely Classical topics previously customary in drama. While the elegant simplicity of the Neo-classical theatre was aimed at the intellect, the drama of the Storm and Stress and of French Romanticism appealed to the eye through its movement and spectacle.

Its effect on the ear was more like an assault. The coarseness of Götz's notorious reply to the Emperor has become proverbial in German. It is typical of the earthiness of the language used by the *Stürmer und Dränger*, who not only portrayed ordinary, lower-class people, but did not hesitate to put into their mouths the kind of speech in which they would most naturally express themselves. So the dialogue of Storm and Stress drama is of a vigour rarely equalled anywhere. Not always can it be as scintillatingly inventive as in Karl Moor's outbursts at the beginning of *Die Räuber*, but it is always varied, reflecting differences of social atmosphere in its tone and vocabulary, and admitting common parlance onto the German stage in an early anticipation of nineteenth-century realism. *Götz von Berlichingen* is a superb example of the genre in its alternation between the refined, slightly precious, diplomatic exchanges at court, the cruder, more direct conversations at Jaxthausen, and the peasants' down-to-earth colloquialisms. Perhaps the only other play of the period to match *Götz* in brilliance and subtlety of dialogue is *Die Soldaten* by the highly gifted poet Lenz who succeeds admirably in catching the semi-educated phraseology of the simple home as well as the soldiers' breezy vulgarity. But even a relatively undistinguished play such as Wagner's *Die Kindermöderin* rises to a high level of linguistic vividness as it ranges from the waitress's cheap jargon to the butcher's terminology and the dialects of the policemen and the washerwoman. The replacement of stage German by natural German was in fact one of the major achievements of the Storm and Stress, a genuine act of liberation.

To see any counterpart to this in the French Romantic theatre may at first seem far-fetched because many of the plays remained in verse (as against the prose of the Storm and Stress), and what is more, they largely upheld the elevated tone and oratorical tradition of French Neo-classicism. This is only too evident as the lengthy set-piece speeches roll forth. Yet it would be equally mistaken to under-estimate the amount of novelty in them. Firstly, in some plays prose is used, and it is used well with real flexibility, as in Vigny's *Chatterton* and in *Antony* by Alexandre Dumas. Secondly, where the Alexandrine is retained, its form is considerably loosened by unaccustomed breaks in the line and frequent *enjambements* which bring it much closer to the rhythm and movement of natural speech. Finally, turns of speech that seem quite innocuous to us today, such as Doña Sol's endearment to Hernani, 'Vous êtes mon lion superbe et généreux' ('You are my proud and valiant lion' – Act III, scene iv), were as profoundly shocking to Frenchmen of 1830 as were Götz's phrases to the Germans of the 1770s. The actress who played the part of Dõna Sol categorically refused to pronounce the offending words.

Any doubts as to the revolutionary impact of the modifications introduced into drama by the French Romantics are dispelled by Théophile Gautier's account of the first performance of *Hernani*.[23] The opening phrases of the play:

> Serait-ce déjà lui?—C'est bien à l'escalier
> Dérobé.

were, Gautier recalls, in themselves a challenging gauntlet thrown
into the arena on account of 'ce mot rejeté sans façon à l'autre vers, cet
enjambement audacieux, impertinent même'[24] ('this word un-
ceremoniously cast into the following line, this daring, indeed impertinent *enjambement*'). With the positioning of one single word therefore
'la querelle était déjà engagée'[25] ('the dispute was already in the open').
And worse was yet to come: when the king asks 'Est-il minuit?' he
receives the reply, 'Minuit bientôt' ('Is it midnight?' – 'Nearly midnight'). Gautier admits that even in 1874 it was hard to conceive the
storm aroused by this simple line: 'On le trouvait trivial, familier, in-
convenant; un roi demande l'heure comme un bourgeois et on lui ré-
pond comme à un rustre: *minuit*. S'il s'était servi d'une belle périphrase,
on aurait été poli; par exemple:

> . . . l'heure
> Atteindra bientôt sa dernière demeure.'[26]

('It was considered trivial, familiar, unfitting; a king asks the time like
an ordinary man and is given an answer such as one would give a peasant: *midnight*. If a fine periphrasis had been used, it would have been
polite and polished; for example:

> . . . the hour
> Will soon enter its final abode.')

Gautier's words, which are as much of a surprise to us today as were
the reactions of the 1830 audience to him in his day, very clearly bring
out the force of innovations that seem to us quite modest. In the context of French theatrical expectations of 1830, however, they were as
daring an act of liberation as was the language of the Storm and Stress
in the Germany of its day. In this sense there is a counterpart
relationship, although the differing framework of tradition in the two
countries leads to a divergence of form and degree in the fundamentally similar rebellious desire for creative renewal.

    This is in fact true in areas beyond the linguistic and the formal.
Comparing the rebelliousness of the *Sturm und Drang* and of French
Romanticism as a whole, it is evident that the Germans went much
further in practice than the French. The French it was who elaborated a
more complex theory of rebellion and reform. Yet in spite of the advances they undoubtedly made, their dramas are relatively timid beside
the extremism in both theme and form of many of the products of the
Storm and Stress. This difference may be connected with the respective

roles of melodrama in the two literatures. Mention has already been made of the flourishing undercurrent of melodrama in later eighteenth-century Germany and in early nineteenth-century France and of its precipitate on the legitimate theatre. It is arguable that the plays of the *Stürmer und Dränger* admit more of the shock effects of melodrama than those of their French counterparts. In France the popular theatre of the boulevards was still fairly strictly segregated from the serious drama of the established *Comédie française*, so that there was less leakage from the one to the other than in Germany where no great, lofty theatrical tradition existed. The French Romantics were, of course, imbued with melodrama, but not to quite the same extent as the *Stürmer und Dränger*, particularly the lesser ones such as Wagner and Klinger. In any case, the melodramas of Pixérécourt are better handled than those of Kotzebue as regards action, theatrical effectiveness and dialogue. This larger ingredient of rather poorer melodrama in many of the plays of the *Sturm und Drang* may well account for their extremism as compared to the French Romantic theatre. But whatever the differences in degree or the reason for them, the rebellious drama of the French Romantics is clearly a counterpart in both theory and practice to that of the Storm and Stress some fifty years earlier. It is a counterpart largely of similarity with mere occasional traces of polarity.

IV

The correspondence between the two movements is just as evident in the introverted melancholy that is their other face. At first sight this tendency to a sentimental softness seems a strange partner to the vigorous, rather noisy rebelliousness that is so much in the forefront of the Storm and Stress and of French Romanticism. The paradox is more apparent than real. From the psychological angle, the two facets are obviously complementary, like the cyclic phases of mania and depression. Where there is high exuberance, there is also often abject self-doubt: the world-conquering rebel, when he is thwarted by society and becomes aware of his impotence in the world of action, only too easily retreats from the scene of his defeat, and turns inwards on himself to become the victim of his own agonized self-questioning. What is more, flight of this kind is in itself a species of rebellion; the drop-out's rejection of the social norms is as much an expression of despair (and self-despair) as of revolt.

This is the case with the Storm and Stress and the French Romantic hero too: Werther and René have both withdrawn literally and figuratively into the forests in consequence of their revulsion from the social standards and habits of their time and class. René is quite explicit in his dismissal of the social round:

> Je voulus me jeter pendant quelque temps dans un monde qui ne me disait rien et qui ne m'entendait pas. Mon âme, qu'aucune passion n'avait encore usée, cherchait un objet qui pût l'attacher; mais je m'aperçus que je donnais plus que je ne recevais. Ce n'était ni un langage élevé ni un sentiment profond qu'on demandait de moi. Je n'étais occupé qu'à rapetisser ma vie, pour la mettre au niveau de la société. Traité partout d'esprit romanesque, honteux du rôle que je jouais, dégoûté de plus en plus des choses et des hommes, je pris le parti de me retirer.[27]

> (For a while I wanted to plunge into a world which did not appeal to me nor understand me. My soul, still innocent of passion, sought an object of attachment; but I saw that I was giving more than I was receiving. Neither lofty language nor deep feeling were expected of me. I had to cut my life down to size in order to bring it to society's level. Regarded everywhere as a dreamer, ashamed of the role I was playing, more and more disgusted with things and men, I decided to withdraw.)

Similarly, in his very first letter to Wilhelm (4 May 1771) Werther comments bitterly on the sloth and perversity that cause so much misery within the court and bourgeois society in contrast to the open-hearted friendliness of the peasants, and specially the children in his village haven. Later his indictment of society becomes considerably more virulent after his final, utterly disastrous attempt (at the beginning of book II) at integration into the life of a small court. From the first day, and certainly long before his disgrace for a purported *faux-pas*, he fulminates with contempt for the hollow formalism and petty rivalries of court life: 'Und das glänzende Elend, die Langeweile unter dem garstigen Volke, das sich hier nebeneinander sieht!', he exclaims on 24 December; 'Die Rangsucht unter ihnen, wie sie nur wachen und aufpassen, einander ein Schrittchen abzugewinnen'[28] ('And the ostentatious misery, the boredom among all these horrible people thrown together here! The pursuit of rank that makes each strive to gain a march on the other at every waking moment!'). He continues scoffing

in the same vein in the following letter (8 January 1772): 'Was das für
Menschen sind, deren ganze Seele auf dem Zeremoniell ruht, deren
Dichten und Trachten jahrelang dahin geht, wie sie um einen Stuhl
weiter hinauf bei Tische sich einschieben wollen! ... Die Toren, die
nicht sehen, dass es eigentlich auf den Platz gar nicht ankommt und
dass der, der den ersten hat, so selten die erste Rolle spielt!'[29] ('What
sort of people are these, whose whole being resides in ceremonial,
whose whole thought and effort for years on end aims at moving one
chair further up at table! ... Fools who do not realize that the seat at
table is of no importance, and that he who occupies the first seat seldom
plays the leading role!'). These outbursts are strongly reminiscent of
the attacks on the jostling for rank in *Hernani*, where a slip of the king's
tongue in addressing a noble as 'comte' ('count') is pounced on as a cue
for advancement. Neither Werther nor René presumes to have the
strength to change this state of affairs, as do Götz and Karl Moor, Ruy
Blas and Antony. Instead of trying to bring down the castle of society,
they turn their backs on it, but this flight is merely another form of that
rebelliousness that inspires the extroverts to action.

The two facets of the Storm and Stress and of French Romanticism
are linked by another important factor, and again it is the same in both
movements. The introverted melancholy, like the rebelliousness, in
each case has its ultimate source in an over-estimation of the individual.
Among the men of action this is immediately apparent; in challenging
society, they place themselves above its laws, confident not only of
their own powers but also of their right to this exceptional position.
Hence the tendency of the *Stürmer und Dränger* and of the French
Romantics to exalt greatness of every kind, including the greatness of
the outlaw; even though he may finally come to grief, he still stands
out as a heroic example, a late instance of the grand warrior and an
early one of the superman. With the introverted melancholic too the
emphasis is on the unique individual, though no longer on his stirring
deeds; it is his intimate feelings and responses, his inmost tensions and
dreams that are the focus of his life. His endless self-analysis stems from
the identical conviction of his own importance as the rebel's defiant
stance. In a sense indeed, the introvert is also trying to break out of his
confines by his endeavours to fathom his own unhappiness; yet,
ironically, all he succeeds in doing is to explore and map the confines
of his ego. If the man of action is the prototype of the superman, the
introvert offers the blueprint for the anti-hero. Both characters
crystallize following the new assertion of the rights of the individual,

the new appreciation of the uniqueness of the particular phenomenon that was as fundamental to French Romanticism as to the Storm and Stress.

This cult of particularity leads directly to that primacy of direct experience that is so loudly proclaimed by both the *Stürmer und Dränger* and the French Romantics. One of the first to posit personal experience as the basis for living and for education as well as for artistic activity was Johann Georg Hamann (1730–88), whose defiance of accepted modes of thought and of behaviour, together with his devotion to inner, intuitive convictions, was one of the starting-points for the Storm and Stress. Throughout his aphorisms Hamann repeatedly dwells on the necessity of 'lebendige Erfahrung'[30] ('live experience') as the only valid guide, adding that the lyric poet 'ist der Geschichtschreiber des menschlichen Herzens'[31] ('is the chronicler of the human heart'), a definition as acceptable to the French Romantic poets as to Hamann's contemporaries in Germany. His own frankly idiosyncratic manner – 'mein spermologischer Stil'[32] ('my spermatological style'), as he wittily termed it – seems to exemplify his arguments in favour of an essentially subjective approach in its eccentric verve that echoes and reinforces the originality of his ideas. His advice to think less and to live more ('Denken Sie weniger und leben Sie mehr!')[33] might have served as a motto to Herder who lamented the deadening effects of his studious upbringing and existence in his *Journal meiner Reise im Jahre 1769*, and preached the same exaltation of direct experience as Hamann. From Hamann to Herder to the young Goethe the creed passed along a chain of friendship until it was bodied forth in a living figure in Goethe's Faust. Reputedly based in part on Herder, Faust is driven by the urge to escape from his academic prison and, above all, to experience life at first-hand:

Schau alle Wirkenskraft und Samen
Und tu nicht mehr in Worten kramen.[34]

(See the world's real force and seed
And no longer rummage in mere words.)

It is in return for the promise of genuine, direct and varied experience that he makes his pact with Mephistopheles. In this glorification of live experience, specifically the personal experience of the human heart, Faust reflects Goethe's own attitude at this period. 'Mir ist alles lieb und werth was treu und starck aus dem Herzen kommt' ('I love and prize all that comes straight and pure from the heart'), he wrote to Anna Luise Karsch on 17 August 1775.[35] These words virtually sum up one whole segment of the aesthetics of the Storm and Stress: the view of art as immediate, tempestuous, spontaneous self-expression. To quote Goethe's own words again, feelings cannot be described except 'mit dem Feuerblick des Moments' (' in the fiery gaze of the moment'). This phrase comes from a lengthy letter written to Auguste von Stolberg[36] over a span of five days, 14–19 September 1775; its ecstatic exclamations in choppy, agitated sentences typify the emotional, personal, often confessional, and either really or apparently uncontrolled manner of the Storm and Stress.

That characterization is equally apposite to French Romantic writing. The overlap between the two movements at this point is such as to amount to a virtual interchangeability, certainly as far as the theory is concerned. Faust's 'Gefühl ist alles'[37] ('feeling is the be-all and end-all') was the prime tenet of the French Romantic poets. It rings out like a chorus: for Musset 'l'art, c'est le sentiment'[38] ('art is feeling'); according to Hugo, 'la poésie, ce n'est presque que sentiment'[39] ('poetry is almost entirely feeling'), while Lamartine claims, in the first preface to his *Méditations poétiques*, that poetry is a cry from the heart, an intensely personal form of catharsis. When the critic Alexandre Soumet, reviewing Hugo's *Nouvelles Odes* in *La Muse Française* (no. 9, March 1824), ranked 'le génie des émotions' as the poet's primary quality, he was formulating a conception of poetry as valid for the Storm and Stress as for the French poets of his own generation.

Such difference as exists between the German poets of the 1770s and their counterparts across the Rhine in the 1820s in the expression of emotion is more a matter of degree and of emphasis than of principle. As in the drama, the French tended to be more vociferous in theory, yet more restrained in practice than their German predecessors. In spite of the French Romantics' purported ambition to burn the paper with the fiery intensity of their outpourings, their writings remain more coherent, in fact more shapely than those of the *Stürmer und Dränger*, among whom the danger of an emotion running riot to the point of self-destruction was so acute that several fell victim to it, as witnessed by the suicide of Lenz and the life-long instability of Hamann and Gerstenberg. Nor was Goethe himself exempt, as has been shown by Barker Fairley who coined that telling phrase 'emotion running riot'[40] to describe the 'excited, irrational, mercurial mood' characteristic of the youthful Goethe and of his 'companions in chaos', as he calls the

Stürmer und Dränger. The vehement emotive urge could topple into an uncontrolled subjectivism, a state of anarchy equally disastrous to the artist personally and to his work. Among the French Romantics this threat appears to have been less menacing, perhaps because they never totally lost the support of tradition. Even through the act of rejection, that tradition nonetheless remained present, albeit subconsciously. The so-called failure of the French Romantics to make a radical break with their native tradition thus had its advantages for it exerted a moderating influence; conversely, the more absolute freedom of the *Stürmer und Dränger*, however desirable ideally, proved in practice full of pitfalls.

The dangers of 'emotion running riot', of uncontrolled subjectivity turning into an introverted melancholy, are illustrated in *Werther* and *René*. These two works have so often been compared[41] that the fundamental similarity between them in the delineation of the Romantic hero has become a critical commonplace. The *Weltschmerz*, the *mal du siècle* that dogs Werther and René alike springs from their imprisonment within themselves. The counterpart relationship is so evident that there is little need to elaborate on it here. Two points, however, should be emphasized in the present context. First, it is important to bear in mind that Chateaubriand's novel appeared in his *Génie du Christianisme* in the section entitled 'Du vague des passions'; René was intended as a cautionary figure, to some extent as an anti-Werther. The story ends with old Souël's sensible diagnosis of René's troubles and his unpalatable prescription for a cure. Whether René took his medicine or not is open to conjecture. His reported death in battle is ambivalent: does it mean that he had renounced his self-centred existence to make common cause with other men, or did he remain a lonely dreamer to the end, as seems to be implied in the novel's closing sentence: 'On montre encore un rocher où il allait s'asseoir au soleil couchant'[42] ('A rock is still shown where he used to sit at dusk'). Ironically, and to Chateaubriand's chagrin, René, like Werther, was interpreted by his contemporaries as an ideal; so much so that Chateaubriand came to regret ever having written the novel. This befell Goethe too, who tired in later life of being typecast as the author of *Werther*. But there can be no doubt that at the time of composition Goethe was far more deeply and personally involved in his Werther than Chateaubriand ever was in René. Goethe's letters up to the very moment of his departure to Weimar read as if they had flowed from Werther's pen: his heart is 'auf den Wogen der Einbildungskraft und überspannten Sinnlichkeit

Himmel auf und Höllen ab getrieben'[43] ('driven up to heaven and
down to hell on waves of imagination and overexcited sensuality'); or
again: 'ich lasse mich treiben, und halte nur das Steuer dass ich nicht
strande. Doch bin ich gestrandet, ich kann von dem Mägden nicht ab'[44]
('I am letting myself drift, I am holding the rudder only to avoid the
rocks. But I am on the rocks, I cannot break loose from the girl'). That
image of the rudder is an illuminating one: Goethe came alarmingly
close to losing his grip on the rudder, whereas Chateaubriand, with the
backing of his Christian faith and his traditionalism, kept a much firmer hold. Once again the *Sturm und Drang* proves more extreme than
its French equivalent.

The second footnote that must be added to the customary comparison of *Werther* and *René* is a chronological one of particular
relevance to the argument in favour of a counterpart relationship between the Storm and Stress and French Romanticism. *René* appeared
thirty-one years after *Werther*. Were this an isolated fact, it would be of
small importance. But *René* is the focal point of a whole cluster of
novels exploring the *mal du siècle* in the first three decades of the
nineteenth century in France, just as *Werther* is the leading example
associated with eighteenth-century *Weltschmerz*. It is already present in
the writings of the group known as the *Göttinger Dichterbund* ('the
Göttingen circle of poets'), as W. Rose has shown in his study *From
Goethe to Byron: the Development of 'Weltschmerz' in German Literature*
(London: Routledge, 1924). With the *Sturm und Drang* and specifically
with *Werther*, the malady reached its peak and, by and large, also its
end, for *Weltschmerz* is not epidemic among the German Romantics as
it was among the French. The fame of *Werther* spread rapidly to
France; between 1776 and 1797 alone fifteen translations and editions
were published. But the critical reception in these early days was
sharply divided between the reservations, even attacks of the *têtes froides*
(the cool heads) and the gushing enthusiasm of the *âmes sensibles* (the
sensitive souls). It was not until the early years of the nineteenth century that *Werther* was given serious critical attention, and even then the
liveliness of the opposition testifies to its controversial novelty. Further
versions and elaborations continued to appear along with a spate of
original novels of the same cast: Mme de Staël's *Delphine* (1802), Mme
de Krudener's *Valérie* (1803), *René* (1805), Constant's *Adolphe* (1807),
Sénancour's *Obermann* (1820), to mention only a few outstanding ones.
The time-lag of some thirty to fifty years between the corresponding
tendencies on the opposite banks of the Rhine is very much in evidence
here.

It is discernible too in the trend to ironize the traditional melancholy anti-hero that comes, in both the German and the French movement, after the crest of the wave. *Der Waldbruder* (1776) by Lenz and Musset's *La Confession d'un enfant du siècle* (1836) are counterparts in so far as each is distinctly mocking in tone. Herz ('heart'), the 'sylvan brother' of Lenz's novel, has gone into the country to seek happiness in a simple peasant life *à la Rousseau*; his friends see him as 'einen neuer Werther'[45] ('a new Werther'). But unlike Werther, who is portrayed predominantly at his own evaluation and in his own words, Herz is also presented to us through the eyes of others, for *Der Waldbruder* comprises a multiple exchange of letters in the manner of the eighteenth-century epistolary novel. So Herz is repeatedly termed a fool ('Narr') by various of the writers who ridicule his attitudes and his emotional involvements. Herz is in fact caught up in a tragi-comedy in which he is the victim of his landlady's machinations as well as of his own errors when he falls in love with the author of certain letters and mistakenly identifies another lady as the object of his love. The parallel with Don Quixote is strongly hinted in the final letter when Herz is referred to as the 'irrender Ritter'[46] ('the knight who roams, makes mistakes and is tinged with madness' – the German adjective implies all these meanings). Musset's Octave evokes the same blend of scorn and sympathy as Herz. On the surface he appears more as the duper than as the duped, as the manipulator rather than the manipulated, yet at a deeper level he is as much the victim of his misapprehensions as Herz. He too has a shrewd insight into the degeneracy of his times, but in spite of his worldly wisdom and his purported detachment, he falls into errors psychologically as preposterous as those of Herz. The two novels are related through their satirical undertone. That such satire was directed against the introspective hero in Germany in 1776 and in France in 1836 forms an interesting footnote to the counterpart relationship between the *Sturm und Drang* and *romantisme*.

The affinity that has so far been illustrated largely in the drama and the prose of the two movements is also manifest in their lyric poetry. The extraordinarily high esteem of the individual, of his special experiences and feelings, together with the reiterated insistence on complete freedom of expression, fostered a climate conducive to a brilliant flowering of lyric poetry in both countries. Historically this blossoming fulfils the same role in the Germany of the 1770s as in the France of the 1820s: the release of the poetic imagination and of personal emotion from their imprisonment in a sterile, mechanical versifying that had for years produced shapeless description of an almost ingeniously boring flatness. There are, as always, exceptions to this sweeping condemnation; no one would deny the intrinsic worth of, say, Chénier or Günther. But equally, no one acquainted with the poetry immediately preceding the Storm and Stress in Germany and the Romantic movement in France could fail to be struck by the refreshing novelty that both introduced. The early poems of Goethe and the lyrics of Lenz, like those of Lamartine, Hugo, Musset and Vigny, were a gust of fresh air that swept out many of the old cobwebs.

Apart from the similarity of their historical function, the lyrics of the *Sturm und Drang* and of *romantisme* are thematically and technically interconnected. Community of theme, it might be argued, is weak evidence of their counterpart relationship since theirs are the common themes of all major lyric poetry: love, joy, grief, pain at parting, in short the exultation and the despair of the human heart. Likewise, an objection could be raised against citing the essential subjectivity of these poems as proof of their affinity on the grounds that subjectivity is fundamental to the lyric genre. In part at least these are valid standpoints, although the subjective illumination of the traditional lyric themes by the poets of the Storm and Stress and of the French Romantic movement was of so particularly intense and so directly personal a kind that a claim in favour of their uniqueness would not be misplaced. Be that as it may, there can be no doubt whatsoever as to the special role of nature in the lyric of both groups. In this the French Romantics were as much innovators as the *Stürmer und Dränger*, and what is more, their innovations were along identical lines. In place of the visual word-pictures of nature previously customary, the *Stürmer und Dränger* and the French Romantics gave an impression that offered no precise details, but that glowed with emotion instead. For theirs was not only a living nature, but also a nature that partook of the poet's vicissitudes, acting as a framework to his musings, and, above all, as a mirror to his moods. The interpenetration of man and nature is so habitual in the poetry of Goethe, Lenz, Lamartine, Hugo and Vigny that it hardly needs illustration. To name only the best known, Goethe's *Mailied*, *Ganymed*, *An den Mond* and *Herbstgefühl*, Lenz's *Wo bist du itzt, Ach, bist du fort?*, *Die erste Frühlingspromenade*, Lamartine's *L'Isolement*, *Le Lac*, *L'Automne*, *Le Soir*, *Le Vallon*, Hugo's *Ce qu'on entend sur la montagne*, *Vois, cette branche est rude*, *O Terre! ô merveilles*, *Tristesse d'Olympio*, *A Villequier*, Vigny's *La Mort du loup*, *La Sauvage*, *La Maison du berger*: all these poems, and many more besides, testify to the organic links between the individual and the sentient nature surrounding him. Often the poet finds in his profound empathy with nature a partner to his exuberance or a response to his longing for consolation; and even when nature seems out of tune with his psyche, he turns to her in his quest for the meaning of his suffering. In this vital new role assigned to nature at the very core of the poem as an extended reflection of its dominant theme there is a close parallel between the lyric of the Storm and Stress and that of French Romanticism.

Their technical affinity stems from the shared ideal of poetry as spontaneous utterance that was as cardinal a tenet of the *Sturm und Drang* as of *romantisme*. The strings of the human heart, to use Lamartine's telling image, were to replace the conventional lyre of Parnassus so that poetry gushed forth straight on to the page in an unchecked improvisation. Whether this was really the case is a moot point, and this is not the place for an inquiry into the processes of artistic creation. What is important in the present context is that the Storm and Stress and French Romanticism subscribed in their theory to a remarkably similar concept of lyric poetry as the free expression of personal feeling. Curiously, in neither movement did the freedom so vociferously proclaimed lead to the actual shattering of the recognized poetic moulds. That was to happen later in both literatures, with the *Frühromantik* and Symbolism respectively, as we shall see. In the Germany of the 1770s and the France of the 1820s, in spite of the arrogation of liberty, conscious control still persisted in poems that favoured regular verse, rhyme and rhythm schemes. Indeed the poetic forms seem to have imposed a certain rein on the emotion that ran riot in prose.

Here too the correspondence between the Storm and Stress and French Romanticism continues, at least up to a point. For as in the drama, the *Stürmer und Dränger* were more daring than the French Romantics when it came to the translation of theory into poetic practice. The diction in the lyrics repeats the divergence between the German and the French poets already noted in the language of their respective dramas. The vocabulary of the Storm and Stress is simpler, barer, more homely, yet at the same time also more stark than that of their French counterparts who tended to cling to the high-flown phrase, the lofty periphrasis, the deliberately *recherché* image. As a result, French Romantic poetry has the greater harmony, but this beauty in itself has the effect of blunting the emotional impact, for the smoothness of form, however alluring, somehow intrudes between the poet and the reader in the communication of feeling. The poetry of the Storm and

Stress, on the other hand, while less gracious in surface appearance, derives its strength from that very directness that is its salient quality. The difference emerges most clearly if we compare the way Lamartine and Lenz expressed their grief at a parting. Lamartine's *L'Isolement* culminates in this finely chiselled stanza:

> Que me font ces vallons, ces palais, ces chaumières?
> Vains objets dont pour moi le charme est envolé;
> Fleuves, rochers, forêts, solitudes si chères,
> Un seul être vous manque, et tout est dépeuplé!

> (What mean these valleys, these mansions, these cottages to me?
> Futile objects that hold no delight for me;
> Rivers, rocks, forests, beloved nooks of solitude,
> One being is absent, and all is empty!)

This is the corresponding stanza in Lenz's *Ach, bist du fort?*:

> Wie ist die Munterkeit von ihm gewichen!
> Die Sonne scheint ihm schwarz, der Boden leer,
> Die Bäume blühn ihm schwarz, die Blätter sind verblichen,
> Und alles welket um ihn her.

> (How cheerfulness has left him!
> The sun seems black to him, the ground empty,
> The trees blossom darkly, the leaves are tarnished,
> And everything is fading around him.)

In both cases nature is the correlative of the poet's sense of desolation, but whereas the seductiveness of Lamartine's Alexandrine lies in its resonant grandiloquence, Lenz's far less accomplished lines are touching through their artlessness. So in the lyric, as in the drama, the *Sturm und Drang* has the vigour and freshness that are the prerogative of a nation in its literary youth, while French Romanticism has the refinement that is the heritage of a polished tradition. It is this difference of background that accounts for the element of polarity among the multiple affinities in the counterpart relationship between the two movements.

It is tempting to go on exploring and illustrating the resemblance between the Storm and Stress and French Romanticism. But this essay aims to be suggestive and stimulating rather than exhaustive. I hope by now to have shown that in essence the two movements are sufficiently alike to warrant my thesis: that French Romanticism is a counterpart to the Storm and Stress. The curious interchangeability of critical comment on the two movements further supports this contention. Goethe's diagnosis of French Romanticism in conversation with Eckermann on 11 June 1825 as 'eine grosse Gährung' ('a great ferment'), and again on 14 March 1830 as a 'heftiges Fieber' ('a violent fever') is strikingly appropriate to the *Sturm und Drang*. Conversely, phrases chosen to characterize French Romanticism, such as 'bruyant, théâtral', 'sa recherche du cas exceptionnel, du contraste criant', 'son mépris de la tradition et des conventions'[47] ('noisy, theatrical', 'its cult of the exceptional, of the screaming contrast', 'its scorn for tradition and conventions'): all these fit the Storm and Stress to perfection. Or, starting from the German side, Pascal's verdict that 'this new start was, in some respects, convulsive and immature'[48] is obviously apposite to French Romanticism. Likewise, to take one final example, the entry under *Sturm und Drang* in *A Handbook to Literature* can virtually be read as a definition of French *romantisme*:

> In essence the *Sturm und Drang* movement was a revolt from classical conventions and, particularly, an expression of dissatisfaction with the tenets of French classicism. The writing was characterized by fervor and enthusiasm, a restless turbulency of spirit, the portrayal of great passion, a reliance upon emotional experiences and spiritual struggles and was intensely personal.[49]

The weight of evidence in favour of the affinity between the Storm and Stress and French Romanticism is such that a mathematician would surely at this stage use the formula: q.e.d.

V

Unlike the mathematician, the literary critic must probe further beyond the proven proposition. The vital question to be asked at this point is: *why* was the French literature of the early nineteenth century a counterpart ('ein Widerschein' – 'a reflection', was Goethe's word) to trends in Germany some fifty years earlier? As is so often the case with questions of this kind, a variety of answers may be given. All are correct in so far as all contribute to an understanding of the situation, but it is only from the combination of apparently disparate factors that the whole picture emerges. Three elements are crucial: the extent, quality and timing of familiarity with German literature in France; the common ancestry of the Storm and Stress and French Romanticism in Shakespeare and Rousseau; and finally the problem of the hidden appeal of the *Sturm und Drang* to the French poets of the early nineteenth century. Each of these is obviously a vast topic whose outlines can here only be adumbrated in an attempt to evaluate its significance for the counterpart relationship between the Storm and Stress and French Romanticism.

The first of the three, i.e. the extent, quality and timing of French cognizance of German literature, is probably the easiest to assess. There can be no doubt that it was predominantly the ideas and writings of the *Stürmer und Dränger* which were known in France in the late eighteenth and early nineteenth centuries. French acquaintance with German literature at this time was a strange patchwork of ignorance, suspicion and enthusiasms. A reading of the French critics of the period shows that the gaps and misjudgements are as surprising as the crazes for such writers as Gessner, Uz, Hagedorn, Bürger and Kotzebue. Sainte-Beuve's comment that Goethe was 'un demi dieu honoré et deviné plutôt que bien connu'[50] ('a demi-god revered and intuited rather than really known') seems valid for German literature as a whole. The process of transmission was frankly haphazard; no reliable account of German literature was available in France until A. Loève-Veimars' *Résumé de l'histoire de la littérature allemande* of 1826, nor had most of the French Romantic poets a really sound knowledge of German. During the revolutionary period France was in any case virtually closed to German imports; thus Johann Friedrich Reichardt, a young German philologist who spent the winter of 1800–1 in Paris, lamented in *Un Hiver à Paris sous le Consulat 1802-1803* (ed. A Laquiante, Paris: Plon, 1896) that German literature was almost unknown, only a few people having heard of Monsieur Schéet (*sic*)! Philippe-Albert Stapfer's *Archives littéraires d'Europe*, designed to encourage the exchange of ideas between France and other European countries, was sadly short-lived (1804-7). Travellers' reports, then as later one of the chief sources of information, tended to be of somewhat dubious reliability. Charles de Villers published a whole series of works on German topics (*La Philosophie de Kant* in 1801, *Essai sur l'esprit et l'influence de la réformation de Luther* in 1804, *De la manière essentiellement différente dont les poètes français et les allemands traitent l'amour* in 1806, *Constitutions des trois villes libres-anséatiques Lubeck, Brêmen et Hambourg* in 1814), while Benjamin Constant, who spent January and February 1804 in Weimar, recorded his impressions of Goethe, Schiller, Wieland, Herder, Voss and Kotzebue in his *Journaux intimes*.[51]

On that visit to Germany Constant was accompanying Mme de Staël, the foremost traveller and reporter of the period. Because of her feud with Napoleon, her massive account of German manners, thought, literature and arts had first to be published in England, but by the second decade of the nineteenth century *De L'Allemagne* was infiltrating into France. Mme de Staël gives wide coverage of German literature, and her judgements are often extraordinarily shrewd. Her book was for a long time one of the main documents about Germany not only in France but also in England and the United States, and as such it played a leading part in shaping the Romantics' view of German literature. For this reason Mme de Staël's preferences and her misconceptions proved of far-reaching import. Let there be no mistake: wide though her coverage is, and shrewd though her judgements are, her picture of German literature is nonetheless a highly selective one. A scrutiny of the poets she writes about quickly reveals her bias: *De L'Allemagne* contains whole chapters on Wieland, Klopstock, Lessing and Winckelmann, Herder, Goethe, Schiller and Zacharias Werner, while further chapters (or half-chapters) are devoted to each of Goethe's and Schiller's major plays, including *Faust*. The other writers discussed in some detail are Bürger, Kotzebue, Klinger, Matthias Claudius, Iffland, Voss, Jacobi, Matthison, Tieck, Jean-Paul (Richter) and A. W. Schlegel, with a passing phrase for Friedrich Schlegel. An impressive list certainly, but as impressive for its omissions as for its inclusions. For in reading *De L'Allemagne* it is important to remember that Mme de Staël was not just giving a personal survey of recent writing in Germany. Her underlying motive was the presentation of German literature as a *Romantic* literature, in contrast to the Classical literature of France. This is not the place to analyse the ramifications of her distinction, let alone its validity. But her ulterior theme of German literature as a Romantic literature must be emphasized because it was to have a deep influence in France, and because it must lead to some reassessment of *De L'Allemagne* as an intermediary. Mme de Staël's individual judgements often hit the nail on the head, but her *total* picture of German literature is not free of distortion. Writing in the first decade of the nineteenth century about German Romantic literature, she never mentions either Novalis or Wackenroder, the major poets of the *Frühromantik*, nor does she show any real awareness of Friedrich Schlegel's significance. In the early years of the nineteenth century the works of Novalis, Wackenroder and Friedrich Schlegel were perhaps still too recent to be widely known at a period that had not our modern machinery for instant publicity. On the other hand, from

1803 until her death in 1817 August Wilhelm Schlegel was one of
Mme de Staël's closest friends and tutor to her sons, and she would
certainly have learned about the *Frühromantiker* from him. Her library
at Coppet contained a fine selection of German Romantic works, of
which she was by no means ignorant. The inevitable conclusion is
that she had a strong innate predilection for the *Stürmer und Dränger*;
with her dynamic energy and emotional wilfulness, she was herself,
after all, very much of a *Sturm und Drang* character. And it is interesting to note that of the three Romantic writers whom she did in-
clude – Werner, Tieck and Jean-Paul – at least two (Werner and
Tieck) have much in common with the *Stürmer und Dränger*, far more
than either Novalis or Wackenroder.[52]

As a result then largely of *De L'Allemagne* it was the *Stürmer und
Dränger* who not only became known in France in the early nineteenth
century, but known specifically as the German Romantics. French interest in the *Sturm und Drang* at this period has been thoroughly
documented by comparative research. Fernand Baldensperger's *Goethe
en France* (Paris: Hachette, 1904) demonstrates the overriding popularity of *Werther* which was matched only by Schiller's *Die Räuber*, as
Edmond Eggli has shown in *Schiller et le romantisme français* (Paris:
Gamber, 1927). Charles Dédéyan's investigations in *Victor Hugo et
l'Allemagne* (Paris: Minard, 1964) have revealed that Hugo read almost
exclusively *Sturm und Drang* writers, notably Schiller. Nor is it surprising that the French discovery of Herder dates from 1827–8 when
Quinet translated the *Ideen zur Philosophie der Geschichte der Menschheit*.
Henri Tronchon in his minutely detailed inquiry into *La Fortune intellectuelle de Herder en France* (Paris: Rieder, 1920) ponders repeatedly
on the puzzle of the late infiltration of Herder into France without
realizing that it forms part of a total picture of retardation. After a
lengthy period of ignorance, and after the delay occasioned by the
Revolutionary Wars which bred distrust of anything that came from
the enemy, a natural curiosity about German culture (heightened indeed by the barriers of enmity) blossomed into a veritable fashion. In
this change Mme de Staël's *De L'Allemagne* played a leading role;
above all, it was instrumental in popularizing the *Sturm und Drang* in
France just as the emergent French Romantic groups were mustering
their forces for battle. A major impact for the development of French
Romanticism thus came from Germany, not however from the German *Romantik*, as is often assumed with a cavalier disregard for the
chronological facts, but from the Storm and Stress which was eagerly
received into the France of the 1820s.

This French attraction to the Storm and Stress must in turn prompt a further question: why did the French poets of the early nineteenth century feel so drawn to this particular period of German literature? To answer this merely by reference to their acquaintance with the Storm and Stress through Mme de Staël's choice of material in *De L'Allemagne* is an over-simplification. For a foreign influence is never warmly welcomed and activated, like yeast in the dough, unless there is a state of preparedness in the host country. An attraction, such as the French felt for the Storm and Stress, generally stems from an inner, possibly sub-conscious, sense of affinity. Wherein lay the roots of that affinity?

One possible answer lies in the common ancestry of the *Sturm und Drang* and of *romantisme*. Both were deeply indebted to Shakespeare and to Rousseau. Many of the similarities between the two movements are due to their derivation from the same sources. Yet this shared worship of Shakespeare and absorption in Rousseau are in themselves expressions of that underlying unity of ideal between the Storm and Stress and French Romanticism that motivated their choice of these two mentors. Moreover, the reactions to Shakespeare, the parallel yet differing tensions in Germany and in France in the late eighteenth and early nineteenth centuries, open up another aspect of the counterpart relationship between the two literatures.

Shakespeare's entry into Germany was sudden and spectacular. In the earlier half of the eighteenth century, 'Sasper', as he was sometimes called, was little known and even less admired, although Johann Elias Schlegel and Bodmer did have a more positive reaction than Gottsched's horror at the irregularity of *Julius Caesar*. The turning-point in Shakespeare's fortune in Germany clearly came in Lessing's seventeenth *Literaturbrief* of 1759, in which an attack on Gottsched's dramatic principles and methods precedes an appraisal of Shakespeare that speaks of his masterpieces, his genius, his naturalness. The key-notes of the Storm and Stress interpretation of Shakespeare were thus already sounded soon after the middle of the eighteenth century. Nor did the Germans have to wait long for the first translation, that of Wieland, who gave them twenty-two plays between 1762 and 1766. With Lessing's mature criticism in the *Hamburgische Dramaturgie* (1767) the question of Shakespeare and of the observation of rules was fused with the problem of the creation of a German national theatre. Shakespeare's stardom as the fountain-head of the new German drama is symbolized by his position at the feet of the goddess of Truth on the new curtain of the theatre in Hamburg in 1773. It was in Hamburg and in Berlin that several Shakespeare plays were first performed in Germany: *Hamlet* and *Othello* in 1766, *The Merchant of Venice* in 1777, *King Lear* and *Richard II* in 1778 and *Macbeth* in 1779, under the direction of the great actor-producer Schröder, who was inspired by the Shakespeare recitations of an English actor he had met in 1758. With the Storm and Stress, admiration for Shakespeare grew into an unqualified cult, as is seen in Herder's and Goethe's rhapsodic essays. He was worshipped as the prototype of the free and natural genius and cast as the liberator of the German muse in the crusade for a national literature. In the *Frühromantik* at the turn of the century the emphasis shifted from the emotional greatness and emancipated technique, the focal points for the *Stürmer und Dränger*, to a more subtle appreciation of Shakespeare's artistry and imagination. So the attitudes to Shakespeare mirror the changes in literary tastes and ideals through the eighteenth century, each group interpreting the plays of Shakespeare through the spectacles of their own expectations.

This indeed holds true across the Rhine too. However, in direct consequence of the warring countercurrents in later eighteenth- and early nineteenth-century France, Shakespeare's fate was much more chequered, and his naturalization much tardier than in Germany. Here again the difference is evident between, on the one hand, a country anxious for advance and therefore open to innovations and, on the other, a nation so steeped in its own traditions that it is sceptical, indeed fearful of any radical departure from them. Yet in the earliest stages French reaction to Shakespeare was similar to that in Germany: a compound of curiosity, some grudging admiration and considerable bewilderment. The first impression in both countries was of a barbarian genius as he was often called. This ambivalence is typified by Voltaire's verdict in the *Lettres philosophiques*: 'Shakespeare avait un génie plein de force et de fécondité, de naturel et de sublime, sans la moindre étincelle de bon goût, et sans la moindre connaissance des règles'[53] ('Shakespeare was a genius full of verve and inventiveness, of the natural and the sublime, without the least trace of good taste and without the slightest knowledge of the rules'). But whereas in Germany genius soon came to be prized as the supreme attribute of the creative poet, in France it was distrusted as the foe of good taste. The reception of Shakespeare on the two banks of the Rhine reflects this dichotomy. Long after his elevation to the role of national hero in Germany, he continued to be profoundly suspect in France. Letourneur's translation of 1776 won its way into drawing-rooms and libraries rather than into theatres. Ironically, it seems to have made less friends than enemies for Shakespeare among the French who were horrified, on closer acquaintance with the text, at such vulgarities as a reference to a handkerchief, or 'a mouse stirring' in a tragedy, not to mention the subversiveness of portraying a mad king on the stage! A desire to acclimatize Shakespeare to France by a process of taming him inspired the work of Jean-François Ducis (1733–1816), who nurtured a passionate admiration for the English dramatist, without, however, any knowledge of English nor any real understanding of his works. So Ducis remodelled Shakespeare, arranging him to current French taste and custom by replacing action with narrative and *confidants* and by attempting to squeeze his plays into the unities. At least his emasculated versions brought the plays (*Hamlet* in 1769, *Romeo and Juliet* in 1772, *King Lear* in 1783, *Macbeth* in 1784, *Othello* in 1792) into the theatre where they evoked both applause and sarcastic opposition in this bowdlerized form.

That opposition grew after the turn of the century, and so did the admiration, when Shakespeare became a centre of controversy in the emergence of the Romantic movement. This is the point at which French reaction diverges most sharply from that in Germany, where there was no parallel to the French phobia of Shakespeare as a threat to the native heritage, as the assassin, so to speak, of Racine and Corneille. Shakespeare's adherents were even castigated as bad citizens, detractors of France. Not that this discouraged them, for Shakespeare had an increasing following. By the early years of the nineteenth century already the movement, the picturesqueness, the fantastic and startling elements had been assimilated into French melodrama. Yet as late as 1822 a company of English actors performing *Othello* in the original were literally driven off stage by a barrage of apples, oranges and eggs – and such conspicuous waste of good food by the thrifty French is surely the most telling comment on the strength of feeling against Shakespeare. This was the episode that prompted Stendhal's *Racine et Shakespeare* which crystallized the conflict between the traditionalists and the progressives. For the French Romantics as for the *Stürmer und Dränger*, Shakespeare came to stand as a cipher for liberty in the fight against the stale and the outmoded. As in Germany, his name was adopted as a slogan, though relatively little was known of his works. Again as in Germany, he acted as a stimulus to the evolution of a new theatre modelled on the freedom of his dramatic form. To Hugo and to Vigny, who adapted *Romeo and Juliet* and *The Merchant of Venice* and translated *Othello* into his *More de Venise* (1829), Shakespeare was as much the symbol of genius and freedom as he had been fifty years earlier to Herder, Goethe and Gerstenberg. The second English troupe to visit Paris, in autumn 1827, met with a rather more cordial reception. Potent though Shakespeare's influence undoubtedly was in the later 1820s and early 1830s, even then the battle had not been conclusively won. When Macready and his company came to Paris in the winter of 1844–5, the French were still so shocked by *Othello, Macbeth* and *Hamlet* that Gérard de Nerval voiced this bitter complaint in *L'Artiste* (22 December 1844): 'Les acteurs anglais nous reviennent avec Shakespeare, et nous trouvent retournés au point où ils nous avaient laissés! . . . Ce qu'on craint à Paris, c'est le mot propre, c'est l'action vraie; mieux vaut la gravelure déguisée, ou le coup de poignard académique' ('The English actors have come back with Shakespeare, and find us just where they had left us! . . . In Paris the plain word and the true act are feared; better a coarse term slightly veiled, or an academic stab in the back'). Nerval's comment underlining the slowness of Shakespeare's infiltration into France indirectly illumines once more the time-lag characteristic of the Franco–German relationship at this period. But the fundamental parallel between the German *Stürmer und Dränger* and the French Romantics is again manifest in their common idealization of Shakespeare.

If Shakespeare was the patron saint of the *Stürmer und Dränger* and of the French Romantics, Rousseau might be called their father. While no writer matched the idolatry accorded to Shakespeare, Rousseau undoubtedly aroused impassioned enthusiasm and made a deep impact on the *Stürmer und Dränger* and the French Romantics. *La Nouvelle Héloïse* was one of the most popular novels of the time: it is reputed to have run to over sixty editions in France before 1800; it was translated into German by Gellius in 1761, discussed in the same year by Moses Mendelssohn in his *Briefe die neueste Litteratur betreffend*, and propagated by Formey, a minister of the French Protestant church in Brandenburg who took it upon himself to adapt the novel to the Christian spirit. Throughout the Storm and Stress there are numerous references to *La Nouvelle Héloïse* as well as to *Emile*. Herder so strongly recommended Rousseau to his fiancée that she even learnt French in order to read him. Lenz called *La Nouvelle Héloïse* 'das beste Buch, das jemals mit französischen Lettern ist abgedruckt worden'[54] ('the best book ever printed in French'), and like Herder and Goethe, undertook a pilgrimage to Clarens and Meillerie. For Klinger it was *Emile* that was the book of books; in spite of his difficulties in reading Rousseau only with much help from the dictionary, he never ceased to extol him, making explicit mention of him in a number of his works. Goethe and Schiller too partook in the mode for Rousseau (Schiller wrote a panegyric on Rousseau shortly after his death in 1778), although they were probably less deeply involved than some of their contemporaries. But the authors of *Werther* and *Die Räuber* undoubtedly cherished a very real sympathy for Rousseau.

Rousseau's influence in France is so vast that it cannot be neatly encapsulated in a survey such as this. It is not merely a matter of enthusiastic reception by, for instance, the young Chateaubriand and Lamartine. His effect was comparable to that of Freud or Marx in our own day in so far as their ideas are everywhere palpably present, indeed all-pervasive, yet at the same time almost perversely defiant of exact notation. Dédéyan, among others, has attempted to summarize all that the Romantic movement owes to him:

sentiment de la nature avec l'amour des paysages de lacs, de montagnes, de la vie rustique et primitive, rêve, rêverie et imagination se développant dans ces cadres enchanteurs, mal du siècle, aussi avec ses désenchantements, ses orages, ses révoltes et ses désirs d'évasion dans l'espace et dans la mort. Amour et passion, sensibilité religieuse, exaltation du moi et des puissances du moi, altruisme humanitaire et esprit d'enfance, voilà ce que nous offre le solitaire misanthrope et bon, qui rayonne en tant de disciples et qui demeure un des pères du romantisme européen.[55]

(feeling for nature, a love for landscapes of lakes and mountains, for rustic and simple life, dreams, dreaminess and imagination, nurtured in these enchanting surroundings, as well as the storms, rebellions and disillusionments of *mal du siècle* with its desire to escape afar or into death, love and passion, religious feeling, exaltation of the ego and its powers, humanitarian altruism and the spirit of childhood, this is what is offered to us by the misanthropic, good hermit, who shines forth in so many disciples and who remains one of the fathers of European Romanticism.)

Extensive though this list is, it is by no means exhaustive, for over and above these thematic strands, Rousseau's style and approach are of paramount importance. Lyricism and radical subjectivism are the true hallmarks of his writing and these are the qualities that passed on to the

Romantics. Every one of the great French Romantics walks, consciously or unconsciously, in the footsteps of the *promeneur solitaire*, whose attitudes and expression coloured French literature well into the nineteenth century.

Looking at Rousseau's works and also at his life, it is not hard to fathom his appeal to the *Stürmer und Dränger* and the French Romantics. For he stands as a living example of that dichotomy of rebelliousness and introversion characteristic of the two movements. In his colourful conflicts with the society of his day, in his championship of the freedom of the individual and in his social criticism he is the prototype of the storming rebel; at the same time his surrender to his own feelings, his perception of nature as a *paysage-état d'âme* and the music of his prose style clearly foreshadow the softer, melancholy aspects of the outsider under stress. It was Rousseau's dual message of sentiment and revolt that evoked such resonance among the *Stürmer und Dränger* and the French Romantics. The affinity between the two movements is underscored by their common response to Rousseau. The sequence of cause and effect is potentially confusing at this point; it is not so much that the Storm and Stress and French Romanticism resemble each other because they derive from the same sources, but rather their affirmation of the same sources is an expression of their inner likeness. It is, in a sense, a complete circle: the shared ancestry of the *Sturm und Drang* and of *romantisme* in Shakespeare and Rousseau, while fostering the connection between them, is also an indication of their parallelism. Had they not been counterparts, they would hardly have been attracted to the same models.

So in the last resort, although it is a significant comment on their alikeness, the shared ancestry of the Storm and Stress and of French Romanticism does not account for the affinity any more than does the work of such intermediaries as Mme de Staël in disseminating knowledge about the *Sturm und Drang* in France. These are outer, contributory factors that furthered the affinity. For all their importance, however, they leave unanswered the basic questions: why were the adherents of the Storm and Stress and of French Romanticism attracted to similar sources? why were the French Romantics fascinated by the *Stürmer und Dränger*? To answer these questions by pointing to the profound similarities between the two movements would in effect be to offer a non-answer that would bring us no nearer to the resolution of the underlying problem posed earlier: why does the French literature of the early nineteenth century represent a counterpart to trends in Germany some fifty years before? Perhaps such questions of causality lie beyond the domain of the literary critic. But to confine the study of literary history to the mere compilation of facts is surely a stultifying approach. The facts cry out for interpretation, even if that interpretation must needs to some extent be speculative and personal.

To my mind, the affinity between the Storm and Stress and French Romanticism stems from the coincidence of the inner predicament facing German poets in the mid-eighteenth century and the French in the early nineteenth century. Considering the differences in background that have repeatedly been noted, this may seem a startling contention. But beneath the outward divergence of attendant circumstances there lurks at the hard core an identical problem: that of breaking out of the dead-end of an effete Neo-classicism that threatened to stifle genuine creativity. Both literatures were sinking into a morass of staleness. The paths which had led the Germans and the French into this sterile impasse were admittedly quite different, as was the timing. But the final effect was exactly the same: an acute sense of frustration, particularly on the part of the young, together with a thirst for a new start. From the deep-seated dissatisfaction with the *status quo* came the impetus to seek a new life and a new literature. Though that quest manifested itself primarily in a blustering, often apparently negative rebelliousness, its true aim was the elaboration of an acceptable life-style and of a productive aesthetic. For this reason the theme of renewal, personal, social and artistic, is so prominent among the *Stürmer und Dränger* and the French Romantics. The re-structuring of human life and thought along more fertile lines is the *leitmotif* that unifies Hamann's aphorisms as well as the manifold deliberations in Herder's *Journal meiner Reise*. Similarly Hugo, in his survey of the three epochs of human history in the *Préface de Cromwell*, sees the advent in his own day of a new religion, a new social order and a new type of poetry. Stendhal's point of departure, in *Racine et Shakespeare*, is the need to evolve a dramatic form appropriate to the year 1823. And all the heroes of the *Sturm und Drang* and of *romantisme*, extroverts and introverts alike, from Faust onwards, are in reality engaged on a search for a *modus vivendi* in accord with their own personality instead of playing the standard role expected of them under the old social system. 'Notre époque est une époque de renaissance', Vigny proclaimed in 1829 in the *Lettre à Lord xxx*.[56] And so was the *Sturm und Drang*. That is the basis of the affinity and the source of the parallels between them.

The recognition of this fundamental community illumines many facets of their relationship. For instance, experimentation, particularly in dramatic but also in narrative form, is an integral part of that process of renaissance. From this also devolves their common interest in Shakespeare and Rousseau as the leading examples of adventurous non-conformism. Thus the French Romantics were so potently attracted to the *Stürmer und Dränger* because they recognized in them kindred spirits, elder brothers who had grappled with, and to some extent managed to conquer those very problems that they themselves were facing. In both countries the tension was between the progressive apostles of innovation and the conservative adherents to the *status quo*. The conflict was more acute and protracted in France because of the greater strength of its entrenched Neo-classical traditions, but in essence the French Romantic movement aimed at the same break-out as the *Sturm und Drang*. The parallelism of their historical predicament with that of the Germans in the mid-eighteenth century nurtured the enthusiasm of the French for the Storm and Stress in the early nineteenth. And it is this parallelism that is at the heart of the affinity between the two movements: trapped in a similar dead-end, the young of both groups attempted the same means of escape by either outgoing rebelliousness or by withdrawal into an introverted melancholy. The similarity of character and ideals springs from a like response to the same challenge: the necessity for radical renewal. So in the 1820s French literature was undergoing the same development as German literature had done in the 1770s. That this situation came to a head some fifty years later in France than in Germany is a direct consequence of the various retarding forces at work on the Western side of the Rhine. French literature in the early nineteenth century was as much in need of a revivifying electric shock as was German literature in the mid-eighteenth century, and this in effect was what the *Sturm und Drang* and *romantisme* amounted to.

                                    VI

This counterpart relationship between the Storm and Stress and French Romanticism had very important implications reaching far into the nineteenth century. Both were relatively short-lived movements; in this too they resemble each other. The vehemence of their active rebelliousness as of their brooding emotionalism was so intense that it could not be sustained for any length of time. Both are comparable to a

period of adolescence, at once self-assertive and self-questioning, alter-
nating between confidence and despair in their search for identity and
their need for self-expression. This adolescence, and particularly its timing in Germany in the 1770s and some fifty years later in France, left its
mark on the subsequent development of nineteenth-century literature.

The after-effects are discernible first in the tendency known as
Realism that was dominant on both sides of the Rhine around the middle of the century. The situation in regard to Realism is in many ways a
repetition of that Pre-romantic phase of the later eighteenth century
when similar trends were apparent in France and Germany without the
existence of a true counterpart relationship (see pp. 7–15). For in
Realism the German version did not in fact correspond to its French
equivalent in spite of their contemporaneity and their common
starting-point in the portrayal of the world of appearances. Here the
French are without rivals, unless it be the English – certainly not the
Germans. Their so-called Poetic Realism, represented in the works of
Keller, Stifter, Storm and Droste-Hülshoff, was an attenuated strain,
considerably softened by its strong poetic colouring. Nineteenth-
century German Realism has many highly interesting and idiosyncratic
writers; apart from those already cited, mention need only be made of
Meyer, Gotthelf, Raabe and Freytag, but none of these is a world giant
of the stature of Balzac, Flaubert or Zola. Conceding the provinciality
– literal and metaphorical – of mid-nineteenth-century German
writing, historians of German literature have tried to site the archime-
dean point of German Realism towards the end of the century. Fon-
tane's late novels of the 1890s are often seen as the climax of German
Realism, or even Thomas Mann's *Buddenbrooks* (1901). This is not the
place for a critical discussion of such judgements; suffice it to say that
they underline the indisputable fact that Realism was slower off the
mark and less vigorous in Germany than in France. This is all the more
surprising in that many of the features of Realism are already plainly
present in the drama of the Storm and Stress. In his analysis of *Kabale
und Liebe* in *Mimesis*, Erich Auerbach points to the bourgeois milieu, the
emphasis on truthfulness, the natural speech, the local colour and the
mingling of styles as characteristic of Realism; these traits are equally
prominent in *Götz von Berlichingen*, *Die Soldaten*, *Der Hofmeister*, and
even *Die Kindermörderin* in spite of its melodramatic hue. But these
beginnings of Realism did not mature in Germany because they were
overlaid and superseded at the turn of the century by a speculative and
metaphysical Romanticism that became as deeply ingrained in the Ger-

man tradition as Neo-classicism had been in the French. So the history
of German literature in the nineteenth century is a record of its struggle
with Romanticism in much the same way as French literature in the
previous century had endeavoured to come to terms with its past. And
just as French Romanticism was then impeded by the burden of its
heritage, so German Realism never quite cast its Romantic shadow. In
its poetic quality resides its strength as well as its weakness.

Circumstances were rather different in nineteenth-century France
owing in part to the relative place and character of its Romantic movement in its literary evolution. For French *romantisme* was in essence and
in effect a Storm and Stress, as I have tried to show. Like its German
counterpart, French Romanticism contained a pronounced element of
Realism, above all in its drama which aspired to naturalness and
cultivated local colour. From the nascent mimeticism of its *romantisme*
there is a straight line of development to the Realism, indeed to the
Naturalism, of the mid-nineteenth century, without the intervention of
the alien *Romantik* that broke the continuity in Germany. Hence the
Storm and Stress character of the Romantic movement in France and its
lateness contributed significantly to the vigour and preponderance of
French Realism.

There is a corollary to that proposition. While the nature of the
Romantic movement in France was such as to foster the growth of
Realism, it was a less propitious breeding-ground for certain other
trends. The emphasis on naturalness, for instance, while encouraging
Realism, tended on the other hand to keep bolder flights of imagination in check. As a result, those currents of transcendental idealism that
were given free rein in the German *Frühromantik* were considerably
retarded in France. So another diagonal counterpart relationship came
into being: between German Romanticism and French Symbolism.

IV

German Romanticism and French Symbolism

I

The relationship between the *Frühromantik*[1] of the opening years of the nineteenth century and the French Symbolism of the 1880s and 1890s is in itself a counterpart to that between the *Sturm und Drang* and French Romanticism. The affinities that link this later pair as well as the time-lag separating the two movements seem to reiterate the earlier conjunction. Coming to this further set of counterparts is somewhat like hearing an echo. But just as an echo is not really a direct repetition, so the connections between the *Frühromantik* and Symbolism are no mere reduplication of the foregoing situation. To mention only one differentiating factor, the outer circumstances had changed in the course of the nineteenth century in so far as the French had a better acquaintance with German literature in 1890 than in 1830. Also, the analogy between the *Frühromantik* and Symbolism resides more in a community of underlying tendencies and problems than in the parallelism of individual works such as can be traced between the *Sturm und Drang* and French Romanticism. This mutation has its source in the character of the two later movements themselves, as we shall see. But since the term 'counterpart' includes in its meaning some contraposition alongside the reiteration, its use is fully justified in the present context. So a counterpart exists not only between the *Sturm und Drang* and French Romanticism and between the *Frühromantik* and French Symbolism respectively, but also between these pairs. Thus a coherent pattern begins to emerge of the structural dynamics of Franco–German literary relationships in the nineteenth century.

Before engaging in more detailed analysis of the filiation between

the *Frühromantik* and French Symbolism, it might be well at this point
to offer a brief summary of those resemblances that suggest the comparison. Just as Symbolism was 'a second flood of the same tide as
Romanticism', to use Edmund Wilson's illuminating image,[2] so the
Frühromantik represents a second wave to the *Sturm und Drang*. The two
movements occupy similar positions in the relative development of
French and German literature, taking up the heritage from an earlier
generation to elaborate and propel it far beyond its original scope. In
the same way as Baudelaire was credited with having found the way to
rejuvenate Romanticism,[3] so the *Frühromantiker* can in like fashion be
said to have revived the *Sturm und Drang*, although in both cases, of
course, it is a matter of only certain elements. In each country the
original momentum of the previous generation had been overlaid by a
deviant development; in Germany the Weimar *Klassik* had blunted the
onslaught of the Storm and Stress, while in France first the Parnasse
had made formal perfection its centre of gravity, and subsequently
Naturalism had introduced all manner of scientific and social considerations into the realm of art. So the *Frühromantik* and French Symbolism came to be cast into parallel historical roles. While continuing
and outdoing the *Sturm und Drang* and *romantisme* respectively, they
were at the same time also reacting against a present that struck them as
uncongenially pedestrian. This is, needless to say, no judgement on the
intrinsic worth of German Classicism or Biedermeier, the Parnasse or
Naturalism; it is merely a statement of the position as perceived by
the *Frühromantiker* and the Symbolists. They are clearly counterparts in
their rejection of the present, their harking back to the past, and
perhaps most of all in their orientation to the future in the widest sense.
Their poetic manifestoes – Friedrich Schlegel's *Athenäum*, Novalis's
Blütenstaub collection, René Ghil's *Traité du verbe*, Jean Moréas's
Manifeste du symbolisme – are primarily formulations of intent,
programmes for what is to come. It is significant that Friedrich
Schlegel defined Romantic poetry in the *Athenäum* (no. 116) as 'eine
progressive Universalpoesie' ('a progressively universal poetry') whose
very essence lies in its constantly evolutionary character ('noch im
Werden'). Likewise Mallarmé envisaged true poetry as 'la poésie
future'[4] to be realized, he hoped, in *Le Livre*, that absolute opus that
assumed almost mythic proportions as the ultimate purpose of his
strivings. Charles Morice too, in *La Littérature de tout à l'heure*, looked
forward to that 'Livre futur' – note again the deliberate use of a capital
letter – which is the subject of the climactic chapter of his work and

which is presented as the eventual goal of all poetic aspiration. It is surely this fixation on the future that accounts for some of those features of the *Frühromantiker* and of the French Symbolists that are frequently criticized: the uncertainty and incoherence of their doctrines, the incessant flux and flow of their notions, that curious sense of floating that provoked Camille Mauclair's stricture in *La Nouvelle Revue* of October–December 1897: 'Le symbolisme comme école est insaisissable' ('Symbolism as a school is ungraspable'), a criticism that is equally relevant to the *Frühromantik*. For this reason Edmund Wilson's image of fluidity ('a second flood of the same tide') is particularly apposite.

The future to which the *Frühromantiker* and the Symbolists alike aspired was not conceived in temporal and spatial terms as a practical Utopia. In contrast to the first wave of European Romantics – the *Stürmer und Dränger* and the French Romantics – who hoped to ameliorate this world through their social criticism, the second generation sought, with reckless grandeur, to create a new world. The impetus for this endeavour sprang from the transcendental idealism that was the common foundation of both movements. Rarely – if indeed ever – in literary history has transcendental idealism exerted such force as in the *Frühromantik* and in French Symbolism. Herein resides the quintessence of the parallelism between the German poets and thinkers of the 1790s and 1800s and their counterparts across the Rhine more than half a century later. From this central communality of belief are derived many of the resemblances between the two groups; their philosophic creed and their artistic practices devolve from that transcendental idealism that forms the kernel and the mainspring of their existence as recognizable artistic phenomena. The absolute worth of creative activity, the postulate of consciousness as the source of that creativity, and the autonomy of art: all these fundamental tenets that link the *Frühromantik* and the French Symbolism are expressions and consequences of their basic transcendental idealism.

Nowhere is the effect of this transcendental idealism as decisive as in shaping their conception of art and of the artist. As the path of access to the superior realm, art becomes the pivot of the design. Friedrich Schlegel, for instance, described Romantic poetry as 'Transzendentalpoesie',[5] for the be-all and end-all of this supreme 'Poesie der Poesie' is the perception of the ideal within and beyond the real. An identical view of poetry and its function was repeatedly adumbrated by Mallarmé for whom poetry alone gave meaning to life in so far as it represented a channel to a higher spirituality. Using the more concrete images of the grave and paradise, Baudelaire voiced the same notion when he wrote: 'C'est à la fois par la poésie et *à travers* la poésie, par et *à travers* la musique, que l'âme entrevoit les splendeurs situées derrière le tombeau' and can 's'emparer immédiatement, sur cette terre même, d'un paradis révélé'[6] ('It is at one and the same time by means of and *through* poetry, by means of and *through* music, that the soul catches a glimpse of the splendours beyond the grave' and can 'come into possession, here and now, of a paradise opened up by revelation'). Various other aspects of the philosophy of art shared by the *Frühromantiker* and the Symbolists follow from this conception of poetry as the conductor of the transcendental. Imagination, the organ for perceiving the transcendental, became 'das Höchste und Ursprünglichste im Menschen'[7] ('man's highest and deepest capacity'), 'la reine des facultés' ('the queen of all faculties'), to cite the title of Baudelaire's essay in the *Salon de 1859*. And the technical means whereby the imagination mediates its vision of the yonder, namely the symbolic image, then assumed its central position in the aesthetics of both movements. 'La poésie symbolique cherche à vêtir l'Idée d'une forme sensible' ('Symbolical poetry seeks to clothe the Idea in a palpable form'), Jean Moréas proclaimed in the Manifesto that appeared in *Le Figaro* on 18 September 1886 and that marked the establishment of French Symbolism as a literary school. Wellnigh a century before in the *Vorlesungen über schöne Kunst und Literatur*, held in the winter of 1801–2, August Wilhelm Schlegel had clearly stated that beauty was a symbolic representation of the infinite and could in the finite world be conveyed 'nur symbolisch, in Bildern und Zeichen'[8] ('only symbolically, in pictures and signs'). Hence the writings of the *Frühromantiker* and of the French Symbolists abound in references to hieroglyphics, a favourite term because it suggests expression in symbolical pictures. The predominance of symbols also leads to the multiplicity of levels characteristic of the works of both groups; the shifts from the world of reality to that of imagination in, for example, *Heinrich von Ofterdingen* and *Le Bateau ivre*, are achieved through a web of flexible, expansive images that glide without apparent transition from one realm to the other. The traditional structure of the work of art is thereby dissolved into a loosely woven fabric of associative, suggestive images, musical in organization. It is, moreover, the primacy of transcendental idealism that accounts for the attraction of the *Frühromantiker* and of the French Symbolists to the exploration of myths, legends, *Märchen* as incarnations of that supernatural, spiritual sphere they longed to enter.

If the imagination is the antenna for sensing the transcendental, the artist's role may be compared to that of the active receiver–transmitter. He is the focal point of the whole system because he alone is endowed with the mysterious gift of perception and the magical capacity to translate his vision into symbolic images. So he is, in Mallarmé's words (in a letter to Henri Cazalis, 14 May 1867), a direct descendant of the alchemists of yore ('les alchimistes, nos ancêtres'), or as Novalis put it even more plainly: 'Der Künstler ist durchaus transzendental'[9] ('the artist is wholly transcendental'). In their exaltation of the artist the *Frühromantiker* and the French Symbolists intensified the conception already prominent among the *Stürmer und Dränger* and the French Romantics. While the earlier generation had cherished the artist as a genius quasi-divine in his creative powers, the second wave raised him virtually to the rank of a divinity. For both the French Symbolists and the *Frühromantiker* art had become a religion, and it was surrounded with all the mysticism and ritual associated traditionally with the practice of religion. Only this religion of aestheticism sought to reveal not so much eternal truth as absolute beauty. It was this beauty that the artist as seer could behold in the ineffable moments of in-sight and that he then endeavoured to convey in symbolic images.

The counterpart relationship between the *Frühromantik* and French Symbolism is thus manifest in their historical position within their respective native traditions, in their common idealistic basis, in their conception of art and the artist and in their literary techniques too. So many of the characterizations of the salient features of French Symbolism are applicable, *mutatis mutandis*, to the *Frühromantik* in exactly the same way as analyses of the *Sturm und Drang* fitted *romantisme*. Take for example A. G. Lehmann's summary of the customary definition of Symbolism:

> that the symbolists were pre-occupied by the nature of music and its relation to poetry; that they were anti-intellectuals or mystics; that they thought art was in some sense symbolical or symbolist (as opposed to 'representative'); that they popularized *vers libre*, and by implication attacked all rigid formalism in art.[10]

If the specific reference to the French form of *vers libre* is replaced by the equivalent German technical innovation of the *Mischgedicht*, the portrait could well be of the *Frühromantik*. The parallel holds true even in the highly specialized field of language. Leo Spitzer's outline of the Symbolists' linguistic aims is astonishingly apposite to the *Frühromantik*:

1. Der Ausdruck soll weniger deutlich, unbestimmter, verschwommener,
2. er soll verinnerlicht,
3. er soll wohllautend werden,
4. er soll überraschend wirken,
5. er soll abkürzen und so der Sprache neue Möglichkeiten eröffnen.[11]

(1. Expression is to be less precise, vaguer, more fluid,
2. it is to be internalized,
3. it is to sound harmonious,
4. it is to spring surprises,
5. it is to abbreviate and thereby create new linguistic possibilities.)

This seems a better statement of the practices of Friedrich Schlegel, Novalis and Wackenroder than is found in any study specially devoted to their style.

There is thus a close identity between the two movements. And it is as deep as it is far-ranging, extending beyond external, beyond even philosophic similarities right to the existential roots. For the *Frühromantik* and French Symbolism are fundamentally akin in that both are the product of a mode of experience, a way of apprehending reality, essentially an attitude to life rather than just a literary school or a philosophy of correspondences that finds its outlet in a particular use of symbols. Starting from an urge to renew poetry, both evolved into a metaphysical quest to re-shape the universe when the aesthetic synthesis expanded into a search for total harmony. If they seem revolutionary or eclectic, it is because they sought to re-discover and re-establish the true order of the world. And that true order resided, in their eyes, solely in inner values. The process of internalization, initiated by the introspective strand of the Storm and Stress and French Romanticism, here reached its ultimate consummation – a triumph that ironically turns into a defeat, as we shall see.

II

So striking a parallel as that between the *Frühromantik* and French Symbolism could hardly fail to attract the critics' attention. Just as Goethe had been aware of the counterpart relationship between the Storm and Stress and the French Romantics, so various contemporaries of the Symbolists in the early 1890s commented on the new movement's German affiliations. Verlaine's well-known blustering verdict should perhaps not be taken too seriously:

> Le symbolisme? . . . comprends pas . . . Ça doit être un mot allemand . . . hein? Qu'est-ce que ça peut bien vouloir dire? Moi, d'ailleurs, je m'en fiche. Quand je souffre, quand je jouis ou quand je pleure, je sais bien que ça n'est pas du symbole. Voyez-vous, toutes ces distinctions-là, c'est de l'allemandisme; qu'est-ce que ça peut faire à un poète ce que Kant, Schopenhauer, Hegel et d'autres Boches pensent des sentiments humains![12]

> (Symbolism? . . . don't understand . . . It must be a German word . . . eh? What on earth can it mean? I, for my part, don't care. When I suffer, when I feel joy or when I weep, I know that isn't a symbol. See, all those distinctions, they are Germanicisms; what can it matter to a poet what Kant, Schopenhauer, Hegel or other Krauts think about human feelings!)

This outburst was provoked by that first literary opinion-pollster, Jules Huret, who has faithfully recorded it among the more solemn replies in his *Enquête sur l'évolution littéraire*. Nonetheless, discounting Verlaine's anger, it is worth mention as an example of the early association of Symbolism with things German; here are the beginnings of that tendency to consider Symbolism 'comme l'efflorescence spontanée d'un parasite étranger'[13] ('as the spontaneous eruption of a foreign parasite'). This is a curious repetition of the French distrust of Romanticism as an outside threat to the indigenous tradition. With Symbolism the phobia never became as acute as it had been in the earlier years of the century, although in this instance too it was in part a reflection of the French sense of insecurity following the rout in 1870 at the hands of the Germans, in the same way as the fear of Romanticism had been the expression of French concern at the possible erosion of their traditional cultural leadership in Europe after the overthrow of the old system and the downfall of the new with Napoleon's defeat. The two situations and French reaction to them reveal a counterpart within French literary history.

But there were more serious discussions in the early 1890s of the relationship of Symbolism specifically to German Romanticism than

Verlaine's salvo. Several came from German critics obviously anxious
to claim credit for Germany for the new poetic movement across the
Rhine. However, these are mostly passing, rather superficial allusions as
in Paul Remer's article, 'Die Symbolisten. Eine neue literarische Schule
in Frankreich' in *Die Gegenwart* (25, 1890), or in K. A. Klein's
analysis of the sources of Stefan George's poetry in the *Blätter für die
Kunst* (no. 2, December 1892); Oskar Walzel indeed, in the *Jahresbericht*
of 1891, urged that the topic be more fully investigated. His plea was
superfluous, for in that year already an article had appeared, written by
a Frenchman, that not only was then, but still remains, one of the best
summaries of the relationship between the *Frühromantik* and French
Symbolism: Jean Thorel's 'Les Romantiques allemands et les symbolistes français' that was published in the September 1891 issue of
Entretiens politiques et littéraires (pp. 95–109). In a leisurely, almost
amateurish tone, yet with extraordinary perspicacity, Thorel explores
'la resemblance frappante que présente le mouvement symboliste avec
un mouvement littéraire qui eut un retentissement considérable en
Allemagne à la fin du siècle dernier et au commencement de celui-ci:
nous voulons parler des manifestations d'art et des oeuvres dues à
l'école romantique allemande'[14] ('the striking resemblance between the
Symbolist movement and a literary movement that had considerable
fame in Germany at the end of the last century and at the beginning of
this one: I refer to the artistic manifestations and works of the German
Romantic school'). After some general reflections on patterns of
cultural change and development, Thorel goes on to list many of the
features common to the two movements: idealism, freedom of the imagination, flight from formal plasticity, obscurity, emphasis on the
musical qualities of language, religious feeling, and even the severity of
critics *vis-à-vis* both groups of poets. Curiously and quite inexplicably
– except for its relative inaccessibility nowadays – Thorel's article
evoked no resonance in spite of Albert Saint-Paul's praise of it in his
Portraits du prochain siècle in 1894. Even more curiously it still failed to
spark any response following its rediscovery in 1910 by Tancrède de
Visan who gave a summary of Thorel's ideas in an article also entitled
'Le Romantisme allemand et le symbolisme français' in *Mercure de
France* (88, 16 December 1910). Visan had little to add other than his
surprise at the neglect of this promising field.

That neglect was in fact to persist for many a long year, possibly
because comparatists in the early phase of the discipline, still under the
sway of nineteenth-century positivistic scholarship, were far more avid

to collect external data than to investigate inner organic connections. This then was the period of the big compilations of the foreign trade between various national literatures. In the area of Franco–German literary relations the closing years of the nineteenth and the beginning of the twentieth century brought a series of weighty studies crammed with factual information (not always of impeccable accuracy!) and lamentably lacking in any real understanding of the structure or dynamics of the Franco-German link: Theodor Süpfle's *Geschichte des deutschen Kultureinflusses auf Frankreich* (Gotha: Thiememann, 1888); *Geschichte des deutschen Kultureinflusses auf Frankreich bis 1870* by Fritz Meissner (Leipzig: Renger, 1893); Virgile Rossel's *Histoire des relations littéraires entre la France et l'Allemagne* (Paris: Fischbacher, 1897); and, still in the same vein though later, Louis Reynaud's *L'Influence allemande en France au XVIIIième et XIXième siècle* (Paris: Hachette, 1922). Sadly none of these monuments of scholarship followed up Thorel's imaginative *aperçu*.

In the last fifty years, however, various critics have touched on the connection between German Romanticism and French Symbolism, often in a comment marginal to a specialized analysis of some particular aspect of nineteenth-century Franco–German literary relations. In an article on 'Novalis et le Symbolisme français' S. Braak for instance pointed out that 'il existe entre le Symbolisme et le romantisme allemand . . . une certaine analogie de forme et de fond'[15] ('there is a certain community of form and of matter between Symbolism and German Romanticism'), but he sees the filiation primarily in such lesser poets as Maurice de Guérin, Marceline Desbordes-Valmore, Sainte-Beuve and Villiers de l'Isle-Adam. Pierre Moreau stops on the brink with the tantalizing remark 'Aussi est-ce dans le symbolisme, – un critique l'a dit, – qu'il faut chercher en France l'analogue du romantisme allemand'[16] ('Thus it is in Symbolism – as a critic has said – that the French analogy to German Romanticism must be sought'). The critic is identified as Tancrède de Visan, and there the matter is left. Enid Duthie was rather more definite: 'Le lien entre le romantisme allemand et le symbolisme français est d'abord et surtout le lien entre deux idéalismes'[17] ('The link between German Romanticism and French Symbolism is above all a link between two idealisms').

All these are scattered, almost casual remarks. The significant breakthrough to an intuition of the underground workings of the Franco–German rapport did not come until Albert Béguin's highly sensitive *L'Âme romantique et le rêve*. Béguin focuses on what he calls the 'lineage

of interior Romanticism'[18] ('cette tradition de romantisme intérieur')
that lurked in France beneath the sound and fury of the official Romantic movement of the early nineteenth century. He illustrates the continuity of this 'interior Romanticism' from Rousseau and the
eighteenth-century occultists (Saint-Martin, Restif de la Bretonne)
onwards through Sénancour, Nodier, Maurice de Guérin, Nerval,
Hugo, to Baudelaire, Mallarmé, Rimbaud and Proust, and he identifies
theirs as 'une poésie qui . . . nous paraîtra étrangement voisine de celle
que voulut saisir, que ne saisit pas toujours le romantisme allemand'[19]
('a poetry that . . . will appear curiously close to that which German
Romanticism sought, not always successfully, to grasp'). Although
Béguin's approach is largely thematic, his analyses transcend the limitations of his method to achieve an exciting chiaroscuro effect that admittedly, and perhaps inevitably with such a subject, begs as many
questions as it answers. Yet Béguin's book is in many ways unique, not
least for the potency of its suggestiveness, even if this is at the cost of a
certain elusiveness.

Recent critics in this field have by and large been more specific, but
narrower. E. L. Stahl has shown that 'the German Romantics were one
of the sources of French symbolism',[20] while Lieselotte Dieckmann
concluded that 'the symbolists' metaphor of the hieroglyphic receives
from the romanticists its true perspective'.[21] In an original reversal of
the customary sequence Marianne Thalmann in *Die Zeichensprache der
Romantik* (Heidelberg: Lothar Stiehm Verlag, 1967) interpreted the
German Romantics as *de facto* Symbolists in their use of ciphers as structural and thematic vehicles of expression. Her references forward to
Baudelaire, Mallarmé and Valéry strongly hint that the German
Romantics pre-empted the French poets' tenets and practices. Werner
Vordtriede's revealing work, *Novalis und die französischen Symbolisten*,
had indeed already uncovered the source of some strands of the Symbolist aesthetic in the writings of Novalis. More important, Vordtriede
realized that: 'In Frankreich geschah etwas, was in Deutschland
ausblieb. Novalis' Nachfolge ist in Frankreich viel echter und legitimer
als in Deutschland selbst'[22] ('In France there took place what failed to
happen in Germany. Novalis's succession is much more genuine and
legitimate in France than in Germany itself'). It is this heritage from the
Frühromantik that underlies the striking resemblance between the two
movements noted by Jean Thorel, and that also contributes in no small
measure to the counterpart relationship that unites them so intimately
in spite of the long outer separation in time.

III

How much did the French know about Germany and especially about German literature and thought in the second half of the nineteenth century? This becomes a pertinent question if the French Symbolists are to be regarded as the heirs to German Romanticism.

Like many such apparently simple questions, it proves by no means simple to answer. The transmission of ideas, let alone the controversial subject of national image, cannot be quantified to yield neat and incontrovertible conclusions. The degree and depth of one nation's comprehension of another is in the last resort beyond objective measure, yet it is this dimension of quality that alone matters in the final balance. All too often, however, comparatists have been tempted to infer an influence from the sheer quantity of contacts between nations.

Granted these reservations, it is nonetheless possible to state with some assurance that on the eve of Symbolism the French were better informed about their neighbour across the Rhine than at the dawn of *romantisme*. Mme de Staël's *De l'Allemagne* certainly initiated a profound change of attitude towards the Germans who were no longer dismissed with a supercilious smile as peculiar barbarians. As curiosity about this strange land and its culture grew, the journey of exploration to Germany became almost a part of the educational ritual for many eminent Frenchmen: Quinet, Jean-Jacques Ampère, Michelet, Taine, Lerminier, Blaze de Bury, Saint-René Taillandier, Philarète Chasles, Victor Cousin, Hugo, Nerval, to name only a few. Following Mme de Staël's example with the pen too, a number of these travellers recorded their impressions so that the middle of the century witnessed a plethora of reports on various aspects of German life: Ampère's *Littérature et voyages* (1833), *Notices littéraires et politiques sur l'Allemagne* (1834) by Saint-Marc Girardin as well as his *Souvenirs de voyages et d'études* (1852–3), Lerminier's *Au delà du Rhin* (1835), *Etudes sur l'Allemagne* (1839) by Michiels, Matter's *L'Etat moral, politique et littéraire de l'Allemagne* (1846–7), Mme Blaze de Bury's *Voyage en Autriche, en Hongrie et en Allemagne* (1851), *Voyage au pays du coeur* (1853) by Eggis, Nerval's *Souvenirs d'Allemagne* (1853), Xavier Marmier's *Voyage pittoresque en Allemagne* (1858–9), Blaze de Bury's *Salons de Vienne et de Berlin* (1861). It would obviously be unwise to attach too great a significance to this outburst of travel literature, most of which has fallen into well-deserved oblivion. In some cases the titles already arouse suspicion (e.g. *Voyage au pays du coeur* – *Journey to the Land of the Heart*; *Voyage pittoresque en Allemagne* – *Picturesque Journey to Germany*), conjuring up an idealized travelogue with a sentimental emphasis on superficial prettiness. However, the number of these books does in itself testify to a very live interest in Germany that was to develop later in the century into a real fascination as Frenchmen stared in astonishment at Germany's emergence as a major European power following its unification and industrialization. And even if many of the travellers were naïve, some at least were gifted with shrewd insight. Outstanding among these is Edgar Quinet who lived in Germany from 1826 to 1837 and came to know many of its intellectual leaders as well.

Travel in the other direction abounded too, particularly after the political upheavals in Germany in 1830 and 1848. Heinrich Heine and Ludwig Börne are the most famous residents in the German colony in Paris that was estimated by the middle of the century to number eighty to a hundred thousand. German was taught in schools and universities, and German prestige was high in artistic and intellectual matters: Beethoven, Gluck, Mozart and Wagner were performed in the concert and opera houses; Winterhalter was the court painter, and the centenary of Schiller's birth in 1859 was celebrated at court with great ceremony. Many Frenchmen extolled the virtues of German civilization: Renan was a staunch advocate of Franco-German co-operation because he believed that France had much to learn from Germany in religious liberalism and in higher education. Taine too was profoundly impressed by German scholarly achievements in philosophy, history, linguistics and archaeology, while the historian Gabriel Monod called Germany the second home of every thinking man. This was a far cry indeed from the tendency to despise all things German in the early years of the century.

The growing interest in German culture was both reflected in, and fostered by, the increasing number and prominence of journals devoted to the study of German philosophy, religion, politics and philosophy of history as well as literature. These were a more reliable source of information than the largely subjective reports of individual travellers. The relative success of these journals offers some outer measurement of public response. Thus it is revealing that the *Archives littéraires de l'Europe* survived only from 1804 till 1807. Likewise the *Bibliothèque germanique* failed in 1805 and fared little better in 1826 in spite of the support of Georges Cuvier, Victor Cousin and Philippe-Albert Stapfer. But the *Revue des deux mondes*, founded in 1831 after the demise of the Romantics' *Le Globe*, went from strength to strength. From 1857 onwards it was supplemented by the *Revue germanique*, established by the Alsatians Charles Dollfus and Auguste Nefftzer on the pattern of the *Revue britannique*. It is worth noting that the *Revue germanique* subsequently changed its name to *Revue germanique et française* in order to emphasize the linking of the two cultures so felicitously implied in the name *Revue des deux mondes*. The importance of the *Revue des deux mondes* as a bridge across the Rhine can hardly be over-estimated: through its regular series of generally well-informed and always favourably disposed articles by such contributors as Quinet, Michelet, Jean-Jacques Ampère, Blaze de Bury, Xavier Marmier, Lerminier, Philarète Chasles and Saint-René Taillandier, it was instrumental in bringing German ideas into wide circulation in France. Moreover, the very positive attitude of this respected journal, that found so much to admire in Germany, further enhanced the prestige of German civilization in mid-nineteenth-century France.

Among the articles on German culture in the *Revue des deux mondes* and the *Revue germanique* as well as in sundry other journals (e.g. *Mercure du XIXième siècle*, *Revue de Paris*, *Revue encyclopédique*, *Revue critique*, *Revue contemporaine*, *Journal des débats*, *Revue de l'instruction publique*) that participated in the fashionable exploration of the land beyond the Rhine, the majority were devoted to facets of German thought. Between about 1830 and 1870 it was much rather German philosophy – philosophy of history, of religion, of science – than German literature that was the focus of attention in France. There is no need to underline the significance of this bias for the transmission of transcendental idealism from the *Frühromantiker* to the French Symbolists. This concentration on philosophy as Germany's principal distinction may also help to explain why Novalis and Friedrich Schlegel were known primarily as mystical thinkers, the image of them projected also by Mme de Staël and Carlyle. The vogue for German philosophy became increasingly manifest from the 1830s onwards, coinciding with the spate of travellers' reports and the establishment of the *Revue des deux mondes*, but coming after the peak of French Romanticism. Here again it is amply evident that the true counterpart relationship is not between the two movements known as *Romantik* and *romantisme* respectively. By 1844 Heine could, in his *Deutschland*

(Kaput V), claim of the French:

Sie philosophieren und sprechen jetzt
Von Kant, von Fichte und Hegel

(They philosophize and now discuss
Kant, and Fichte and Hegel)

– though the seriousness of his testimony is somewhat undermined by
the following two lines in which he puts forward this further proof of
German influence on the French:

Sie rauchen Tabak, sie trinken Bier
Und manche schieben auch Kegel

(They smoke tobacco, they drink beer
And some even play skittles)

By 1844 the French certainly could have read Kant and could have
some familiarity at least with Fichte and Hegel. Kant's works had appeared in French translation some ten years previously already: in 1831
L.-F. Schön had published a volume entitled *Philosophie transcendentale
ou système d'Emmanuel Kant*; the following year saw the appearance of
Principes métaphysiques de la morale, traduits de l'allemand d'Emmanuel Kant
by Charles Tissot, who was also responsible for the *Critique de la raison
pure* of 1835–6. In the next decade Jules Barni offered renderings of
Kant's major works: *Critique du jugement* in 1846, and in 1848 *Critique de
la raison pure* together with *Fondements de la métaphysique*. Barni's version
of the *Critique de la raison pure* of 1869 marks a second and deeper stage
in the appreciation of Kant in France that is of direct relevance to the
formation of Symbolism. Whereas earlier he had been suspect as a
sceptic, by the 1870s he came to be esteemed above all for the loftiness
of his thought and its independence of traditional religiosity. The
idealism of Kant was, according to Henri Régnier, 'la clé métaphysique
de la plupart des esprits de la génération qui compose l'école
symboliste'[23] ('the metaphysical key to most of the minds of the
generation that makes up the Symbolist school'), as it had been in Germany almost a century before the key to the *Frühromantik*. This common paternity of the *Frühromantik* and French Symbolism in Kant
parallels the indebtedness of both the Storm and Stress and French
Romanticism to Shakespeare and Rousseau.

No other German thinker, with the possible exception of Hegel, had
as strong and as lasting an effect in France as Kant in the mid-

nineteenth century. Several histories of German philosophy dating from this period take Kant as their starting-point: the *Histoire de la philosophie allemande* (1836) by the Breton Barchou de Penhoën, Ott's *Exposé critique des systèmes depuis Kant jusqu'à Hegel* (1844) and Joseph Willm's *Histoire de la philosophie allemande depuis Kant jusqu'à nos jours* (1846–9). Victor Cousin's role in the introduction of German thought into France in both his teaching and his writings is so well known as to require little comment. On his first extensive visit to Germany in 1817 at the age of twenty-five, Cousin met the brothers Schlegel, Hegel, Solger, Schleiermacher and Goethe. The impact of German philosophy found an immediate precipitate in his lectures in Paris the following year, the *Cours de philosophie, professé à la faculté des lettres pendant l'année 1818*. From then on he maintained close contacts with many leading German thinkers and scholars including Hegel, Schelling, Schleiermacher, Savigny, Creuzer, Humboldt, Förster and Varnhagen von Ense. His official mission to Germany to study the school system on behalf of the French government resulted in his *Mémoire sur l'instruction secondaire dans le royaume de Prusse* (1827). His critique of Kant's *Kritik der reinen Vernunft*, published in 1842, was deemed by Schelling the finest expose of Kant's system. In his later years Cousin was alternately credited with, or castigated for, having brought German thought into France. While the consequences of Cousin's work may be a matter of opinion, the facts of his manifold and discerning intermediacy across the Rhine are beyond contest.

The ethical idealism of Kant became tinged with transcendental mysticism through the insinuation of three further German thinkers of considerable importance in the evolution of Symbolism: Schelling, Eduard Hartmann and Schopenhauer. *Extraits philosophiques de Schelling*, compiled and translated by Charles Benard, was published in the mid-1850s almost simultaneously with Grimblot's rendering of the *Système de l'idéalisme transcendental*. There is therefore firm ground for the supposition that the Symbolists were familiar with Schelling's mystical philosophy of nature, a corner-stone of the *Frühromantik* and of the whole Symbolist theory of *correspondances*. Hartmann's *Philosophie des Unbewussten*, which appeared from 1869 onwards, was translated into French in 1877. As for Schopenhauer's *Die Welt als Wille und Vorstellung*, it was so current in France in the 1870s and 1880s as a result of Théodule Ribot's book *La Philosophie de Schopenhauer* (1874) and a veritable avalanche of articles that Cantacuzène's translation seemed almost superfluous when it finally appeared in 1886. Perhaps it is well to be reminded by this curious incident of the innate haphazardness of the process of transmission.

The infiltration of German literature into France in the course of the nineteenth century was slower than that of German philosophy and just as unpredictably inconsistent as in the previous phase at the time of *romantisme*. For instance the *Hochromantik* came to be known much sooner and more readily than the *Frühromantik*. E. T. A. Hoffmann, whose reception in France has been traced by Elizabeth Teichmann in *La Fortune de E. T. A. Hoffmann en France* (Geneva: Droz, 1961), enjoyed an almost immediate and enormous success from his first introduction in the late 1820s; in the early 1830s, following the translation of his complete works in twenty volumes, his fame probably surpassed that of Goethe and Schiller, and he became in the eyes of the French *the* German Romantic. Equally popular was the German *Lied*, the lyrics of poets such as Mörike, Uhland, Rückert, Lenau, La Motte-Fouqué and of course Heine. Several collections succeeded each other in a close cluster towards the middle of the century, encouraged perhaps by the success of Nerval's translations in the *Revue des deux mondes* of April, July and September 1848. The growth of interest in German literature in France is revealed by the fact that Nerval's first edition of *Poésies allemandes* in 1830 had been little noticed. Then suddenly within the space of some twenty years came a whole spate of anthologies and studies: Nicholas Martin's *Poètes contemporains de l'Allemagne* in 1848 and 1860, Paul de Lacour's *Bouquet de Lieder* in 1856 and *Rhythmes et Refrains* in 1864, the *Ecrivains et poètes de l'Allemagne* by Saint-René Taillandier in 1861, Chatelain's *Fleurs du Rhin* in 1865, and in 1868 Edouard Schuré's *Histoire du Lied*, to mention only a few outstanding works.

This preference for the *Hochromantik* is not surprising; the tales of Hoffmann, the lyrics of Uhland and Mörike and the dramas of Zacharias Werner are more easily accessible than the subtle refinements of Novalis and Wackenroder or the complexities of Friedrich Schlegel. A number of references to Friedrich Schlegel, Tieck and Novalis are scattered in journals and reviews of the first half of the century, and several major works were in fact translated at a relatively early date: Mme Necker de Saussure's version of August Wilhelm Schlegel's *Vorlesungen über dramatische Kunst und Literatur* had appeared in 1814; Tieck's *Sternbald* was translated by the Baronne de Montolieu in 1823, and in 1825 Friedrich Creuzer's *Symbolik und Mythologie der alten Völker* by J. D. Guigniaut; 1829 brought Friedrich Schlegel's *Geschichte der alten und neuen Literatur*, and 1835 parts of *Lucinde* in the *Revue germanique*. The same journal, then under the enlightened guidance of Xavier Marmier, introduced fragments of Novalis's *Hymnen* in 1829, prompted perhaps by Carlyle's essay of the same year which hailed Novalis as a figure of outstanding importance; further works of his were published by Têtot Frères in 1837. But all these passed unheeded. There was quite simply no awareness in France of the significance of the *Frühromantik*. As far as the French were concerned, German Romanticism continued to be Goethe, Schiller, Bürger, Werner, i.e. the poets launched by Mme de Staël, plus Hoffmann and the *Lied*.

A turning-point might have come in 1833 with Heine's *Die Romantische Schule*, which had its origins in a series of articles for *L'Europe littéraire*. It was Heine's avowed aim, as sugested by his initial title 'De l'Allemagne depuis Madame de Staël' ('About Germany since Madame de Staël'), to correct the portrait of his native land presented in *De L'Allemagne* which – to quote his opening sentence – had remained 'die einzige umfassende Kunde welche die Franzosen über das geistige Leben Deutschlands erhalten haben' ('the only comprehensive statement that the French have received about Germany's cultural life'). This would surely have been the opportunity for that well-informed, judicious account of the *Frühromantik*, indeed of the entire Romantic movement, lacking in France. But Heine was not the man to fulfil that task. Though he obviously had an incomparably wider and deeper knowledge of German Romanticism than Mme de Staël, his total picture is, if anything, even more distorted than hers. For he allowed himself to be so carried away by his bitter sarcasm as to make a mockery of the Romantics. To take two specific examples in areas that were to be of prime importance for the Symbolists: Jacob Böhme and Novalis.

The vignette of Böhme is worth quoting in full:

Unter den Verrücktheiten der romantischen Schule in Deutschland verdient das unaufhörliche Rühmen und Preisen des Jakob Böhme eine besondere Erwähnung. Dieser Name war gleichsam das Schiboleth dieser Leute. Wenn sie den Namen Jakob Böhme aussprachen, dann schnitten sie ihre tiefsinnigsten Gesichter. War das Spass oder Ernst?

Jener Jakob Böhme war ein Schuster, der Anno 1575 zu Wörlitz in der Oberlausitz das Licht der Welt erblickt und eine Menge theosophischer Schriften hinterlassen hat. Diese sind in deutscher Sprache geschrieben und waren daher unsern Romantikern um so zugänglicher. Ob jener sonderbare Schuster ein so ausgezeichneter Philosoph gewesen ist, wie viele deutsche Mystiker behaupten, darüber kann ich nicht allzu genau urteilen da ich ihn gar nicht gelesen; ich bin aber überzeugt, dass er keine so gute Stiefel gemacht hat wie Herr Sakoski. Die Schuster spielen überhaupt eine Rolle in unserer Literatur, und Hans Sachs, ein Schuster, welcher im Jahre 1454 zu Nürremberg geboren ist und dort sein Leben verbracht, ward von der romantischen Schule als einer unserer besten Dichter gepriesen. Ich habe ihn gelesen, und ich muss gestehen, dass ich zweifle, ob Herr Sakoski jemals so gute Verse gemacht hat wie unser alter, vortrefflicher Hans Sachs.[24]

(Among the lunacies of the Romantic school in Germany the incessant glorification and praise of Jacob Böhme deserves special mention. This name was something of a shibboleth for these people. When they pronounced the name Jacob Böhme, they put on their most pensive expressions. Was this in jest or in earnest?

This Jacob Böhme was a shoemaker who was born in Wörlitz in Oberlausitz in the year 1575 and who left a mass of theosophical writings. They are in German so that they were readily accessible to our Romantics. Whether this odd shoemaker was such an excellent philosopher as many German mystics maintain, I cannot judge too well since I have not read him; but I am convinced that he did not make as fine boots as Mr Sakoski. Shoemakers altogether play an important role on our literature, and Hans Sachs, a shoemaker who was born in Nuremberg in the year 1454 and spent his life there, was extolled by the Romantic school as one of our best poets. I have read him, and I must confess that I doubt whether Mr Sakoski ever made such good verse as our excellent old Hans Sachs.)

This is typical of Heine's method in its aggressive momentum from the very opening words onwards, its satirical intent and, most damaging of all, its reduction of the elevated to the ridiculous by the use of pedestrian details as a transition to deflect the serious into the absurd. Here it is the ludicrous comparison of Böhme as a shoemaker to a Mr Sakoski which is the crux of his destructive analysis. He then cleverly conceals his hatchet activity, at least partially, under the cover of a pseudo-earnest rumination on the role of shoemakers in German literature, specially Hans Sachs, but this too is undercut by the reiterated reference to Mr Sakoski.

Heine's approach to Novalis is fundamentally the same, though rather more discrete at the outset and therefore perhaps all the more insidious in that its sensible beginning disposes the reader to accept what follows. The first two of the five pages devoted to Novalis in *Die Romantische Schule* (Book II, section 4) are hardly exceptionable: some biographical data quickly lead to a discussion of *Heinrich von Ofterdingen*, of which the opening paragraph is cited. Indeed, Heine's poetic comment on the quotation reveals the finesse of his sensitivity to Romantic writing when he so chose. From that point on, however, the whole nature of his presentation changes, but so unexpectedly and with such apparently authentic reportage that the unwary may not know where to draw the line between fact and fantasy. Certainly the contemporary French reader would hardly have realized the manipulation. Novalis's Sophie, sketched as a stylized, ethereal fairy-tale beauty, is contrasted with her plump, jolly, practical, high-bosomed sister who delights in the tales of Hoffmann. True or false? The caricature is sufficiently subtle not to disturb the unsuspecting reader. Further on, with the digression into minutiae about swans, their migration to Africa, their death by arrows identified by Professor Blumenbach as African, etc., the excursion into extravagance is barely veiled. And on the narrator's own return from the far South, the news of the sister's switch from Hoffmann to brandy for sustenance in her sorrow at Sophie's impending death verges on the burlesque. The plausible and the nonsensical are cunningly intertwined. For example, Novalis did refer to Sophie as an angel during her tubercular decline, but since *Ofterdingen* was not published until after Novalis's own death, she could hardly have been reading the volume bound in red leather with gold lettering that the narrator now has in his hand, much less could she have 'sich die Schwindsucht herausgelesen'[25] ('got consumption from reading it'). Those final pathetic touches – the red leather volume, the poplar shading Sophie's grave – are carefully designed to stir up sympathy and to lull disbelief. Yet, as in the portrait of Jacob Böhme, Heine has in fact ended with a travesty of Novalis by contaminating his sublimity with comic nonsense that is well enough disguised to take the ignorant reader in.

Die Romantische Schule amounts to a sardonic persiflage. Far from acting as a corrective to *De L'Allemagne*, it only compounded the misconceptions, and in the worst possible manner for it is the product of calculated malice, whereas Mme de Staël's shortcomings were the fruit of inadvertency. No French reader of *Die Romantische Schule* could derive from it any inkling of the true significance of the *Frühromantik*. If recognition of the poets and ideas of the *Frühromantik* was so long delayed in France, the fault must in part at least be attributed to Heine and his viciously misleading technique of reduction. No wonder that it was not until the second half of the nineteenth century, and then by indirect routes, that the *Frühromantik* really penetrated into France.

One of these indirect routes was via England, more specifically via Carlyle's *Sartor Resartus* which appeared in the same year as Heine's *Die Romantische Schule*. Like Heine's work, Carlyle's is a satire, but it is devoid of the guile that makes Heine so deceptive a guide. Carlyle's account of the mystical German philosopher, Professor Diogenes Teufelsdröckh of Weissnichtwo (Knownotwhere) is full of good-natured whimsicality. Though Carlyle makes use of his detached position as the fictitious editor of the Professor's writings to poke fun at Teufelsdröckh, beneath his banter he in fact gives a penetrating insight into German transcendentalism:

> All visible things are emblems; what thou seest is not there on its own account; strictly taken, is not there at all: Matter exists only spiritually, and to represent some Idea, and *body* it forth. Hence Clothes, as despicable as we think them, are so unspeakably significant. Clothes, from the King's mantle downwards, are emblematic, not of want only, but of a manifold cunning Victory over Want. On the other hand all Emblematic things are properly Clothes, thought-woven or hand-woven: must not the Imagination weave garments, visible Bodies, wherein the else invisible creations and inspirations of our Reason are, like Spirits, revealed, and first become all-powerful; — the rather if, as we often see, the Hand too aid her, and (by wool Clothes or otherwise) reveal such even to the outward eye?
>
> Men are properly said to be clothed with Authority, clothed with Beauty, with Curses, and the like. Nay, if you consider it, what is Man himself, and his whole terrestrial Life, but an Emblem; a Clothing or visible Garment for that divine ME of his, cast hither, like a light-particle, down from Heaven? Thus is he said also to be clothed with a Body.
>
> Language is called the Garment of Thought: however, it should rather be, Language is the Flesh-Garment, the Body, of Thought. I said that Imagination wove this Flesh-Garment; and does not she? Metaphors are her stuff.[26]

Such a passage lends credence to the contention made by Francis Viélé-Griffin in the first issue of *Entretiens politiques et littéraires* (1 April 1890) that Carlyle had provided, in the idealistic opinions of Professor Teufelsdröckh, the most satisfying statement of the role of the symbol.

Carlyle's work was readily appreciated in France from an early date onwards: in 1846 Antoine Dilmans drew attention to *Sartor Resartus* in an article in the *Revue indépendante* to be followed three years later by Montégut's contribution to the *Revue des deux mondes*. By the 1860s Carlyle's fame in France reached its peak with Taine's series in *Débats* (subsequently published in 1864 under the title *L'Idéalisme anglaise: étude sur Carlyle*), Milsand's *Esthétique anglaise* (1864) and the translation of Carlyle's works as from 1865. Through Carlyle's absorption in Fichte as well as Kant these two leading exponents of idealism gained wider currency in France. Carlyle was also the first outside Germany to give serious attention to Novalis. It seems a prime example of those paradoxes in which international literary relations abound that it should have been a Scot who was one of the earliest and most effective mediators between the *Frühromantik* and France.

Thus during the major part of the nineteenth century the French still had at best only a partial and haphazard image of Germany. With good reason Jean-Marie Carré has branded it a 'mirage'. His clever survey of Franco-German relationships in *Les Ecrivains français et le mirage allemand* (Paris: Boivin, 1947) outlines a changing series of such 'mirages': for Mme de Staël in her hostility to the Napoleonic tyranny Germany was the land of freedom, candour and enthusiasm; to Hugo and the poets of the Restoration, weary of the Neo-classical niceties, it was the land of fantasy, lyricism and inspiration; Victor Cousin in his fight against materialism saw it as the land of pure idea, the home of metaphysics; to Michelet with his dream of bringing French history to life, Germany denoted a viable philosophy of history; and to Renan in his longing for precision it represented the personification of philology and science. Even discounting the streak of political intent that makes Carré's book an admonition to the French after the defeat of 1940, his arguments are highly persuasive. Certainly under the Second Empire the French struggle against imperialism and clericalism encouraged the fashioning of a distorted picture of Germany as the fatherland of Luther, Kant, Hegel, Strauss and Feuerbach, a citadel of liberalism, emancipation, science and free-thinking. This new vision was nothing other than an updated version of Mme de Staël's wish-child; stylized and above all idealized, it fulfilled French needs, but was far removed from reality. The dangers of this *germanolâtrie* (idolizing of Germany) were first understood by Edgar Quinet who sensed the changes in Germany and

clearly spelled out the threat to France in his article 'De l'Allemagne et
de la révolution' which appeared in the *Revue des deux mondes* (1
January 1832). Quinet's warnings, however, either went unheeded or
were deplored as unfounded pessimism. What prevailed was the per-
sistent romanticizing of Victor Cousin and his disciples who elaborated
on, and indeed intensified, Mme de Staël's view of Germany as the
home of idealism *par excellence*. Not even the so-called *Année terrible*,
1870, could wholly shatter this illusion. Paradoxically, the Germans'
victory enhanced their prestige; from their defeat the French concluded
not only the need for reform in France but also the superiority of German scientific and military systems. And so, after an initial period of
hesitation and disenchantment, the belief in German supremacy in
practical organization as well as in idealist thought gained new
strength.

Between about 1830 and 1870 therefore the French had at their disposal many more sources of information about Germany than in the
opening decades of the century. The multitude of travellers' reports,
the journals, the translations, the vogue for German philosophy and
science: all these indicate that admiration for Germany had well and
truly ousted the earlier contempt of the 'civilized' French for their 'barbarian' neighbours. But if it was a richer picture, it was still very far
from a balanced one. While German philosophy was highly esteemed,
German literature continued to be largely neglected. *De l'Allemagne*,
reprinted no less than thirteen times between 1835 and 1869, still
remained the standard source of information, and the writers whom
Mme de Staël had championed – Goethe, Schiller, Jean-Paul, Werner
– were regarded, with the notable addition of E. T. A. Hoffmann, as
the leading German men of letters. Of the existence, let alone the
significance of the *Frühromantik's* aesthetics and works the French
remained in ignorance for an amazingly large part of the nineteenth
century. Here once again we come up against the time-lag between the
two countries that was already so striking in the earlier periods and that
determines the structure of Franco-German literary relationships between 1770 and 1895.

IV

It is Wagner who was the linchpin in the advent of the *Frühromantik*
into France. In certain respects Wagner's role as an intermediary bet-

ween the *Frühromantik* and French Symbolism forms a counterpart to that of Mme de Staël between the Storm and Stress and French Romanticism; in both their impact in France and their function as mediators bridging the Rhine they are patently comparable. There is, however, also a cardinal difference: whereas Mme de Staël merely gave an account of the Storm and Stress, Wagner's works can be regarded as the embodiment of German Romanticism. Thus at one and the same time he presented and represented German Romanticism in France. It is this that makes him of such crucial importance in the dynamics of Franco-German literary relationships.

The history of Wagner's reception in France has been so fully documented[27] that a brief résumé will suffice here. Contrary to common belief, Wagner did not conquer France at one great onrush. There were vicissitudes, including another of those time-lags characteristic of Franco-German transmissions. The earliest mentions of Wagner in France date from about the middle of the century: on 12 September 1843 in the journal *Débats* Berlioz gave brief reports on *Rienzi* and *The Flying Dutchman* which he had seen in Dresden; again in *Débats* on 18 May 1849 Liszt wrote about *Tannhäuser*, while in the following year Nerval contributed to *La Presse* of 8 and 9 September an account of Liszt's production of *Lohengrin* at which he had been present the previous month in Weimar. This first phase of Wagner's introduction into France was completed by Gautier's appraisal of a performance of *Tannhäuser* in Wiesbaden in the *Moniteur universel* of 29 September 1857. Wagner was thus relatively little known in Paris at the time of his visit in 1859. Concerts of his music were badly received as indeed was the first performance of an opera of his in France: *Tannhäuser* in March 1861. There were exceptions to the general coldness: one of them was Challemel-Lacour whose translations of four libretti (*Tannhäuser, Lohengrin, Tristan and Isolde* and *The Flying Dutchman*) together with some of Wagner's theoretical writings appeared in 1861. But by far the most ardent apostle of Wagner in France was Baudelaire, to whom Wagner's music was nothing short of a revelation. His substantial article, 'Richard Wagner et *Tannhäuser* à Paris' in the *Revue européenne* of 1 April 1861 marks a decisive turning-point in several respects. Not only was it the first passionately enthusiastic appreciation of Wagner in France; it also signifies a real breach in French artistic sensibility, the incursion of new elements full of possibilities for the future. The words are Baudelaire's own as he jubilantly proclaimed 'l'idée est lancée, la trouée est faite, c'est l'important'[28] ('the idea has been launched, the opening made, that is what is important') and expressed his faith in

> la possibilité de tentatives nouvelles dans le même sens, et que dans un avenir très rapproché on pourrait bien voir non pas seulement des auteurs nouveaux, mais même des hommes anciennement accredités, profiter, dans une mesure quelconque, des idées émises par Wagner, et passer heureusement à travers la brèche ouverte par lui.[29]

(the possibility of new endeavours in the same direction, and that in the very near future we might see not only new writers but even established men deriving some advantage from the ideas put forth by Wagner, and successfully going through the breach he has opened up.)

It was to be almost another twenty-five years before Baudelaire's visionary hopes were to be fulfilled in the Symbolist movement. In the meanwhile there were a few concert performances of Wagner's music and some scattered articles, notably Edouard Schuré's 'Le Drame musical et l'oeuvre de M. Richard Wagner' in the Revue des deux mondes of 1869, the first attempt at a global assessment, together with the first reference to the idea of the Gesamtkunstwerk, the total work of art. But the circle of enthusiasts was small, and they were obliged to make pilgrimages abroad to see Wagner's music-dramas on stage.

It was as a consequence of one such pilgrimage that the Wagnerian fever finally reached France. In 1882 the Bayreuth production of The Ring was seen in London by Edouard Dujardin. The impression was as electrifying as that of Tannhäuser on Baudelaire some twenty years earlier: 'l'oeuvre répondait évidemment aux plus profonds besoins de mon inconscient'[30] ('the work clearly satisfied the deepest needs of my subconscious'), Dujardin commented many years later. The premiere of Parsifal in Bayreuth also in 1882 and Wagner's death in 1883 provoked an upsurge of interest in him in Paris; the 1883–4 concert season included a fair amount of Wagner's music in the repertoire. This was the background for the Revue Wagnérienne that was founded and edited by Dujardin and that wielded an influence quite out of proportion to its brief life-span (1885–8). It numbered among its collaborators Catulle Mendès, Edouard Schuré, Téodor de Wyzewa, René Ghil, Gérard de Nerval, Joris-Karl Huysmans, Villiers de l'Isle-Adam, Charles Morice, Houston Stewart Chamberlain, Verlaine and Mallarmé. Initially intended as a collection of information for

Wagnerians, it quickly deepened beyond this original scope. As Dujardin explained,

> L'objet de la *Revue Wagnérienne* ne fut pas, comme d'aucuns le crurent, de propager l'oeuvre wagnérienne, mais d'en pénétrer et d'en faire connaître la signification profonde. Pour parler sans nuances, nous voulûmes, Chamberlain et moi, répandre notre découverte: Wagner grand musicien? la chose était trop évidente; mais Wagner grand poète; mais Wagner grand penseur; et surtout Wagner créateur d'une nouvelle forme d'art.[31]

> (The aim of the *Revue Wagnérienne* was not, as some thought, to promulgate Wagner's works, but to come to understand them and to make their deeper meaning known. To put it plainly, we wanted, Chamberlain and I, to broadcast our discovery: that Wagner was a great musician? that was too obvious; but that Wagner was a great poet; but that Wagner was a great thinker; and above all that Wagner was the creator of a new form of art.)

The importance of the *Revue Wagnérienne* lay in its shift of focus from Wagner the musician on to Wagner the prototype of the experimental artist engaged in a quest for the absolute. It is in this context that Wagner formed so vital a model for the Symbolists. Baudelaire had already sensed this in his article of 1861, but never had the underlying significance of Wagner's work been formulated as explicitly as by the *Revue Wagnérienne*. That Moréas's Symbolist Manifesto appeared one year after the establishment of the *Revue Wagnérienne* is surely more than a coincidence. Through the intermediacy of the *Revue Wagnérienne*, which had grasped the full import of his undertaking, Wagner became the catalyst to the Symbolist movement.

What then was the ultimate source of his impact? Dujardin's exposition of the aims of the *Revue Wagnérienne* suggests a partial answer: it was not so much Wagner the musician as Wagner the poet and explorer of new artistic paths that attracted the Symbolists. In certain respects the situation bears a distinct resemblance to that at the beginning of the century: the emergent Symbolists were as dissatisfied with the reigning plastic formalism of the Parnasse as the young Romantics had been with the sterile rigidity of an outworn Neo-classicism. In the resolution of the predicament Wagner stands as a counterpart to the Storm and Stress: in both instances the stimulus from across the Rhine was so avidly welcomed in France because it nurtured a longing for innovation already strong in latent form. A most telling explanation of Wagner's appeal is contained in that phrase of Dujardin's that has already been cited: 'l'oeuvre répondait évidemment aux plus profonds besoins de mon inconscient' ('the work clearly satisfied the deepest needs of my subconscious'). Like the Storm and Stress in the earlier part of the century, Wagner held out to the French exactly what they sought at this point of their development: a new form of art.

That new art form is encompassed in the term *Gesamtkunstwerk*. It denotes a work that embraces the various media: the musical in the score, the literary in the libretto, and the pictorial in the stage-setting, as well as the diverse modes of the dramatic, the epic and the lyrical. Through its address to all the senses simultaneously it has a powerful effect on the audience which is irresistibly drawn into its realm, a nebulous region of medieval sagas, Germanic myths and fairy-tale strands, the appropriate setting for the enactment of elemental human passions. With its innate mysteriousness as well as its skilful use of haunting repetition in the device of the symbolic *leitmotif*, the Wagnerian music-drama casts an undeniable spell. The audience experiences more than a new art form, more even than the creation of a whole new world; the ultimate effect of the *Gesamtkunstwerk* is that of a religious ritual.

This new art form came in many ways close to fulfilling the aspirations earlier harboured by the *Frühromantiker*. Whether Wagner was, as Max Nordau has described him, 'der letzte Pilzling auf dem Dünger der Romantik'[32] ('the last mushroom on the dungheap of Romanticism'), or its final glorious flowering: that is a matter of opinion. But that he took up the heritage of German Romanticism is beyond dispute. Wagner's antecedents have been traced – by André Coeuroy in *Wagner et l'esprit romantique* (Paris: Gallimard, 1965) – to Herder, Goethe, Schiller, Hölderlin, Eichendorff, Novalis, Tieck, Wackenroder and Hoffmann. Another attempt to follow the lineage from the Romantics to Wagner was made by Paul Arthur Loos in *Richard Wagner. Vollendung und Tragik der deutschen Romantik* (Bern: Francke, 1952) through a series of thematic links in these areas: the artist and society, the isolation of the narcissistic ego, the experience of love and friendship, the portrayal of womanhood, sympathy with death, the cult of the past, dream and sleep, man's relationship to nature, the proximity of art and religion, madness and disease, infinite longings, etc. Such an analysis does not really reach the heart of the affinity. Wagner did indeed exploit and popularize many of the topics and attitudes associated with the German Romantics. But his historical importance as the carrier and summation of Romanticism springs from a deeper community of ideal. The Wagnerian *Gesamtkunstwerk* approaches as nearly as is probably feasible the attainment of the *Frühromantik*'s artistic programme. Or to put it the other way round, the so-called *Mischgedicht* (mingled poem) of the *Frühromantik* seems almost the blueprint for the *Gesamtkunstwerk* in its striving for a free mingling of the genres and the arts. Wagner was also treading in the footsteps of the Romantics in his elaboration of a new mythology fashioned mainly out of Germanic material, his preference for the *Märchen*, his consistent patterns of symbolic images, his intensity and elevation, and last but by no means least, the harmonic fluidity which is his element as much as it had been that of the *Frühromantiker*. Friedrich Schlegel's outline for Romantic art as 'a progressive universal poetry' comes closer to realization in Wagner's music-dramas than in any creative work of the *Frühromantik* itself. Wagner thus came to act as a luminous filter for the transmission of the *Frühromantik* to France.

More than any other subsequent document Baudelaire's paean on Wagner shows an appreciation of him as a Romantic artist; it was not by chance published within the framework of *L'Art romantique*. Starting from the impact of a performance of *Tannhäuser*, Baudelaire presents an apprehension of art that is remarkably similar to the ideal of Friedrich Schlegel, Novalis and Wackenroder. Art is essentially a religious celebration, in which the artist is equated with the priest; it induces an intoxicating sense of elevation as the participant is raised to a higher realm of spiritual beauty. This mystical revelation is conceived and described in terms of a release from this world and a dream-like ascension into an infinite expanse of brilliant light:

Je me souviens que dès les premières mesures, je subis une de ces impressions heureuses que presque tous les hommes imaginatifs ont connues, par le rêve, dans le sommeil. Je me sentis délivré *des liens de la pesanteur*, et je retrouvai par le souvenir l'extraordinaire *volupté* qui circule dans *les lieux hauts* (. . .). Ensuite je me peignis involontairement l'état délicieux d'un homme en proie à une grande rêverie dans une solitude absolue, mais une solitude avec *un immense horizon* et une *large lumière diffuse; l'immensité* sans autre décor qu'elle-même. Bientôt j'éprouvai la sensation d'une *clarté* plus vive, *d'une intensité de lumière* croissant avec une telle rapidité, que les nuances fournies par le dictionnaire ne suffiraient pas à exprimer *ce surcroît toujours renaissant d'ar-*

deur et de blancheur. Alors je conçus pleinement l'idée d'une âme se
mouvant dans un milieu lumineux, d'une extase *faite de volupté et de
connaissance*, et planant au-dessus et bien loin du monde naturel.[33]

(I remember that, from the opening bars onwards, I experienced one
of those happy sensations that nearly all imaginative men have
known, in dreams, or in sleep. I felt freed of the *bonds of weightedness*,
and I found again in memory that extraordinary *voluptuousness*
current in *high spots* (...). Then involuntarily I thought of the
delightful state of a man given to a great reverie in an absolute
solitude, but a solitude with an *immense horizon* and a *tremendous
widespread light; immensity* without any decor beyond itself. Soon I had
the feeling of a more brilliant *brightness, and intensity of light* growing
with such speed that all the nuances in the dictionary would not suffice to express *this constantly renewed superaddition of glow and whiteness.*
Then I fully understood the idea of a soul moving in a luminous
space, of an ecstasy *compounded of voluptuousness and knowledge*, and
floating above and very far from the world.)

Baudelaire's response to Wagner is, parenthetically, very reminiscent
of the archetypal Romantic experience of music conveyed in
Wackenroder's *Herzensergiessungen eines kunstliebenden Klosterbruders*:

indem . . . die ganze Gewalt der Töne über seinem Haupte daherzog,
– da war es ihm, als wenn auf einmal seiner Seele grosse Flügel
ausgespannt, als wenn er von einer dürren Heide aufgehoben würde,
der trübe Wolkenvorhang vor den sterblichen Augen verschwände,
und er zum lichten Himmel emporschwebte. Dann hielt er sich mit
seinem Körper still und unbeweglich, und heftete die Augen
unverrückt auf den Boden. Die Gegenwart versank vor ihm; sein In-
neres war von allen irdischen Kleinigkeiten, welche der wahre·Staub
auf dem Glanze der Seele sind, gereinigt; die Musik durchdrang
seine Nerven mit leisen Schauern, und liess, so wie sie wechselte,
mannigfache Bilder vor ihm aufsteigen. ... Tausend schlafende
Empfindungen in seinem Busen wurden losgerissen, und bewegten
sich wunderbar durcheinander. Ja bei manchen Stellen der Musik endlich schien ein besonderer Lichstrahl in seine Seele zu fallen; es war
ihm, als wenn er dabei auf einmal weit klüger würde, und mit
helleren Augen und einer gewissen erhabenen und ruhigen Wehmut,
auf die ganze wimmelnde Welt herabsähe.[34]

(as the whole force of the music swelled around him, – he felt as if suddenly the great wings of his soul spread, as if he were being lifted from a bare heath, the gloomy curtain of clouds disappeared from his mortal eyes, and he were floating up to heaven. Then he kept his body still and his eyes glued to the ground. The present faded away from him; his innermost being was purified of all earthly trivialities which are like dust on the splendour of the soul; the music penetrated his fibres with soft shudders, and as it changed, brought various pictures before him. . . . A thousand feelings dormant in his breast were roused and stirred within him in wondrous fashion. At some points in the music a special ray of light seemed to enter his soul; he felt as if he were suddenly becoming much wiser and were looking down on the whole teeming world with brighter eyes and a certain lofty, calm melancholy.)

Different though the expression may be in its balance of sensuality and abstraction in the two instances, the phenomenon is palpably the same.

But to this emotional reaction to the music Baudelaire allies a rational understanding of its underlying ideology also. Thus he offers a symbolical interpretation of the action of *Tannhäuser*[35] that reveals a thorough awareness of the role of myth and legend as a universalizing force in Wagner's music-dramas. What is more, he has grasped that from the fusion of thought and sound stems the synesthesia that distinguishes Wagner's work and that was to become one of the characteristic hallmarks of Symbolist poetry. Such mingling inspires too the notion of the *Gesamtkunstwerk*, 'la *coïncidence* de plusieurs arts, comme l'art par excellence, le plus synthétique et le plus parfait'[36] ('the *coincidence* of several arts as the outstanding, the most complete and perfect art'). Above all, Baudelaire is acutely conscious of Wagner's complex historical position and function which he is able to formulate with brilliance: impelled by his 'dégoût du présent'[37] ('disgust for the present'), he sought in the past his brevet ('légitimation') for the creation of *'la musique de l'avenir'* ('*the music of the future*') which draws 'dans une forte dose, de l'esprit romantique'[38] ('in large measure on the Romantic spirit'). In these few brief pages, truly remarkable for their insight, Baudelaire has summarized into a cohesive pattern the motivating factors of Wagner's art. At the same time he has, unconsciously perhaps, foreshadowed the tendencies of the Symbolists whose stance could aptly be defined in those phrases coined for Wagner. Baudelaire's essay is therefore not only crucial for the reception of Wagner in France, but also highly suggestive of the nature of the link between Wagner and the Symbolists.

For, like Wagner, the Symbolists were driven by their rejection of the present to search in the past and in remoter spiritual regions for nourishment for their art of the future which also rose out of the well of Romanticism. So just as the French Romantics had recognized their kinship with the *Stürmer und Dränger*, in counterpart, the Symbolists sensed their own affinity to Wagner and what he represented. In both cases the relationship grew from an inner congruence. It was because they saw a reflection of their own aspirations in Wagner's art that the Symbolists were attracted to him; his work struck them as an anticipation of their own, of 'l'oeuvre, aussi, qui se préparait chez nous' ('the art, too, towards which we were moving in France'), to quote Dujardin's words from his very perspicacious survey of the development of French poetry in his article, 'Richard Wagner et la poésie française contemporaine'.[39] The same state of readiness existed for Wagner in the France of the 1880s as had done for the Storm and Stress in the 1820s. Each in turn was welcomed so warmly because each corresponded to the French needs of the moment, each strengthened and confirmed tendencies and aspirations already present, though still dormant.

It was not his music, nor indeed any single aspect of Wagner that fascinated the Symbolists as much as the total significance of his endeavour and the philosophy of art inherent in it. It is easy enough to point to certain features of Wagner that were to recur in Symbolist writings: the remote, the legendary, the mystically erotic; the cult of the priest-artist; the mythification of action; the fusion of the arts; the use of the *leitmotif*, etc. But these isolated strands are of considerably lesser importance than the impact of Wagner as a whole. 'On aperçut derrière l'orchestrateur incomparable un poète et un métaphysicien comme l'Allemagne n'en avait plus vu depuis Goethe' ('Behind the incomparable orchestrator we saw a poet and a metaphysician such as Germany had not had since Goethe'), Camille Mauclair wrote in his 'Souvenirs sur le mouvement symboliste en France 1884–1897' which appeared in *La Nouvelle Revue* of 15 October 1897. Of special interest in the present context is his next remark: 'Cette oeuvre allégorique et philosophique se révéla comme un produit direct de l'idéalisme allemand' ('This allegorical and philosophical work turned out to be a direct product of German idealism'). The centrality of Wagner to French Symbolism can hardly be better illustrated than by that strange diagram that Charles Morice drew for his *La Littérature de tout à l'heure*:[40] Wagner's name, in capital letters, stands in the very middle, the focal point from which lines radiate outwards to Baudelaire,

Mallarmé, Verlaine, Rimbaud, Villiers de l'Isle-Adam, Huysmans and Judith Gautier. In characteristically rhapsodic manner Morice exclaims: 'Inutile aussi d'affirmer davantage de quel précieux et grave poids la pensée wagnérienne pèse et toujours pèsera, féconde! sur les esprits engagés dans la voie lumineuse'[41] ('No need to emphasize further how precious and consequential a load Wagner's thought is and always will be, ever fruitful! for those embarked along the luminous way').

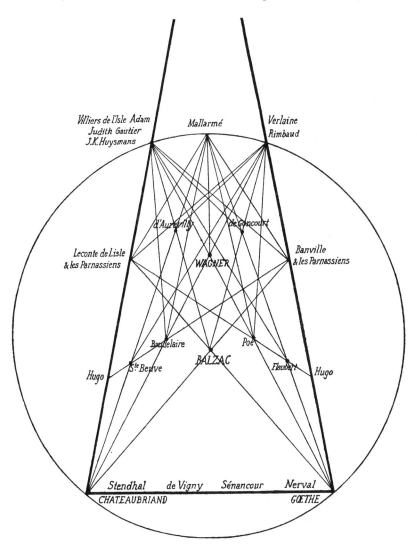

What then was the import of this 'load' of Wagnerism, as it was called? Gradually its multiple layers become apparent. In the first place Wagner was a cipher, almost a slogan-like rallying name for the emergent Symbolist movement, rather as Shakespeare had been for the *Stürmer und Dränger* and the French Romantics. For a while at least he acted as a unifying force, a flag for the aesthetes in their opposition to the materialists. Secondly, proceeding from this first function, he served as a model; his music-dramas were concrete proof of the possibility of an art radically other than the reigning realistic orientation of the Parnasse and Naturalism. Wagner's aesthetics drew on an entirely different tradition – that of Romanticism – to which Wagnerism helped to give a new lease of life in France. For this reason his name is starred in capital letters in René Ghil's *Traité du verbe* as if it were in itself a kind of symbol, as indeed it was:

> Pour une oeuvre une et que ne sent d'immortelle beauté l'om-
> nivoyant Génie qu'autant qu'elle symbolise, unir et ordonner
> magistralement soumises et épurées toutes les artistiques expressions:
> c'est de WAGNER sonné par les victoires l'atlantique entreprise.[42]

> (For a total work whose eternal beauty the all-seeing Genius senses
> in as far as it becomes symbolical, unify and dispose all the artistic
> means, purified and masterfully placed: that is the Atlantic under-
> taking of WAGNER hailed for his victories.)

Onto Wagner, the emblem of the daring pioneer, the Symbolists pro-
jected their own artistic hopes and ideals. Many of the articles on Wagner in the *Revue Wagnérienne*, such as Mallarmé's 'Richard Wagner. Rêverie d'un poète français' (1, no. 8, 8 August 1885) and Dujardin's 'Considérations sur l'art wagnérien' (3, nos. 6–8, July–August 1887), take Wagner as a pretext for an exposition of the Sym-
bolist programme. This point has already been made by a number of critics. 'What was wanted in the *Revue Wagnérienne*', A. G. Lehmann has pointed out, 'was less Wagner's doctrines set out accurately, than arguments to reinforce symbolist tendencies with the prestige of his name.'[43] Or, even more explicitly, Haskell M. Block has contended that the *Revue Wagnérienne* was important 'for its illumination of the aims and values of the French writers themselves, who used Wagner as a mirror and image of their own theories and aspirations.'[44] Wagnerism was thus an integral part of the Symbolists' quest for their own path. This then was Wagner's third role in the birth of the Symbolist movement: in addition to being a cipher and a model, he acted as

a kind of midwife. For onto Wagner, the 'Précurseur à l'Oeuvre d'Art de l'avenir'[45] ('the Herald of the Work of Art of the future'), as Dujardin called him, the Symbolists projected all their hopes for realizing their own dreams which ran so much in his wake.

And here we reach the quintessence of Wagner's significance for developments in France. With his theories of art and his music-dramas that tendency that Béguin has called *romantisme intérieur* finally came into its own in a land whose own Romantic movement had largely been a matter of externals, i.e. a question of dramatic and poetic technique rather than an existential mode of experience. Baudelaire already had asserted in the *Salon de 1846* that 'Le romantisme n'est précisément ni dans le choix des sujets ni dans la vérité exacte, mais dans la manière de sentir' ('Romanticism resides neither in the choice of subject matter nor in exact truth, but in a way of feeling'), to which he added that observation of supreme importance: 'Ils l'ont cherché en dehors, et c'est en dedans qu'il était seulement possible de le trouver'[46] ('They sought it in externals, and it is only within that it can be found'). Although written of painters, this is equally apposite to the history of French literature. The poets and dramatists of the 1820s had sought the touchstone of Romanticism in externals. Only slowly, with the mature Victor Hugo, with Gérard de Nerval and with Baudelaire himself did the 'way of feeling' assume primacy, a change of attitude that was reflected in a turn towards the inner world, the world of the imagination. Through Wagner that inner world of myth, dream and fantasy, which is the world of the *Frühromantik*, was triumphantly bodied forth on the stage. With Wagnerism *romantisme intérieur* at last came to the fore in France. The French themselves were to some extent aware of this. In *Le Drame musical*, which ran to three editions in less than twenty years, i.e. 1876, 1885 and 1894, Edouard Schuré hailed Wagner as the very incarnation of idealistic art and one of the great masters of the occult. With the strong resurgence of cults such as Buddhism in later nineteenth-century France as part of the reaction against materialistic Positivism, the religious, archetypal aspects of Wagner's work were particularly welcomed. Thus Wagnerism itself quickly evolved from a rallying-cry and artistic model into a veritable religion: 'Wagner a été pour nous mieux qu'une passion, une religion', Camille Mauclair later recalled; 'Par lui nous avons réellement possédé un esprit de mysticisme collectif'[47] ('Wagner was for us more than a passion, a religion. Through him we really came into a collective sense of mysticism'). This current of mysticism was to be of utmost importance to Symbolism.

Wagner's music-dramas then, projections of an inner world of emotional forces structured by musical principles, brought a new art form into France. In essence this new art form was none other than the *romantisme intérieur* of the *Frühromantik*. It was this that the Symbolists intuitively recognized in Wagner and that prompted their great enthusiasm. Thus through Wagner the way was opened for the infiltration of the *Frühromantiker*. That Novalis, the high-priest of *romantisme intérieur*, at last won appreciation in France just after the high-tide of Wagnerism is far from a coincidence.

V

The *romantisme intérieur* that is at the heart of the *Frühromantik* and of French Symbolism alike is in essence 'an attempt to spiritualize literature'.[48] That phrase of Arthur Symons, coined to characterize Symbolism, is another of those definitions as relevant to the *Frühromantik* as to Symbolism itself. To 'spiritualize literature' means for Symons 'to evade the old bondage of rhetoric, the old bondage of exteriority. Description is banished that beautiful things may be evoked, magically.' The phrase can also bear a wider and deeper connotation in reference to the *Frühromantik* and French Symbolism: it can denote their common endeavour to raise literature above the world of everyday reality and to turn it into an exploration of that higher realm whose existence was posited by transcendental idealism.

The process of spiritualizing literature in this broader sense leads to a certain sequence that is equally pronounced in both movements. The simplest and most illuminating image for this sequence is that of the door. As literature is spiritualized to an increasing degree, certain doors are closed, while simultaneously others are opened. The pattern is one of a continuous progression, and it is identical for the two movements in its positive as in its negative implications. The congruence of the pattern, the closing and opening of the same doors, reveals the extent to which the *Frühromantik* and French Symbolism are linked counterparts.

Both groups with equal deliberateness closed the doors on contemporary reality, and for very similar reasons. Fundamentally their withdrawal expressed a rejection of the world as they found it, the exasperation of an idealism in surroundings not attuned to its ethos. The predicament of the French Symbolists is perhaps more obvious than that of the German Romantics. The second half of the nineteenth cen-

tury marked the apogee of materialism, of a social order that took com-
mercialism to such lengths as to measure human beings by their visible
possessions. This was a society that would deny the artist the right
to his existence, let alone to his creativity, because it served no immediately and tangibly useful purpose. As Mallarmé lamented, in reply
to Jules Huret's inquiries: 'Pour moi, le cas d'un poète, en cette société
qui ne lui permet pas de vivre, c'est le cas d'un homme qui s'isole
pour sculpter son propre tombeau'[49] ('In my view, the situation of the
poet in this society which does not allow him to live is that of a man
who withdraws in order to carve his own memorial'). On occasion, as
in some of Baudelaire's and Verhaeren's poems or in Villiers de L'Isle-
Adam's stories *La Découverte de M. Grave* and *La Machine à gloire*, the
aesthete declaimed his displeasure at the industrial civilization of the
labyrinthine cities with their gruesome slums and distorted values. But
on the whole he preferred to turn his back on all that offended his
delicate sensibility, seeing 'une mosque à la place d'une usine'[50] ('a
mosque instead of a factory'), to cite Rimbaud's words from *Une Saison
en enfer*. Since the superior life of the spirit was impossible within the
confines of the uncongenial workaday reality, the artist disdainfully
repudiated a world that had in any case discarded him. 'Vivre?' Axel
exclaims haughtily in Villiers de L'Isle-Adam's play, 'les serviteurs
feront cela pour nous' ('Live? the servants will do that for us' – Act IV,
scene ii). For Axel such an imperious rejection of the commonplace
was a necessary preliminary to the incomparably more rewarding exploration of the yonder realm of dream and death: 'les réalités' are as
nought beside 'les mirages' of the imagination. Des Esseintes too in
Huysmans' *A Rebours* demonstratively closes the door on the here and
now when he retreats from the horrors of Paris to the idyllic Fontenay-
aux-Roses, where he insulates himself from his outer surroundings in a
dark, silent, luxuriously splendid cocoon of his own making. Not only
the persona of the aesthete was to be protected in this way; language
too was to be segregated into the utilitarian on the one hand and on the
other the 'essential'. The term is Mallarmé's from his *Avant-Dire* to
René Ghil's *Traité du verbe* where he writes of 'le double état de la
parole, brut ou immédiat ici, là essentiel'[51] ('the dual condition of the
word, crude or direct here, quintessential there'). The notorious complexity of the Symbolist style, the syntactical contortions as well as the
lexical eccentricities, may well reflect the revulsion from the ordinary
and the desire to escape into a more refined medium.

If the French Symbolists had ample reason to rebel against the age

into which they were born, the German Romantics seem at first sight
to have lesser grounds for a negative reaction. The closing decade of
the eighteenth century and the early years of the nineteenth were after
all the heyday of German Classicism under the aegis of Goethe and
Schiller. It is tempting, but fallacious, to assume that all the many principalities that made up Germany at that time were as friendly to the arts
as Weimar. Social and economic conditions varied greatly from state
to state and even from year to year, depending as they did to no small
extent on the whims of the individual ruler. Few were as enlightened
as Karl August of Weimar; for most military, sporting or amorous adventures took precedence over cultural pursuits. Philistinism was one
of the major bugbears of the *Frühromantiker* who openly flaunted their
scorn for their pedestrian countrymen. So the German Romantics felt
almost as alienated from their milieu as later the French Symbolists.
'Der Schriftsteller lebt in unseren Tagen in einer Einsamkeit wie noch
nie'[52] ('The writer of today lives in unprecedented isolation'), Tieck
complained in a letter to Solger on 1 February 1813, while Novalis
deplored the 'tiefe Entfremdung zwischen Mensch und Umwelt'
('profound alienation between man and his environment'), adding
elegaically: 'Wir sind aus einer Zeit der allgemein geltenden Formen
heraus'[53] ('We are no longer in a period of universally valid standards'). The *Frühromantiker*'s emphasis on harmony may be interpreted
as a response to the dangers of dualism and fragmentation of which
they were so acutely aware. Under the threats of the French Revolution and the Napoleonic Wars the political conservatism characteristic
of most of the German principalities in the eighteenth century already
was intensified into downright reactionarism. The individual was discouraged, indeed often excluded from political activities, and even
social criticism was suspect as an implied disloyalty. Hence the
Frühromantik is almost wholly apolitical, at least as far as involvement in
the politics of the day is concerned. In this too it forms a counterpart to
French Symbolism which was equally remote from the hurly-burly of
the partisan arena. In the authoritarian climate of Germany after 1789
and especially after 1799 the free expression of ideas was permissible
only in the philosophic and aesthetic field. So the poet was driven to
close the door on contemporary reality in order to seek his self-
realization elsewhere. Different though the circumstances were in early
nineteenth-century Germany and late nineteenth-century France, the
effect was identical: in both instances the artist consciously divorced
himself from a reality inimical to his ideals.

It was, however, not only on the society of their day that the *Frühromantiker* and the French Symbolists closed the door, but also on the dominant literary trends. The sheer desire for novelty, often cited by critics as a mainspring for both movements, should not be over-rated; the *Frühromantiker* and the Symbolists alike were inspired less by a thirst for innovation *per se* than by genuine opposition to the reigning modes of writing. Again this is more readily apparent in the France of the 1880s than in the Germany of the 1790s. In the mid-nineteenth century French literature was by and large on a rationalistic tack. Realism and particularly Naturalism, under the sway of science and Positivism, concentrated on the description of exteriors. This held true in poetry too: in reaction against the effusion of sentiment by the French Romantics and their less gifted imitators, the Parnasse reverted to an over-riding cult of pure form which they came to regard as an end in itself. Poetry became as it had been before the incursion of *romantisme*, only perhaps more so: cold, regular, noble, descriptive, pictorial, technically polished to perfection, but for all its formal beauty dreary to the point of death. The general stagnation of poetic art by the mid-1870s is painfully evident in the third and last collection published under the title *Parnasse contemporain* which fully warrants André Barre's verdict that 'Le Parnasse, c'est en poésie le triomphe des médiocres'[54] ('The Parnasse signifies in poetry the triumph of mediocrity'). Against this back-cloth no wonder that Jean Moréas in the preface to *Les Premières armes du symbolisme* (1889) presented Symbolism as a protest against vulgar, un-idealistic literature and as a search by the soul for the inner meaning beyond the outer appearance. In this revolt against exteriority, against a materialistic bias and against rhetoric, Positivism together with for-malism and even nature were dismissed as foes to the spirituality that was central to the Symbolists' transcendental idealism. 'Il s'agissait de réagir contre la platitude naturaliste qui bornait la littérature de tout ordre à ne plus être qu'un inventaire'[55] ('We had to react against the platitude of Naturalism which limited every kind of literature to being no more than an inventory'), Rémy de Gourmont later commented in his *Promenades littéraires*. This negative aspect of Symbolism, the resistance to the immediate past, acted for a while as a unifying force among the Symbolists. With a touch of cynicism Henri de Régnier suggested to Jules Huret at the time of his *Enquête sur l'évolution littéraire* in 1891 that all those unwilling timidly to follow in the tracks of the Parnassiens and the Naturalists were calling themselves Symbolists. Gustave Kahn subsequently developed the same point:

L'union entre les symbolistes, outre un indéniable amour de l'art, et une tendresse commune pour les méconnus de l'heure précédente, était surtout faite par un ensemble de négations des habitudes antérieures. Se refuser à l'anecdote lyrique et romanesque, se refuser à ecrire à ce va-comme-je-te-pousse, sous prétexte d'appropriation à l'ignorance du lecteur, rejeter l'art fermé des Parnassiens, le culte d'Hugo poussé au fétichisme, protester contre la platitude des petits naturalistes, retirer le roman du commérage et du document trop facile, renoncer à de petites analyses pour tenter des synthèses, tenir compte de l'apport étranger quand il était comme celui des grands Russes ou des Scandinaves, révélateur, tels étaient les points communs.[56]

(The bond uniting the Symbolists, beyond an incontrovertible love of art and a common tenderheartedness towards the unrecognized talents of the past, consisted mainly of a series of negations of earlier practices. To set one's face against the anecdotal in lyric and in prose, to refuse to write in this happy-go-lucky fashion on the pretext of adapting to the reader's ignorance, to reject the Parnassiens' finite art, the cult of Hugo to the point of a fetish, to protest against the minor Naturalists' platitude, to raise the novel above the level of gossip and mere documentation, to give up the little analysis and attempt instead a synthesis, to be aware of important foreign contributions such as those of the great Russians or the Scandinavians, these were the common factors.)

This opposition to the current literary modes was, moreover, instrumental in shaping the Symbolists' practices in various directions. Their imaginative insinuation into the mysteries of the universe is in sharp contrast to the mimetic portrayal of the world's surface that was the aim of the Realists and of the Parnassiens. The *Théâtre d'art* founded in 1891 by Paul Fort fostered a fluid dramatic form that included the recitation of poems and the miming of mythological subjects to a musical accompaniment, as against the documentary, tightly knit plays on contemporary problems favoured by the Naturalists' *Théâtre libre*. A new mythology that drew heavily on the legendary came to oust the Classical mythology cultivated by the Parnassiens. Above all, the poet escaped from the straitjacket of Parnassien metrics, to use Gustave Kahn's vivid image, into the freedom of *vers libre* and the prose poem. *Point de reportage!* (NO reportage!) was the repeated slogan in the Symbolists' condemnation of objective description, the purveying of information, even prose narration itself — all features prominent in the writings of their predecessors. Instead of the factual use of words, a wholly new magical language of evocation was to be evolved; the finite clarity of the Parnassiens was replaced by a deliberate blurring of the contours, a suggestive vagueness, the capacity for expansion into the infinite, fostered by a widespread preference for indefinite plurals and such words as *quelque* and *tout* (*some* and *all*). And if the poetry of the Parnasse with its regular, often elaborate verses appealed predominantly to the eye, Symbolist poetry in its primary emphasis on musicality was addressed rather to the ear and to the imagination.

On the literary as on the social scene the Symbolists had better reason to close the door on much that was current in their age than had the Germans of the 1790s and the 1800s. By the turn of the century German literature had risen to the crest of the wave with the Weimar *Klassik* of Goethe and Schiller. The situation appears to have little resemblance to that which faced the French Symbolists. Yet the *Frühromantiker* too were essentially an opposition party. In philosophy their mystical idealism and striving for harmony combated the vestigial intellectualism and mechanistic dualism of the eighteenth century. Their foe, like that of the Symbolists in their onslaught on Postitivism, was scientific rationalism. Its nineteenth-century incarnation, buttressed by the recent discoveries of the evolutionists, was undoubtedly more formidable, but fundamentally the two movements were fighting the same battle: for the poetic perception and against the rationalistic explanation. Friedrich Schlegel's elevation of beauty (*das Schöne*) above truth (*das Wahre*) clearly reveals the *Frühromantik*'s order of priorities, and that of the Symbolists was to be identical. Both groups with equal conviction turned their backs on rationalism as anathema to the transcendental idealism that formed the basis of their *Weltanschauung*. However, the analogy must not be pushed too far since rationalism had already been subjected to decisive questioning by the Storm and Stress and by Kant, and had in any case never held such firm sway in Germany as in France.

In the field of literature, too, though the *Frühromantiker* were antagonistic to Weimar Classicism, theirs was a more arbitrary stand than that of the Symbolists. For the writings neither of the *Stürmer und Dränger* nor of Goethe and Schiller in their Classical phase can be accused of lacking imagination, as did the works of the lesser French Realists, Naturalists and Parnassiens. Weimar Classicism did tend towards a certain formalism in its use, for instance, of pentameters and hexameters and its return to more traditional forms and subjects in its highly polished dramas. The Romantics by contrast posited a limitless freedom of form as the poet's birthright, as indeed the French Symbolists were to do. Again paralleling the Symbolists, they substituted a new – in their case, Nordic – mythology for the standard Classical one. But it was in matters of attitude that the *Frühromantiker* were most deeply at odds with their predecessors. From the vantage point of their own transcendentalism both the Storm and Stress and Weimar Classicism appeared too down-to-earth: the Storm and Stress in its propaganda on social problems of the day, its interest in the fate of the lower classes, its introduction of commonplace, not to say common language; and Weimar Classicism in its acceptance of the established order, its insistence on the need for integration into the social fabric and its shunning of any extreme in favour of the balanced norm. The message of sensible moderation in *Wilhelm Meister*, for example, deeply incensed Novalis and the Romantics. Nor could they welcome *Hermann und Dorothea* with its glorification of so bourgeois an institution as marriage as a symbol of stability and a bulwark against the cataclysms of the French Revolution. As for *Torquato Tasso*, it undermined the Romantic conception of the poet by revealing his personal weaknesses as well as by acknowledging the demands of society to be wholly justified. Thus the *Frühromantiker* spurned the literature of their day as vehemently as the French Symbolists, though for rather different and possibly less cogent reasons.

From this closing of the doors on contemporary society, thought and literature, it is only a short step to the ivory tower that was the favoured abode of both the *Frühromantiker* and the French Symbolists. The cult of otherness, as Marianne Thalmann has suggested, is a corollary to the revulsion from present reality: 'Er setzt sich von den landläufigen Begriffen ab und bekennt sich zum Anderssein'[57] ('He places himself at a remove from current concepts and proclaims his allegiance to differentness'). Though this comment refers to the German Romantics, it is just as apposite to the French Symbolists. Conversely Anna Balakian's characterization of the French Symbolists as 'one of the closest intellectual alliances in European history'[58] is equally appropriate to the *Frühromantiker*. Both coteries withdrew into private, closed circles where they communicated with their own breed in the special cryptic language of an in-group. Eccentric, anti-social and hostile though they were towards outsiders, among themselves they nurtured a strong *esprit de corps*. The *Frühromantiker*'s cult of

Symphilosophie and *Sympoesie*, as they pleased to name their activities, underlines their ardent sense of community. Even friendship was systematized in Schleiermacher's *Versuch einer Theorie des geselligen Betragens* (*Attempt at a Theory of Social Behaviour*), and what is more, genuine efforts were made to put this into practice by mutual support of each other's work, such as Tieck's handling of Wackenroder's and Novalis's manuscripts after their early deaths, not to mention those frog-catching expeditions to help Ritter! Among the Symbolists, the Tuesday evening meetings at Mallarmé's home in the Rue de Rome in Paris have become quite legendary. Here are Gustave Kahn's memories of those receptions:

> Mallarmé montait les premiers degrés de la gloire, ses mardis soirs étaient suivis avec tant de recueillement qu'on eût dit vraiment, dans le bon sens du mot, une chapelle à son quatrième de la rue de Rome.
>
> Oui, on eût cru, à certains soirs, être dans une de ces églises au cinquième, ou au fond d'une cour, où la manne d'une religion nouvelle est communiquée à des adeptes qui doivent, pour entrer, montrer patte blanche; la patte blanche là c'était un poème ou la présentation par un accueilli déjà depuis quelque temps.[59]

(Mallarmé was beginning to achieve fame, his Tuesday evenings were celebrated with such devotion that one could really speak, in the best sense of the word, of a chapel on his fourth floor in Rome Street.

Indeed, on some evenings, one might have thought oneself in one of those top floor or backyard churches where the manna of a new religion is distributed to the faithful who must show a white paw in order to gain admission; the white paw in this case was a poem or an introduction by a long established follower.)

This cult of the ivory tower sprang from, and at the same time encouraged, the belief in the existence of an élite, specifically the superiority of the creative artist over the philistine masses. The *Frühromantiker* often took this literally: thus Novalis used the image of the statue raised on its pedestal to describe the artist's elevation over ordinary men,[60] while Friedrich Schlegel maintained[61] that the artist is as far above men as men are above the other creatures of the earth. Likewise Mallarmé referred frequently to the élite and to the 'Élu' ('the Chosen' – note the capital letter), the 'individu royal' who is authentically sovereign 'par dons spirituels'[62] ('through his spiritual endowments'). This exceptional creature is a law unto himself, ruled only by

'die Willkür des Dichters' ('the volition of the poet'), as Friedrich
Schlegel put it in the *Athenäum* (no. 116). It is worth noting that several
works of both the *Frühromantik* and French Symbolism treat in one
form or another the myth of the poet's voluntary isolation and his pursuit of a distant and difficult ideal. Among the outstanding examples
are *Heinrich von Ofterdingen, Franz Sternbalds Wanderungen*, 'Das merk-
würdige musikalische Leben des Tonkünstlers Joseph Berglinger' in the
Herzensergiessungen eines kunstliebenden Klosterbruders, many of whose
episodes illustrate the same theme, *Igitur, Narcisse, Paludes*, and *La
Chevauchée d'Yeldis*.

Such artistic autonomy within the ivory tower might, and in fact did,
preclude the majority of readers. Of this the *Frühromantiker* and the
French Symbolists were fully aware, yet they remained disdainfully in-
different to the average reader, closing the door on him as a plebeian
unworthy of admission to the sacred temple of art. This was explicitly
stated by August Wilhelm Schlegel:

> Allein der Dichter braucht nicht für alle zu schreiben, . . .; er kann
> seinen Kreis willkürlich beschränken, und man darf ihm keine
> Unverständlichkeit vorrücken, wenn er nur für die Klasse von
> Lesern verständlich ist, denen er sein Werk bestimmt, er mag sogar
> bei diesen eine beträchtliche Anstrengung des Geistes fordern, wenn
> es der Inhalt mit sich bringt.[63]

> (The poet however does not have to write for all and sundry, . . .; he
> can limit his circle at will, and he should not be reproached with
> incomprehensibility if he is comprehensible only to that class of
> readers for whom his work is destined, and even from them he can
> demand a considerable mental effort if the content of his work is
> such as to require it.)

On the French side, Anatole Baju reiterated the same attitude:

> Peu nous importe que les foules ne nous comprennent pas.
> L'écrivain, soucieux de son art, doit faire abstraction de leur ex-
> istence. C'est à elles de s'élever vers lui, non à lui de s'abaisser vers
> elles.[64]

> (It matters little to us that the masses do not understand us. The
> writer, intent on his art, must disregard their existence. It is up to
> them to raise themselves to his level, not for him to lower himself to
> theirs.)

This haughtiness may be seen as a protest against the popular debasement of literature, but it testifies principally to the belief in the sacredness of art, a cardinal tenet of the *Frühromantiker* as of the French Symbolists. The notion of 'l'Art pour Tous' ('Art for All') is branded by Mallarmé[65] as the prime heresy. Art is to be practised for the élite, and savoured by the élite, in the ivory tower behind closed doors.

VI

Such closing of doors on the undesirable was only a prelude to the true mission of the *Frühromantiker* and the French Symbolists, namely to open doors to some very special sanctums. The idea of entry into an exclusive, enchanted realm is strongly implied in the castles, temples, remote lands, private chambers that so often form the setting in which the characters move: Axel, des Esseintes, Maeterlinck's blind, Hérodiade, Henrich von Ofterdingen, Tieck's Eckbert, Wackenroder's Joseph Berglinger all inhabit strangely rarefied regions. Often the plot portrays an initiation of some sort, or the quest to penetrate an ineffable secret. One of the dominant images of the *Frühromantik* and of French Symbolism is also closely connected with the notion of access: the lifting of a veil. The veil is raised to reveal the hidden object of longing in Novalis's tale about Hyacinth and Rosebud in *Die Lehrlinge zu Saïs* and in Villiers de L'Isle-Adam's *Axel*, and it is from 'sous le voile'[66] ('beneath the veil') that the poem emerges according to Mallarmé. The same image was used too by Friedrich Schlegel in his *Geschichte der alten und neuen Literatur* and by Ferdinand Brunètiere in the *Revue des deux mondes* (1 April 1891) to describe the aims of the *Frühromantik* and of French Symbolism respectively: a lifting of the veil shrouding the ultimate realities beyond the surface appearances.

The doors were to be opened then onto another and higher world attainable only to the élite of refined sensibility. The fervent affirmation of the existence, and indeed superiority, of this other world reveals to the full the transcendental idealism of the Germans around 1800 and the French about 1890. It is an idealism of a distinctive kind, differing from that of earlier groups, including the *Stürmer und Dränger* and the French Romantics who had still hoped, and sometimes even actively sought, to establish their Utopias within this world, perhaps in a new social order on some remote island. By contrast the *Frühromantiker* and the French Symbolists, having to all intents and purposes written off this world, located their ideal on a spiritual dimension, in dream or art, or beyond death. Its apparent evanescence does not, however, render it any less 'real'; quite the contrary in fact, because this Utopia, sited as it is within the individual, is free of physical ties and may therefore unfold in total liberty. The absolute validity of the inner ideal is categorically expounded by Novalis in the sixteenth section of *Blütenstaub*:

> Die Phantasie setzt die künftige Welt entweder in die Höhe, oder in die Tiefe, oder in der Metempsychose zu uns. Wir träumen von Reisen durch das Weltall: ist denn das Weltall nicht in uns? Die Tiefen unsers Geistes kennen wir nicht. – Nach Innen geht der geheimnisvolle Weg. In uns, oder nirgends ist die Ewigkeit mit ihren Welten, die Vergangenheit und die Zukunft. Die Aussenwelt ist die Schattenwelt, sie wirft ihren Schatten in das Lichtreich.

> (The imagination puts the future world either up in the heights, or down in the depths, or in some transsubstantiation. We dream of journeys through the universe: is the universe not within us? We do not know the depths of our souls. Inwards leads the mysterious path. Within us, or nowhere lies eternity and its worlds, the past and the future. The outer world is a world of shadows, it casts its shadows on to the realm of light.)

It is this turning inwards that distinguishes the second generation, i.e. the *Frühromantiker* and the Symbolists, from the first, the *Stürmer und Dränger* and the French Romantics. While the latter had endeavoured to realize their ideal in the outer world through social and artistic reforms, the second wave, with greater pessimism but also higher hopes, admitted its possibility only in a private, inner realm. The difference was most succinctly formulated by Baudelaire, to cite once again his key phrase: writing in the *Salon de 1846* under the heading 'Qu'est-ce que le romantisme?' he is critical of the French who had hitherto looked for Romanticism 'en dehors' ('in externals'), whereas, he points out, 'c'était en dedans qu'il était seulement possible de le trouver'[67] ('it is only within that it can be found'). The shift recommended by Baudelaire had already been accomplished by the *Frühromantiker* in Germany and was to be made in France by the Symbolists.

The exploration of the inner realm, the prospect of discovery, and above all of expansion into domains barely intuited until then held the greatest fascination for the Germans and the French alike. It had obvious antecedents in the love of adventure and the interest in the exotic already common among the previous generation. Italy, Greece, the Orient, the Northern lands of mists or the Southern islands: these earlier goals of travel were ousted now by the even more tempting mysteries of the uncharted inner world. The most extreme instance of the leap into the yonder comes in Novalis's *Hymnen an die Nacht* with their total commitment to a region of dream and vision beyond death. That inner vision is also the guide to Tieck's Christian in *Der Runenberg* although it lures him away from normal paths into eventual madness. Somewhat later the same road is followed by Elis Fröbom in *Die Bergwerke zu Falun* by E. T. A. Hoffmann. In both these tales the dark, recondite world takes the concrete form of the mine. Often the image of the journey serves to denote the quest for the spiritual other realm. So Heinrich von Ofterdingen is outwardly travelling to Augsburg while his inner pilgrimage is towards his artistic calling. Franz Sternbald's picaresque wanderings are likewise part of his search for his ideal. The motif of the journey is common too among the French Symbolists who were as avid to fathom the unknown as their German counterparts. 'Au fond de l'Inconnu pour trouver du *nouveau!*' ('To the depths of the unknown to find the *new!*'): that concluding line of Baudelaire's poem *Le Voyage* might well serve as an epigraph to Nerval's passage through the underworld of his subconscious in *Aurélia*. But the most famous voyage is surely that of *Le Bateau ivre* (*The Drunken Boat*) by Rimbaud who celebrated in *Les Illuminations* 'l'héroïsme de la découverte'[68] ('the heroism of discovery') and the excitement of 'voyages métaphysiques'.[69]

The journey represents one mode of access to the world within; but the primary gateway to its innermost recesses is through the medium of art. Of this the French Symbolists were as certain as the *Frühromantiker*. Art at one and the same time opens the way to the inner world and contains within the perfect work the revelation of the ideal.

> Die Kunst ... schliesst uns die Schätze in der menschlichen Brust auf, richtet unsern Blick in unser Inneres, und zeigt uns das Unsichtbare, ich meine alles was edel, gross und göttlich ist, in menschlicher Gestalt.[70]

(Art opens up for us the treasures of the human heart, turns our gaze inwards and shows us the invisible, I mean all that is noble, great and divine, in human form.)

This fundamental conviction re-echoes throughout the writings of the
Frühromantiker and the French Symbolists. August Wilhelm Schlegel,
for instance, maintained that Romantic art is close to 'dem Geheimnis
des Weltalls'[71] ('the secret of the universe'). For Novalis poetry gives a
portrait 'der innern Welt in ihrer Gesamtheit'[72] ('of the inner world in
its totality'). Like Wackenroder, Baudelaire conceived of the imagination as opening up deep avenues; the word he uses, 'ouvre',[73] parallels
the former's 'schliesst ... auf'. Similarly Mallarmé's belief in 'la
corrélation intime de la Poésie avec l'Univers'[74] ('the intimate connections between Poetry and the Universe') is clearly akin to that of
August Wilhelm Schlegel, and so is Charles Morice's conception of art
as 'le révélateur de l'Infini'[75] ('the revealer of the Infinite').

From these and many similar statements it becomes amply evident
that the *Frühromantiker* and the French Symbolists perceived art as an
essentially metaphysical entity. Here too a distinction must be drawn
between the earlier and this later generation: whereas art was an object
of, and for, improvement to the *Stürmer und Dränger* and the French
Romantics, in the eyes of the second wave it assumed a loftier mien by
far. For the *Frühromantiker* in Germany and the Symbolists in France
crystallized a new conception of art, envisaging it as a mysterious,
almost magical creative act fundamentally other to common human experience. In this mutation the recrudescence of the mystical current
played an important role. After remaining long underground in
Europe during the period dominated by rationalism, it resurfaced in
Germany in the late eighteenth century, and somewhat later in France.
Illuminism, particularly that of Swedenborg, was rife among both the
Frühromantiker and the French Symbolists who were deeply imbued
with the Orphic tradition. Although interest in the occult had already
been quite strong among the *Stürmer und Dränger* and the French
Romantics,[76] it was only with the second wave, i.e. Friedrich Schlegel,
Wackenroder and Novalis in Germany, and Baudelaire, Mallarmé and
Rimbaud in France, that mysticism became decisive in shaping the concept of art and the artist. For the French poets of the later half of the
nineteenth century, as for their German predecessors at the turn of the
century, poetry became a spiritual pursuit, a means for metaphysical
exploration, a key to the portals of the infinite. In the emergence of this
crucial facet of 'interior Romanticism' French Symbolism is clearly a
counterpart to the *Frühromantik*.

Such a transcendental conception of art is the hallmark of both
groups. In his *Ideen zu einer Philosophie der Natur* of 1797 Schelling had

already posited the interpenetration of this and the yonder world in
nature and in art which mediate to us a fleeting vision of the invisible.
The revelatory character of art was further developed in the *System des
transzendentalen Idealismus*: 'so ist die Kunst die einzige und ewige Of-
fenbarung, die es gibt, und das Wunder, das, wenn es auch nur einmal
existiert hätte, uns von der absoluten Realität jenes Höchsten über-
zeugen müsste'[77] ('so art is the sole and eternal revelation that exists,
and the wonder which, even if it had come into being only once,
would have had to convince us of the absolute reality of that Highest').
On this conviction Friedrich Schlegel based his whole system of
aesthetics: all genuine art and poetry partakes in the communion with
the infinite; it is therefore 'eine irdische Hülle und körperliche Ein-
kleidung der unsichtbaren Dinge und der göttlichen Kräfte'[78] ('a
terrestrial cover and a physical embodiment of invisible things and of
divine forces'), or even more directly, with the emphatic italicization:
'Das Wesen der höhern Kunst und Form besteht in der *Beziehung aufs
Ganze*'[79] ('the essence of higher art and form lies in its *relationship to the
whole*'). In the *Athenäum* (no. 238) Friedrich Schlegel expounded the
notion of a special kind of poetry to be known on the analogy with
philosophy as 'Transzendentalpoesie', 'deren Eins und Alles das
Verhältnis des Idealen und des Realen ist' ('whose alpha and omega is
the relationship of the ideal to the real'). The adoration of art as a
superior, sanctified level of being is the repeated theme of various sections of Wackenroder's *Herzensergiessungen eines kunstliebenden Klosterbruders*. But the most fervent apostle of transcendentalism was Novalis
whose aphorisms abound in dicta such as: 'Durch Poesie entsteht die
höchste Sympathie und Koaktivität, die innigste *Gemeinschaft* des End-
lichen und Unendlichen'[80] ('Through Poetry the highest co-feeling
and co-activity, the closest *community* of the finite and the infinite come
about'); or again:

> Der Sinn für Poesie hat viel mit dem Sinn für Mystizism gemein; er
> ist der Sinn für das Eigentümliche, Personelle, Unbekannte, Geheim-
> nisvolle, zu Offenbarende, das Notwendig-zufällige. Er stellt das
> Undarstellbare dar; er sieht das Unsichtbare, fühlt das Unfühl-
> bare.[81]

> (The feeling for poetry has much in common with the feeling for
> mysticism; it is the feeling for the particular, the personal, the
> unknown, the arcane, the revelatory, the perforce adventitious. It

portrays the unportrayable; it sees the invisible, senses the impalpable.)

An attempt to see the invisible and portray the unportrayable actually occurs in Novalis's *Hymnen an die Nacht*.

An analogous belief in the metaphysical dimension of art was one of the chief factors unifying the French Symbolists. Almost without exception poets avowed their allegiance to this creed onwards from Baudelaire's contention that the imagination 'est positivement apparentée avec l'infini'[82] ('is specifically related to the infinite'). In his *Manifeste du symbolisme* Jean Moréas announced that the concrete phenomena of art are only 'des apparences sensibles destinées à représenter leurs affinités ésoteriques avec des Idées primordiales'[83] ('tangible manifestations whose purpose is to epitomize their esoteric affinities with primordial Ideas'). Rémy de Gourmont and Saint-Pol-Roux both identified the absolute as the Symbolist poet's goal. The dramatist too must forge new links between the visible and the invisible, the temporal and the eternal, Maeterlinck demanded in the preface to his *Théâtre*,[84] where he outlined a programme fulfilled in his own lyrical dramas, *L'Intruse, Les Aveugles* and *La Princesse Maleine*. Repeatedly this association of the spiritual and the poetic was underlined:

L'oeuvre du poète symboliste serait donc de découvrir l'idée à travers sa représentation figurée; de saisir les rapports des choses visibles, sensibles et tangibles du monde avec l'essence intelligible dont elles participent; de remonter des effets à la cause, des images aux prototypes, des phénomènes et des apparences aux sens mystérieux.[85]

(The Symbolist poet's task would then be to discern the idea through its concrete representation; to grasp the connections between the visible, palpable, tangible things of this world and the luminous essence in which they partake; to rise from the effects to the cause, from the images to the prototypes, from the phenomena and appearances to the mysterious meanings.)

This metaphysical conception of art was propagated above all by Mallarmé. The pursuit of 'la notion pure'[86] inspired all artistic creativity; its sole manifestation is in Beauty which in turn 'n'a qu'une expression parfaite: la Poésie'[87] ('has only one perfect expression: Poetry'). Hence Mallarmé held the poem to be the instrument of the poet's transcendental vision, and so too he came to formulate his definition of poetry with its strong metaphysical overtones: 'La poésie est l'expression, par le langage humain ramené à son rythme essentiel, du sens mystérieux des aspects de l'existence: elle *doue* ainsi d'authenticité notre séjour et constitue la seule tâche spirituelle'[88] ('Poetry is the expression, in human language reduced to its essential rhythm, of the mysterious sense for some aspects of existence: it thus *endows* our sojourn with authenticity and represents the only spiritual task'). In writing poetry the Symbolists, like the *Frühromantiker*, were thus engaged in a primarily transcendental quest: 'la découverte de la clarté divine'[89] ('the discovery of divine light') as Rimbaud called it in *Une Saison en enfer.*

Their quest could also be described as religious. 'Art métaphysique. Religion esthétique.'[90] Charles Morice intuited the sequence in that brisk pronouncement. Once the propinquity of art to the spiritual essence of things and its capacity for mysterious insight are as fanatically advocated as they were by the *Frühromantiker* and the French Symbolists, art becomes an esoteric rite, in short a religion. Conversely the customary preoccupations of religion – the search for the meaning of life, the relationship with the eternal, hope for the future – are transferred into the domain of art. The work of art was to perform the functions normally ascribed to religion in the revelation of the infinite as well as in the progressive idealization of the world in which we live. Just as the *Frühromantiker* looked forward to the poeticization (*Poetisierung*) of the universe, so Mallarmé in all sincerity believed that the world would be saved by better literature. This radical and literal apotheosis of art, one of the distinguishing features of the *Frühromantik* and of French Symbolism, testifies to the strength of the Illuminist tradition from which it devolves. At the same time it offers a striking illustration of that opening of doors on the inner realm characteristic of both movements.

In keeping with its sacred aura as a religion, art was also credited in the canon of the *Frühromantik* and of French Symbolism with the magical powers of a mysterious rite. Mallarmé actually compared the impact of the incantatory ('incantatoire') poem to that of a fairy or a magician in a piece that bears the significant title *Magie.*[91] This is reminiscent of Wackenroder's description of the artist's activity as 'Verwandlung'[92] ('metamorphosis') and of Tieck's term 'Alchimie',[93] both of which suggest magic. Only a particular kind of poetry can aspire to this effect, the 'higher' poetry in constant communion with the transcendental. This is what Friedrich Schlegel called 'Poesie der

Poesie' and what Charles Morice seems to have had in mind as he
groped for definitions of the new poetry in *La Littérature de tout à
l'heure*. The basic criterion for this type of poetry is its capacity to *create*.
The italicization of that word is Mallarmé's; in stressing the difference
between 'making' ('faire') and 'creating' ('créer'),[94] he made it clear that
only where there is creativity can there be true poetry. Again the
parallel is evident with the *Frühromantik* which was equally insistent on
the primacy of creation in the artistic process: 'Dichten ist Zeugen'[95]
('To write poetry is to create'), Novalis affirmed point-blank. And
Schelling maintained, in the lectures on the philosophy of art he held in
the winter of 1802–3, that all art is a direct repetition of the original act
of absolute creation. The instrument of creativity was always the poetic
imagination which was enthroned as 'la reine des facultés' ('the queen
of faculties'), to use the famous title of one section of Baudelaire's *Salon
de 1859*. It was extolled by Friedrich Schlegel as 'das Organ des
Menschen für die Gottheit'[96] ('man's organ for the divinity'), that is
to say as the path of access to the transcendental realm above and
within us. In this sense the magic conception of the imagination
fostered by the *Frühromantiker* and the French Symbolists represents yet
another means of opening the doors on the yonder, superior reality.

This the imagination may do in two distinct though interrelated
ways. First, by mediating its perception of the infinite to the dwellers
on this earth, translating the other-worldly into terrestrial terms, bringing the dream into the finite. So the supernatural becomes ordinary and
natural to us, Tieck wrote in praise of *The Tempest* in his essay on
Shakespeare's treatment of the wondrous. For Baudelaire too one of
the functions of the imagination was to endow the dream with greater
reality, as he put it in the section on 'Le Gouvernement de l'imagination' in his *Salon de 1859*. But far more important to the *Frühromantiker*
and to the French Symbolists was the imagination's other potential for
opening doors, namely by creating a world of its own. The
Frühromantiker indeed believed quite literally in their own ability to
poeticize the world. 'Die Welt muss romantisiert werden'[97] ('The
world must be romanticized'), proclaimed Novalis, who portrayed
such a gradual transformation in *Heinrich von Ofterdingen* where the
dream becomes a reality and reality a dream: 'Die Welt wird Traum,
der Traum wird Welt' in the poem that introduces the second part of
the novel. Understandably the *Frühromantiker* were none too specific
about the implementation of this poeticization. They envisaged it as a
progressive – and endless – process in which the new would rise like

the dawn out of the night and spread like the rainbow over the sky. Those are the images chosen by Friedrich Schlegel in his *Geschichte der alten und neuen Literatur*. Novalis, in *Blütenstaub* (no. 32), preferred the metaphor of the mission: 'zur Bildung der Erde sind wir berufen' ('we are called to form the earth'), which aptly conveys the mystical devotion with which the *Frühromantiker* endeavoured to open these particular doors. Such a 'divine transposition', moving from the real to the ideal, was also the aim of the French Symbolists. 'Le symbolisme est une transposition dans un AUTRE ordre de choses'[98] ('Symbolism is a transposition into ANOTHER order of things'), according to Charles Morice. The transformation of real objects in Verhaeren's poetry evokes comment from Rémy de Gourmont in his *Promenades littéraires* (iv, 55). There the word 'hallucination' appears which Rimbaud was first to apply to his visions. Rimbaud seems near indeed to the *Frühromantiker* in his expressed desire to invent new flowers, new stars, new languages so as substantially to change life. By and large, however, the French Symbolists were less bent on a total transformation of the world than their German counterparts; they were more interested in the purely artistic workings of the creative imagination for the writing of suggestive poetry than in its power to re-structure the whole universe. Nevertheless in spite of this difference the Symbolists resemble the *Frühromantiker* – and differ from the French Romantics – in regarding the creative imagination as a gateway to another, superior realm. This facet of the 'spiritualization of literature', which occurred in Germany with the *Frühromantiker*, did not become manifest in France until the Symbolists and their immediate precursors.

While the creative imagination is the instrument for opening doors, the active agent is the artist himself. In the conception of the artist's nature and role the parallel between the *Frühromantiker* and the French Symbolists is extremely close. Both envisage him as a Chosen being endowed with an exceptionally penetrating, at times supernatural vision that enables him to pass beyond outward appearances to an intuitive apprehension of the inner essence. He is thus in the physical as well as the metaphorical sense of the word a 'seer' whose primary urge is the exploration of the infinite and whose function is to mediate the wonders of the transcendental. That is the thrust of Novalis's contention that 'Der Künstler ist durchaus transzendental'[99] ('The artist is wholly transcendental'). Such openness to the infinite was, to Novalis as to Friedrich Schlegel and to Rimbaud, the very hallmark of the true artist. Through his innate capacity for revelation – and his intense effort to 'se faire *voyant*[100] ('become *visionary*'), as Rimbaud put it in his famous letter of 15 May 1871 to Paul Demeney, he alone may reach the unknown in an ineffable moment of mystical experience. Rimbaud was apparently the only one conscious also of the darker, more sinister aspects of the artist whom he branded in that same letter to Paul Demeney as diseased, criminal and cursed in a fashion not unlike that of E. T. A. Hoffmann and later Thomas Mann. But such a view is quite uncharacteristic of the Symbolists or of the *Frühromantiker* who never ceased to stress, on the contrary, the poet's lofty, crypto-religious role. The quasi-divine quality of his creativity bestows on him an affinity with God himself, while his mediation of the transcendental leads to frequent comparisons with the priest. 'Dichter und Priester waren im Anfang *eins*, und nur spätere Zeiten haben sie getrennt. Der echte Dichter ist aber immer Priester' ('The poet and the priest were originally *one*, and were separated only in later times. The true poet, however, is still a priest'), Novalis maintained in *Blütenstaub* (no. 77). Charles Morice looked forward to the day when, through Symbolism, 'le Poète ... reprend son rôle sacerdotal des premiers jours'[101] ('the Poet ... resumes the priestly role that was his in earlier days'). The capital letter to denote the poet – like God – is already indicative of the special aura surrounding him. He rises above his individual incarnation to a higher public condition: 'je suis maintenant impersonel', Mallarmé wrote to Henri Cazalis on 14 May 1867, 'et non plus Stéphane que tu as connu, – mais une aptitude qu'a l'Univers Spirituel à se voir et à se developper, à travers ce qui fut moi'[102] ('I am now impersonal, and no longer the Stephen you knew, – but an aptitude of the Spiritual Universe to see and to develop through what was myself'). Beneath the somewhat cryptic formulation, this is a wholehearted affirmation of the poet's powers as a mediator, i.e. as a door-opener.

But a crucial problem confronted the artist at this point: 'Wie kann nun das Unendliche auf die Oberfläche, zur Erscheinung gebracht werden?'[103] ('How can the infinite now be brought to the surface into appearance?'), August Wilhelm Schlegel asked in his *Vorlesungen über schöne Kunst und Literatur*. The answer that he gave in the opening years of the nineteenth century already contains in nucleus the theory of *correspondances* fundamental to Symbolist aesthetics: 'Nur symbolisch in Bildern und Zeichen. ... Dichten [...] ist nichts andres als ein ewiges Symbolisieren: wir suchen entweder für etwas Geistiges eine äussere Hülle, oder wir beziehen ein Äussres auf ein unsichtbares Innres' ('Only symbolically in pictures and signs. ... The art of poetry

[. . .] is nothing other than an eternal symbolizing: we either seek an outer cover for something spiritual, or we relate an external to something invisible and inward'). Throughout the *Vorlesungen über schöne Kunst und Literatur* August Wilhelm Schlegel insists on the key position of the symbol in the work of art: beauty is the symbolic representation of the infinite; the organic relationship between the sign and the object signified is essential if a work is not to be arbitrary; the language of poetry must capture the interconnections between all phenomena in an incessant chain of symbols; and finally, the two worlds, the finite and the infinite, should merge in the symbol that can at one and the same time partake of the sensual and the spiritual. Without exception each of the major writers of the *Frühromantik* subscribed to the ideas so clearly enunciated by August Wilhelm Schlegel. Indeed the argument in favour of the use of symbols follows in logical consequence on the *Frühromantiker's* conception of art: i.e. the decisive hallmark of genuine, 'higher' poetry lies in its attachment to the infinite; since the infinite can be bodied forth only in pictures and symbols, all true art must of necessity be fundamentally symbolical. 'Im Stile des echten Dichters ist nichts Schmuck, alles notwendige Hieroglyphe' ('In the writing of the true poet nothing is merely decorative, everything is an indispensable hieroglyph'), Friedrich Schlegel decreed in the *Athenäum* (no. 173). That term 'hieroglyph', as Marianne Thalmann[104] has pointed out, was popular among the German Romantics. Friedrich Schlegel repeatedly referred to hieroglyphics as images of the divine; his brother August Wilhelm looked forward to the invention of a new system of hieroglyphics to express the inexpressible; Novalis believed that 'Die erste Kunst ist Hieroglyphistik'[105] ('the primary art is the shaping of hieroglyphics'); Franz von Baader, in a diary entry of 19 July 1786, described the hieroglyph as the cipher for the inner essence, while Wackenroder maintained: 'Die Kunst ist eine Sprache . . . sie redet durch Bilder . . . und bedient sich also einer Hieroglyphenschrift, deren Zeichen wir dem Äussern nach kennen und verstehen'[106] ('Art is a language . . . it speaks through pictures . . . and accordingly uses hieroglyphics whose significance we know and understand through their outer appearance'). The frequency of this term in itself already shows the *Frühromantik's* strong disposition towards a conception of poetry as symbolic notation.

This recourse to symbols is more than the solution to the technical problem of translating the infinite into concrete form. It is also a precipitate of the group's *Weltanschauung*: of the belief in the organic animation of the universe, of Schelling's hypothesis that nature is spirit made visible, of the striving for harmony, of the magic idealism that sought to re-create the world. So each pregnant symbol becomes the means not just of conveying the transcendental, but also of reaching for the cosmic unity of all being. Through the progressive coalescence of the separately fashioned symbols, through the continuation in effect of this symbolizing process, that new mythology for which Friedrich Schlegel called was gradually to emerge, giving fresh meaning to man's existence. Like art itself, the symbol came to assume a quasi-religious function as a kind of invocation; in its perfected form it offers trenchant testimony both to the artist's visionary and conceptualizing powers and to his capacity to transform the world.

In this context Wackenroder's *Herzensergiessungen* and Novalis's *Lehrlinge zu Saïs* are of particular importance. Though no explicit theory of symbols is formulated in the *Herzensergiessungen*, the work as a whole rests on the implied assumption of a universal system of analogies. This is most clearly brought out in the section entitled 'Von zwei wunderbaren Sprachen, und deren geheimnisvoller Kraft' ('Of two wondrous languages, and their mysterious power') in which the parallel is drawn between the language of God manifest in nature and the language of the artist whose hieroglyphics fuse (*schmelzen*) the spiritual with the material. The same idea of a fusion underlies *Die Lehrlinge zu Saïs* where it is developed in a more detailed and complex manner. The apprentice's task in this tale of initiation is to learn to per-ceive the secret language of nature, so as eventually to reach the condi-tion of the Master who is able to see 'die Verbindungen in allem, . . . Begegnungen, Zusammentreffen'[107] ('the connections between all things, . . . encounters, cohesions'). The universe has become for him a single unified entity in an ideal state of harmony. Slowly and at times painfully the apprentice has to cultivate eyes to see and ears to hear; like Hyacinth, his paradigm, and like Heinrich von Ofterdingen, he has to acquire understanding of the flowers, the animals, the stones and the stars; he has to open his mind to a comprehension of these 'things' because only through such analogical fusion of all phenomena can the supreme balance of wisdom be attained:

Ist es denn nicht wahr, dass Steine und Wälder der Musik gehorchen und, von ihr gezähmt, sich jedem Willen wie Haustiere fügen? – Blühen nicht wirklich die schönsten Blumen um die Geliebte und freuen sich, sie zu schmücken? Wird für sie der Himmel nicht heiter

und das Meer nicht eben? – Drückt nicht die ganze Natur, so gut
wie das Gesicht und die Gebärden, der Puls und die Farben, den Zustand eines jeden der höheren, wunderbaren Wesen aus, die wir
Menschen nennen? Wird nicht der Fels ein eigentümliches Du, eben
wenn ich ihn anrede? Und was bin ich anders also der Strom, wenn
ich wehmütig in seine Wellen hinabschaue, und die Gedanken in
seinem Gleiten verliere?[108]

(It is not true that stones and forests heed music and, tamed by it, sub-
mit to any will like domestic animals? Do not the most beautiful
flowers really blossom around the beloved, and delight in bedecking
her? Does not the sky become clear and the sea smooth for her? Does
not the whole of nature, like face and gestures, pulse and colours, express the state of each of those higher, wondrous beings that we call
humans? Does not the rock turn into a particular you through my
address to it? And what am I other than the stream when I cast a
melancholy look into its waves, and yield my thoughts to its flow?)

This is reputed to have been one of the French Symbolists' favourite
passages. Its propinquity to Baudelaire's sonnet *Correspondances* is quite
obvious:

La Nature est un temple où de vivants piliers
Laissent parfois sortir de confuses paroles;
L'homme y passe à travers des forêts de symboles
Qui l'observent avec des regards familiers.

(Nature is a temple in which the living pillars
From time to time let cryptic words come forth;
Man passes through a forest of symbols
That watch him with a familiar gaze.)

For Baudelaire and the Symbolists, as for the *Frühromantiker*, the
analogical lines extended in two directions: horizontally between the
phenomena of this world, from colours to sounds, from humans to
streams, and vertically between the transcendental and the terrestrial.
So this world ('ce monde-ci') was regarded as a 'dictionnaire hiéroglyphique',[109] 'un magasin d'images et de signes auxquels l'imagination
donnera une place et une valeur relative'[110] ('a store of images and of
signs to which the imagination will give their due place'). The poet's
function therefore is to act as 'un traducteur, un déchiffreur' ('a translator, a decipherer') who draws on 'l'inépuisable fonds de l'*universelle*

analogie'[111] ('the inexhaustible stock of *universal analogy*') for the comparisons that are the core of his work. In the last resort, Baudelaire concluded, using again the term so current among the *Frühromantiker*, 'tout est hiéroglyphique'[112] ('everything is hieroglyphic'). This profound conviction of the analogical character of the whole universe is, together with the transcendental idealism from which it devolves, one of the foundations of French Symbolism. As such it is so pervasive and also so well-known that there is no need to elaborate on it at any length. The symbol is honoured as 'une espèce de révélation'[113] ('a kind of revelation'), the vessel for the superior insight acquired by the artist in his mystical experience. It is the passage, the open door from one realm to the other, or, in August Wilhelm Schlegel terms, the outer cipher for the inner substance. The idea of a fusion between disparate spheres is present in the verb *mêler* that recurs with such striking frequency in French Symbolist poetry and that has its counterpart in the *schmelzen* of the *Frühromantiker*. Through the subtle, indirect means of the symbol the ideal world that defies description may be mediated in a process of suggestion. '*Suggérer*' was, to Mallarmé, 'le rêve. C'est le parfait usage de ce mystère qui constitue le symbole'[114] ('To *suggest*, that is the dream. It is the perfect use for the mystery represented by the symbol'). Charles Morice was even more explicit when he stressed that 'c'est le caché, l'inexpliqué et l'*inexprimable* des choses'[115] ('it is the recondite, the unexplained and the *inexpressible* aspect of things') that can be conveyed by the suggestiveness of the symbol. This is remarkably close, even in its verbal formulation, to Novalis's belief[116] that poetry alone can see the invisible, feel the intangible and express the inexpressible.

In the role assigned to the symbol as a magical door-opener there is thus a distinct parallel between the *Frühromantiker* and the French Symbolists.[117] A momentous change in the function of the complex of image, metaphor, allegory and symbol took place in both French and German literature, but it was consummated at different times in the two countries. In Germany this change represents one of the factors distinguishing Classicism from Romanticism. The arguments in favour of a division at that particular stage have been cogently advanced by Doris Starr in *Über den Begriff des Symbols in der deutschen Klassik und Romantik* (Reutlingen: Eugen Hutzler, 1964) and clearly illustrated by Bengt Algot Sørensen's collection of texts, *Allegorie und Symbol* (Frankfurt: Athenäum, 1972). The shift in emphasis from Classicism's cult of formal perfection to Romanticism's predilection for infinite progression, together with the resurgence of mystical religious currents, led to a fundamental revaluation of the role of art, the artist, and consequently also the symbol in early nineteenth-century Germany. In France development ensued along the same broad lines, but not until later in the century. Significantly, in *L'Âme romantique et le rêve*, Béguin takes his examples predominantly from among French poets of the second half of the century, whereas his German references are to the early nineteenth and indeed later eighteenth centuries. Here again we encounter that time-lag already so familiar in any juxtaposition of German and French literature in this period. The great divide that occurred in Germany between the *Klassik* and the *Frühromantik* came into effect on the opposite bank of the Rhine between *romantisme* and Symbolism. This does not, of course, mean to imply a lack of continuity in either case; literatures grow by evolution, each successive movement elaborating on those features of its heritage from the past that concur with its own aims and views. But at certain points within and alongside that evolution something more like a revolution breaks in. In Germany this supervened between Classicism and Romanticism; in France between Romanticism and Symbolism. The revolution is of like character in the two instances, though separated by over fifty years: it is towards the 'spiritualization of literature', towards an interiorization, an orientation to the transcendental. As far as the role of imagery, or rather symbols, is concerned, that revolution is still best summarized by M. H. Abrams' illuminating metaphor: from the mirror to the lamp, from the mimetic to the expressive conception. For a true understanding of Franco–German interrelationships in the nineteenth century it is essential to grasp the full import of this mutation, and also its relative timing in the two literatures. The distinction that Anna Balakian makes between Romanticism and Symbolism[118] certainly holds true in reference to French Romanticism; but not to German – nor for that matter to English – Romanticism which is a counterpart of agreement, not of opposition, to Symbolism. The *Frühromantik* was arguably an antecedent to Symbolism, particularly in its perception of the symbol itself.[119]

In some respects the *Frühromantiker* even went much further than their successors. Their gaze was more firmly riveted on the transcendental than that of the Symbolists, who still had eyes for this world too. In spite of its vehement opposition to the Parnasse and its cult of the external, Symbolist poetry nonetheless shows some traces of previous stages in the development of the French lyric, specifically that

of plasticity, for which there is no real counterpart in the history of
German literature immediately prior to the Romantic movement. This
led in turn to a difference in the approach to the infinite. While the
Frühromantiker hoped to attain it by a sudden revelatory discovery, by
one great leap into another world *beyond* the things of the here and
now, the Symbolists expected to penetrate to the infinite *through* the
objects in reality. 'En cherchant dans les choses l'image de l'infini'[120]
('seeking in things the image of the infinite'): this definition of the
process as envisaged by the Symbolists makes it plain that the infinite
was to be sought within the finite. The various *correspondances*, the latent affinities and mysterious identities between things were to provide
the path from the outer to the inner. For the Symbolists therefore the
real was the starting-point for the exploration of the yonder in a way
that it never was for the *Frühromantiker* who looked from the outset
straight into the visionary realm. 'L'Idée, qui seule importe, en la Vie
est éparse'[121] ('the Idea, which alone matters, is unfolded in Life'),
René Ghil proclaimed in his *Traité du verbe*. Note the word 'en' ('in');
the *Frühromantiker* in contrast sited it *outside* the life of this world. It
was their belief that the artist could enter that other dimension by one
thrust of his imagination, whereas the Symbolists placed more emphasis
on the process, the notion of a gradual ascension from the real into the
spiritual. It is worth referring again in this context to that revealing
passage from Georges Vanor's *L'Art symboliste* already quoted earlier,
because it so clearly enunciates the presence of the transcendental
within the physical, as well as the ideal of a continuous upward movement:

> L'oeuvre du poète symboliste serait donc de découvrir l'idée à
> travers sa représentation figurée; de saisir les rapports des choses
> visibles, sensibles et tangibles du monde avec l'essence intelligible
> dont elles participent; de remonter des effets à la cause, des images
> aux prototypes des phénomènes et des apparences aux sens
> mystérieux.[122]

> (The Symbolist poet's task would then be to discern the idea through
> its concrete representation; to grasp the connections between the
> visible, palpable, tangible things of this world and the luminous es-
> sence in which they partake; to rise from the effects to the cause,
> from the images to the prototypes, from the phenomena and ap-
> pearances to the mysterious meanings.)

Because the Idea was thought to have concrete manifestation, there is noticeably more interest in, and more description of, reality in Symbolist poetry than in the writing of the *Frühromantiker*. Baudelaire and Verhaeren are the outstanding examples of poets whose rich notation of the physical world around them forms the basis for their evocation of other domains that lurk beneath the surface. Even in the works of so essentially visionary a poet as Rimbaud it is the graphic image that stands in the forefront; he called one of his collections *Les Illuminations* and subtitled it in English 'coloured plates' as if to draw attention to the visual aspect. And in thinking of Symbolist poetry, it is the images that first spring to mind: the swans, the castles, the gardens, the street scenes, Rimbaud's boat and Mallarmé's faun. By comparison the landscape of the *Frühromantik* is quite blurred, its shadowy figures barely emerging into a delineated shape. In this context a lexical difference that goes beyond the merely verbal is of significance: the contrast between the French choice of the term *Idée* to denote the ineffable, and the German fixation on *das Unendliche* (the infinite), a vaster and vaguer concept. The French Symbolists patently concentrated on the lucid elaboration of specific symbols to a far larger extent than the *Frühromantiker*, whose exclusive transcendentalism predisposed them to the theory of symbolizing, and at the same time, paradoxically, precluded the actual crystallization of precise images. From this disparity stems the divergence in the nature and scope of the works characteristic of the two movements. The French Symbolists, partly because of their greater consciousness of present reality, found their most effective expression in the short flight of the shapely lyric or the brief lyrical drama. The German Romantics, in their ethereal remoteness, tended to embark on longer works that all too often were destined to remain incomplete.

Experimentation with artistic forms represents another of the doors that the *Frühromantiker* and the French Symbolists wanted to open. Their assumption of total liberty for the God-like creative artist had deeper roots than the self-assertive demand for freedom that was part of the rebelliousness of the *Stürmer und Dränger* and of the French Romantics. The adventurousness of the later generation in both literatures sprang rather from the need to find a form appropriate to their transcendentalism: when the vision passed beyond the normal confines of this world, so too must the expression. The problem was, as Béguin has so aptly defined it, how to 'capter au piège du langage des fragments de la vie secrète'[123] ('capture in the trap of language fragments of the hidden life'). One solution lay in the widespread and systematic use of symbols to convey the inexpressible. Various other possibilities were mooted in the theories of the *Frühromantiker* and the French Symbolists, and some were tried in their creative writings: the very liberalized novel based on a freely associative flow; the equally elastic lyrical drama; the prose poem; the interpolation of verse into narrative; the exploration of the musical dimension, etc. Whatever their specific direction, all these technical experiments reveal the same trends already noted in the ideological sphere: a closing of the doors on the conventional, and an expansion into new forms that were to implement an artistic renaissance hand-in-hand with the visionary re-creation of the universe. The frequency of the question as a stylistic and rhetorical device among both groups is again indicative of that opening up under which so much of their activity may be subsumed.

Flexibility and fluidity are the keys to their technique; the *Mischgedicht* (mingled poem) and *vers libre* (free verse) their epitome. Both testify to the emancipation from the accepted older order, be it in genre or in metrical organization. More important, however, than any iconoclasm was the quest for the true 'organic' form that would be in inner congruence with the *Weltanschauung* innate in the work rather than some arbitrary 'mechanical' mould superimposed from without. So the *Frühromantiker* broke out of the Classical segregation of genres and styles just as the French Symbolists threw overboard the established rules of metrics. Each was continuing that loosening of traditional structures initiated already by their predecessors in the *Sturm und Drang* and *romantisme*. But while the earlier pair were primarily making a reckoning with the past in an often angry reaction against the restrictions binding them, the *Frühromantiker* and the French Symbolists were essentially positive and forward-looking in their innovations. As in their use of symbols, so also in their search for organic form and their sense of freedom to express themselves at will they mark a crucial turning-point in the history of aesthetic consciousness. In these two movements the foundations were laid for twentieth-century writing. Here too in this opening-up of the channels for experimentation along every path the French Symbolists are a counterpart to the *Frühromantiker*.

The parallelism between them is as marked in their actual practices as in their overall direction. The mingling of the senses in synesthesia and the mingling of the various genres and arts, commonly associated above all with French Symbolism, is already apparent in the *Früh-romantik*. The equation of poetry and music, for instance, was a familiar idea among the Romantics in Germany long before it attained such prominence in France with the Symbolists. The fusion of sounds, colours and shapes was adumbrated by Wackenroder in his *Phantasien über die Kunst*. Even the famous *audition colorée* (coloured sound-scale) expounded by René Ghil in his *Traité du verbe* and by Rimbaud in his sonnet *Voyelles* was prefigured in August Wilhelm Schlegel's 'Vokalfarbenleiter' ('vocal colour scale'):

A	O	I	Ü	U
rot	purpurn	himmelblau	violett	dunkelblau[124]
(red	purple	sky-blue	violet	dark blue)

The underlying purpose of these somewhat weird techniques was a serious one, and it was much the same for the French Symbolists as for the *Frühromantiker*: the creative opening-up of whole new realms. It was this that determined the predilection of the *Frühromantiker* for the *Märchen*[125] which they regarded as the ideal form wherein to conjure up the wondrous horizons of the imaginative vision. Novalis in particular repeatedly extolled the *Märchen* as 'ganz musikalisch'[126] ('wholly musical'), as 'prophetische Darstellung – idealische Darstellung'[127] ('prophetic representation – ideal representation'), the diametric antithesis to the historical world of reality. The tale of Hyacinth and Rosebud in *Die Lehrlinge zu Saïs* is a simple example of such a *Märchen* with its imperceptible drift into the enchanted wish-fulfilment. A far more complicated one is woven in *Heinrich von Ofterdingen* in its structural arabesque of interrelated tales, each of which moves more deeply into the dream world of Heinrich's destiny as a poet. It is the private, at times wayward, logic of the imagination that inspires these flights into mythic regions. Parallels might well be drawn between the *Frühromantik Märchen* and such works as Mallarmé's *Hérodiade* and *L'Après-midi d'un faune*, Rimbaud's *Bateau ivre* or indeed *Une Saison en enfer*, not to mention many of Maeterlinck's dramas.

If the Symbolists were less articulate than the *Frühromantiker* in their championship of the *Märchen* – a term for which there is significantly no French equivalent – they sought in fact to achieve the same end by means of their language. The innovative use of words was to fulfil for them the function of the *Märchen* in the *Frühromantik*, namely the re-ordering of the world in accordance with the poetic vision. In his brilliantly penetrating analysis of Symbolist syntax, Leo Spitzer has shown that their frequent recourse to neologisms and peculiarities aimed to enlarge the expressive possibilities of French so as to evolve a more fitting medium for their mysterious perception of the universe. Shadowiness and expansiveness ('Ausdehnung') are the outcome of the Symbolists' love of such indefinites as *ou, là-bas, loin, à jamais, le long de, parmi*, all of which avoid the specific in favour of a floatingly suggestive openness. Their departure from traditional syntax, far from being a wilful game, as has sometimes been hinted, proved an essential tool for the communication of their vision. Commenting on Régnier's introduction of the unexpected plural *lunes* (moons), Spitzer shrewdly observes that with this word 'geht der Dichter schon weit über syntaktische Neuschöpfung hinaus: er dichtet die Natur um und gibt ihr mehrere Monde'[128] ('the poet goes far beyond syntactical neologism: he transforms nature and gives it several moons'). Through that apparently artless plural Régnier has transfigured reality into *Märchen* just as surely as Novalis with his projected marriage of the seasons that was to usher in the era of poetic Utopia at the close of *Heinrich von Ofterdingen*. At such points the door is fleetingly ajar on that other domain to which the *Frühromantiker* and the French Symbolists aspired.

VII

But the door was no more than ajar, and that only fleetingly. There is a strong hint of tragic irony in the sequence in which the *Frühromantiker* and the French Symbolists were trapped. For after they had themselves deliberately closed certain doors in order to be better placed to open the magic portals of the higher kingdom of art, very soon in their exploration of the inner chambers of that realm they found themselves facing other doors that stayed, against their volition, obstinately and firmly shut.

How did this come about? A clue towards an answer is contained in a comment of Nietzsche's on German Romanticism. Writing to Georg Brandes on 27 March 1888, he opined that the whole movement had achieved its aim only in music, and in literature had remained merely a promise ('wie diese ganze Bewegung eigentlich nur als Musik zum Ziel gekommen ist [Schumann, Mendelssohn, Weber, Wagner, Brahms]; als Litteratur blieb sie ein grosses Versprechen').[129] At first sight that contention seems a sweeping generalization; it appears to overlook, or at least to minimize, the lasting value of those lyrics and tales for which German Romanticism is famed. But they were largely the product of the *Hochromantik*. Nietzsche's judgement therefore needs some qualification. Once the distinction is drawn, however, between the two phases of the Romantic movement in Germany, his verdict proves devastatingly relevant to the *Frühromantik*, and what is more to French Symbolism also. They did both remain a promise; their grandiose hopes and plans are belied by the relative paucity of their creative harvest. Seminal though their aesthetics were, the new paths frayed by the *Frühromantiker* and the Symbolists were to be trodden by later generations rather than by their own. Their ideas were in the most literal sense *avant-garde* with the result that their fructifying effect was to come more in their future influence than in any present realization.

This helps to account for that disproportion between aspiration and accomplishment that is one of the most obvious – and embarrassing – features of the two movements. Both laboured under the primacy of poetic theory, for though their programmes were expounded with a great outflow of eloquence, they preceded any substantial attempts at writing in the new manner. Moreover the theory itself was hardly designed to give practical encouragement to creative work; all too often in the *Athenäum*, in Moréas's *Manifeste du symbolisme* or in Ghil's *Traité du verbe* the expression is disjointedly dithyrambic, the content disturbingly evanescent. The concern with the cognitive, mystical aspects of art led to endless speculation, to an enclosement in theorizing that was anything other than conducive to artistic productivity. Finally, the view of the nature and function of poetry fostered by the *Frühromantiker* and the Symbolists was such as to exert an almost paralytic effect on the poet. It may be something of an exaggeration to brand it as leading 'unavoidably to literary suicide'.[130] However, in its reiterated hope that poetry would by some mysterious means transfigure the world, it not only came into serious danger of overreaching, but also imposed a dauntingly heavy burden on the poet who was cast in the role of priest-prophet-leader. Paradoxically, through its very loftiness, this conception of poetry militated against the actual writing of poetry since any concrete work was inevitably bound to fall short of a well-night impossible ideal. To this extent the poetic theory of the two movements was ironically self-defeating. It is no coincidence that Mallarmé's monumental *Le Livre* (*The Book*) remained a project on the horizon, nor that Novalis's *Heinrich von Ofterdingen* breaks off abruptly a few pages into the second part, 'Die Erfüllung' ('Fulfilment'). The door was closed on poetic fulfilment; the grandeur of their aspirations condemned the *Frühromantiker* and the French Symbolists to wait in the antechamber of promise.

Many of the poets themselves were conscious of this predicament.
Novalis opened his collection of aphorisms, *Blütenstaub*, with the
crushing confession: 'Wir suchen überall das Unbedingte, und finden
immer nur Dinge' ('We seek everywhere the absolute, and always find
only things'). The fundamental earnestness of that statement is barely
veiled by the play on the verbal connection in German between the
word for 'things' ('Dinge') and 'the absolute', 'the unconditional' ('das
Unbedingte'). Novalis's experience is echoed in Mallarmé's poem *Les
Fenêtres*, where the attempt to pierce the windows of reality so as to attain 'Au ciel antérieur où fleurit la Beauté!' ('the yonder sky where
blossoms Beauty!') suddenly collapses into this terrible acknowledgement:

> Mais, hélas! Ici-bas est maître: sa hantise
> Vient m'écoeurer parfois jusqu'en cet abri sûr,
> Et le vomissement impur de la Bêtise
> Me force à me boucher le nez devant l'azur.

> (But alas! the down-here is master: it haunts and
> Comes to sicken me even in this safe shelter,
> And the contaminated vomit of Stupidity
> Forces me to hold my nose before the azure sky.)

These are prime examples of that syndrome that Paul de Man has outlined in his article 'Intentional Structure of the Romantic Image'.[131]
Briefly, de Man argues that the ambiguity of Romantic poems springs
from the attempt to posit the priority of the imagination, and the subsequent defeat of this poetic defiance in the recognition of the necessary
ontological priority of natural objects. In other words, 'Ici-bas est
maître' ('The down-here is master'), or even more materially, the poet
is aware of finding only 'things' ('Dinge'). Such avowals shake the
very foundations of the *Frühromantik* and of Symbolism. In the act of
reaching out for the absolute the poet admits that it is unattainable, that
the door is closed to him. The intrepid exploration of the outset may
then turn into an anguished retreat, indeed a wandering in a frightening inner labyrinth from which there is no escape exit. Huysmans' Des
Esseintes, Mallarmé's Hérodiade, Maeterlinck's blind creatures, Tieck's
Eckbert and Christian are all victims of that imprisonment in the world
within that is a constant threat to the Romantics. Having shut out this
world to search for some absolute, they may then make the dual bitter
discovery that their ideal is inaccessible, perhaps even illusory, and that

there is no path of return. Not only do they end by living in a void, suspended in a limbo between the reality they have rejected and the ideal they cannot attain; they are also, in consequence, singularly vague and shadowy as representational figures, lacking in flesh and blood to the point of ghostliness. In this respect the *Frühromantik* and French Symbolism are again counterparts. What is more, both are in striking contrast to the clear-cut characterization of the Storm and Stress and French Romanticism.

The note of defeat is more pervasive among the French Symbolists than among the *Frühromantiker*. Mallarmé is the most immediate example of a poet obsessed with the spectre of his putative failure, the fear of sterility, the intrinsic impossibility of his whole enterprise, the clear view into the abyss of nothingness confronting him. These are the repeated preoccupations of his letters and of many of his poems, including *Angoisse, Les Fenêtres, L'Azur, Brise Marine, Tristesse d'été, Soupir*. 'Je fuis' ('I flee') is the recurrent motif; and the characteristic scenery of Mallarmé's poetry, the coldness of the glaciers, the barren trees and the swans, reinforces the prevailing atmosphere of despair. The key figure is that of Hérodiade, the sterile woman resplendent in her own useless beauty, refusing to contaminate herself through contact with ordinary human activity, preserving her purity for its own sake, and pushing aside the dim and deeply disturbing awareness of the emptiness of her existence. Images of man's futility and impotence also dominate Mallarmé's last work, *Un Coup de dés jamais n'abolira le hasard*, whether its ending is interpreted as a flicker of hope at long last, or a message of unredeemable disaster. Mallarmé's despondency is shared by others of the French Symbolists, notably Maeterlinck in the poem 'Oraison' that forms part of his volume *Serres chaudes*; but none matched Mallarmé in intensity of expression save Rimbaud in the savage unmasking of *Une Saison en enfer*. In *Délires II* he recounts what he calls 'l'histoire d'une de mes folies' ('the tale of one of my follies'): 'je croyais à tous les enchantements. J'inventai la couleur des voyelles! . . . Je fixais des vertiges'[132] ('I used to believe in all the enchantments. I invented the colour of the vowels! . . . I used to pin down hallucinations'). All this is noted in the past tense and as if scoffingly – the tale of a folly. For now, *'Je ne sais plus parler!'*[133] (*'I no longer know how to speak!'*), he proclaims with perverse glee in the section that bears the surely ironic title *Matin* (*Morning*). The morning of his awakening is the evening close of his poetic career. It is an awakening that annihilates the beautiful dream, as it does at the end of two poems in *Les Illumina-*

tions, 'Aube' and 'Ouvriers'; after a glimpse of an ideal realm through the shutters of the poetic vision the door is abruptly and brutally slammed shut.

Such negativity is less readily apparent among the *Frühromantiker*. Its relative attenuation is probably due to their single-minded focus on the infinite and their resulting greater remoteness from reality than the French Symbolists'. The difference may also reflect a divergence of mood between the more vigorous hopefulness of the early years of the nineteenth century and the increasing disillusionment throughout Europe in the second half of the century. But even though idealism was paramount among the *Frühromantiker*, it is a schematization simply to contrast them with the *poètes maudits*, as even so perspicacious a critic as Werner Vordtriede[134] has been tempted to do. The darker sides of their endeavour were by no means beyond the ken of the *Früh-romantiker*. The nocturnal aspect of nature (the so-called *Nachtseite der Natur*), to which they were so strongly drawn, could be threatening as well as enticing. The question that is the impetus to exploration may remain tantalizingly without answer for ever; in the *Märchen* we are often ultimately placed before possibilities and mirror images that raise only further queries in a confusion of uncertainties. Even art, which is generally glorified as the source of mankind's salvation, is grudgingly conceded to have its sombre streak too, to be a seductive, forbidden, indeed poisonous fruit, as is admitted in Wackenroder's and Tieck's *Phantasien über die Kunst*. Beneath its surface optimism the *Frühromantik* carried also its grimmer undercurrents, that inverse side that was soon enough to be uncovered by E. T. A. Hoffmann. Romantic idealism could, and did, capsize into romantic agony.[135]

Just as the high hopes of the *Frühromantiker* and of the Symbolists soured into a fearsome intuition of impending failure, so the experiments with new forms tended to backfire, or at best to prove ambivalent in effect. That both groups did win a far greater degree of freedom for the poet is beyond dispute; through his elevation to the rank of a divine creator he was virtually exempted from the norms of ordinary mortals. Even if the price he paid was that of becoming an outcast, he did so willingly, closing the doors with alacrity on the social and artistic establishment in return for the immeasurable gain in liberty. Bound no longer by the conventional hierarchy of genres, nor by the traditional segregation of arts and of sense media, nor by rigidities of prosody, the *Frühromantiker* and the Symbolists could and did range entirely at will. The *Mischgedicht, vers libre*, prose poem, lyrical drama, synesthesia, and approaches to the condition of music represent a significant expansion of the expressive possibilities of literature. The freewheeling elasticity of much twentieth-century experimentation is already anticipated in the tentatives of the German Romantics and of the French Symbolists. The two movements are clearly counterparts to each other in their replacement of the older Classical and Parnassien static ideal of statuesque perfection by the dynamic notion of a pliant perfectibility. This in turn brought with it a totally different expectation from the work of art than had existed hitherto. Instead of endeavouring to attain in its formal impeccability a microcosm of the finite certainty that underpinned its ethos, as the Classical and Parnassien work had sought to do, the Romantic-Symbolist (and also the twentieth-century) work laid its chief stress on its potential, its promise of infinite progression in the future, its quintessential openness to the possibilities of endless evolution. And those possibilities were indeed manifold: stream-of-consciousness narration, the juggling of temporal and spatial order, action painting, novels printed on cards to be shuffled at the reader's pleasure, and so forth. These devolve, I would suggest, from that radical emancipation from form *per se* that took place with the *Frühromantik* and French Symbolism.

Actual problems of form as such were of scant interest to either group. Aesthetics centred on the larger questions of the function and nature of art, or then fell, particularly among the French Symbolists, into the technical details of versification and synesthesia. Little, if any, attention was devoted to concrete considerations of narrative, dramatic or lyrical structure. These were to all intents and purposes crowded out by the overriding concern with the transcendental dimension of art and the mechanics of translating it into symbols; the lesser minutiae of artistic organization paled into unimportance beside these cardinal issues, and so were largely neglected. The interest in exploring and recording mystical experience took precedence over any desire to create form. At best form was secondary, the subservient reflection of, and appropriate vessel for the substance, the inspiration. This order of priorities led to an explicit toleration of even artistic aberrations, as Friedrich Schlegel unabashedly stated in the *Athenäum* (no. 139):

Aus dem romantischen Gesichtspunkt haben auch die Abarten der Poesie, selbst die exzentrischen und monströsen, ihren Wert, als Materialien und Vorübungen der Universalität, wenn nur irgend etwas drin ist, wenn sie nur original sind.

(From the romantic point of view the most curious sorts of poetry, even the eccentric and the monstrous, are of value as preliminary exercises to universality, provided there is in them some grain of originality.)

Novalis too, in *Blütenstaub* (no. 58), championed 'die Verworrenen' ('the confused') on the grounds that they are 'so progressiv, so perfektibel' ('so progressive, so perfectible') in contrast to the finite limitations of the orderly. Jules Laforgue's cheerful acceptance of 'l'anarchie ouverte'[136] ('open anarchy') as the guiding principle of art is strongly reminiscent of Friedrich Schlegel's welcome to 'monstrosities'. Anarchy was mooted again by Rémy de Gourmont when he defined Symbolism as 'une théorie de liberté . . . une absolue licence d'idées et de formes'[137] ('a theory of liberty . . . an absolute license in ideas and forms'); for, he maintained, in distinction to previous literary revolutions, which had been content only to change the captive's fetters from one chain to another, Symbolism, descended as it is from Idealism, will achieve Liberty with a capital L, a liberty that is tantamount at its extreme to anarchy.

Theoretically therefore the *Frühromantiker* and the Symbolists threw the door wide open to any form whatsoever without stricture. What this produced in practice was formlessness, a dissolution into fragmentariness that was as frightening as the cold gaze into the abyss of nothingness of which it was but another aspect. That dissolution became manifest in a variety of guises. The anecdotal, for instance, was often eschewed probably as too pedestrian for 'higher' art, or as too redolent of previous orthodoxy. Through this tendency to discard plot a valuable factor of compositional unity was lost. Exactly what was to replace the story-line never becomes clear; passing reference is made to such elements as mood, feeling, atmosphere, musicality, none of which would seem sufficient to support the weight of a full-length work. This suspicion is confirmed by a glance at some of the characteristic works of the *Frühromantiker* and the French Symbolists. Friedrich Schlegel's *Lucinde*, Novalis's *Heinrich von Ofterdingen*, Mallarmé's *Hérodiade* and *L'Après-midi d'un faune*, Rimbaud's *Une Saison en enfer*, Rémy de Gourmont's 'roman de la vie cérébrale' ('novel of cerebral life') *Sixtine*: all these impose on the reader a burden of decipherment by withholding information necessary for ready comprehension. The delicate shadings of psychic perception, bounteously and subtly though they are delineated in these writings, are in the long run no satisfactory substitute for the architectural composition vital to the epic genre. For this reason the *Frühromantiker* and the Symbolists were more successful in shorter pieces such as the *Märchen*, the prose poem, the lyric, where the intensity of poetic resonance could be sustained for a brief span in a manner that is hardly feasible under the challenge of extensiveness. Thus longer works often tend to splinter into a series of episodes as in Wackenroder's *Herzensergiessungen*, Tieck's *Franz Sternbald*, Novalis's *Heinrich von Ofterdingen*, Huysmans' *A Rebours*, Rimbaud's *Une Saison en enfer* and Gourmont's *Sixtine*. What is more, many remained unfinished, or seem to break off in mid-air. *Heinrich von Ofterdingen* itself, the major poetic product of the *Frühromantik*, was left barely on the brink of its 'Fulfilment' on Novalis's death; similarly, *L'Après-midi d'un faune* has only eighteen lines of the 're-awakening', while *Hérodiade*, announced as a tragedy in three acts, never came to fruition either; as for *Un Coup de dés*, it has been dismissed, not without justification, as no more than 'quelques îles verbales, des *membra disjecta poetae*'[138] ('a few verbal islets, *membra disjecta poeta*').

This problem of the dissolution of form is at its most acute in drama, because it comes up against the practicalities of stage performance. With the exception of Tieck, the *Frühromantiker* avoided drama, aware perhaps of the difficulty of fashioning a form fitting at once to their transcendental vision and to the realities of the theatre. The Symbolists, on the other hand, impelled perhaps by the strong French dramatic tradition, did make the attempt. But theirs is, as Haskell M. Block has so well characterized it, 'a drama of suggestion rather than statement, of inner rather than external movement, of mystery and spirituality',[139] 'a fluid interweaving of the planes of the everyday and the occult, . . . a reduction of the role of the narrative, . . . and an interiorization of dramatic action'.[140] This is not, Block concedes, the stuff of drama: 'the values of suggestiveness, musicality, mystery, reverie, and dream all point to an indifference to character and to human relationships, which have been a central part of the drama from ancient times to the present'.[141] With their lengthy poetic soliloquies, their dearth of movement and action, their frozen tableaux, the shadowiness of their figures, such plays as Villiers de L'Isle-Adam's *Axel*, Maeterlinck's *Les Aveugles, L'Intruse* and *Pelléas et Mélisande* plainly stand in the Romantic lineage of lyrical closet drama, far removed indeed from the lively movement of theatrical action. Here again it becomes amply apparent that it was the capturing of the vision that was of sole importance to the *Frühromantiker* and the French Symbolists. Their transcendentalism led directly to the decomposition of reality, the gradual removal of external substance, and with it the atrophy of the poetic structure necessary to the embodiment of the vision. At that point they were confronted with a menacingly closed door.

Admittedly the *Frühromantiker* and the French Symbolists were unconcerned with the more traditional demands of narrative and drama, and consciously sought instead to introduce new systems. In place of the old method of rational discourse, they preferred what T. S. Eliot was later to call 'the logic of the imagination', whose natural expression is in a sequence of images and ideas linked by association, at its most refined in a web of symbols. This new organizing principle is already adumbrated in Novalis's gropings, startlingly avant-garde at the time they were written:

> Erzählungen, ohne Zusammenhang, jedoch mit Association, wie *Träume*. Gedichte – blos *wohlklingend* und voll schöner Worte – aber auch ohne allen Sinn und Zusammenhang – höchstens einzelne Strofen verständlich – sie müssen, wie lauter Bruchstücke aus den verschiedenartigsten Dingen [seyn]. Höchstens kann wahre Poesie einen *allegorischen* Sinn im Grossen haben und eine indirecte Wirkung wie Musik etc.[142]

> (Narratives, unconnected, yet full of associations, like *dreams*. Poems, simply *fine-sounding* and full of beautiful words – but also devoid of meaning and connection – at most isolated stanzas comprehensible – they must like fragmented pieces [be made up] of the most diverse things. At most true poetry can have an *allegorical* meaning in its totality and an indirect effect like music etc.)

That final phrase in particular must surely have rung in the ears of the Symbolists (bearing in mind the interchangeability of 'allegorical' and 'symbolical' at that time). It seems to echo through Rémy de Gourmont's essay on Mallarmé, for his defence of Mallarmé rests on his use of the associative aesthetic, his suppression of the first element of a comparison in favour of a full record of the second, i.e. the symbolic image.

> Il en résulte une langue nouvelle, imprécise comme le rêve même qu'elle évoque et dont elle ne veut s'astreindre à cerner les contours. Les mots, dans cette seconde manière du poète, sont choisis pour leurs qualités complémentaires, à peu près comme les couleurs par le peintre. Aussi ne faut-il pas analyser la phrase selon la méthode grammaticale, encore moins selon la méthode logique ordinaire, de même

qu'il ne faut pas regarder de trop près les tableaux impressionnistes, même ceux de Claude Monet. L'éducation de l'oeil est plus avancée en France que celle du sens poétique; on fera un peu comprendre la manière de Mallarmé en disant que c'est le Claude Monet de la poésie. Ni ses vers, ni les taches lumineuses du peintre ne peuvent servir à l'enseignement de la grammaire ou à celui du dessin.[143]

(From this springs a new language, as equivocal as the dream itself that it evokes and whose outlines it does not seek to trace. In this alternate poetic manner the words are chosen for their complementary qualities, rather as the painter chooses his colours. Thus the phrase must not be analysed according to the laws of grammar, much less according to the ordinary methods of logic, any more than Impressionist pictures, even those of Claude Monet, must be scrutinized from too close an angle. The education of the eye is further advanced in France than that of the poetic sense; Mallarmé's approach may be better understood by saying that he is the Claude Monet of poetry. Neither his verse nor the painter's luminous areas can serve as primers of grammar or of drawing.)

Gourmont certainly makes his main point which is akin to Novalis's: that Romantic-Symbolist writing, like Impressionist painting, has different aims, uses different means and should be regarded with different expectations than previous poetry. However, his persuasive parallel between the Symbolists and the Impressionists does in turn raise problems. Not only does he overlook the outraged opposition which the Impressionists aroused for many years through the alienating strangeness of their art in the eyes of their contemporaries. He also fails to realize that, in spite of their luminous decomposition of objects, they did, in the very process of illumination, in the colour harmony, achieve a degree of cohesiveness which the Symbolists and the *Frühromantiker* only rarely attained. The disparity may stem in part from the variance of their media: the colours and shapes of the pictorial artist, being further removed from the rational utilitarianism of the word, may be more amenable to re-alignment according to the logic of the imagination than the poet's verbal material. Whatever the reason, both the *Frühromantiker* and the French Symbolists encountered grave difficulties in substituting their new synthetic pattern of images for the architectonic order customary hitherto. Even in works as successful in implementing this innovative mode as Novalis's *Hymnen an die Nacht* and Nerval's *Aurélia* the perplexities of access are not to be underestimated. For the reader must suspend his ratiocinations in order to yield to the stream of imagery, yet at the same time intellectual as well as emotional intuition must come into play for the understanding interpretation of that imagery. Great though the rewards of this manner may be in poetic intensity, its dangers too are signal. It can spawn vague and wandering blurs of imagery, as in the poems of Tieck and Gustave Kahn, an amorphousness unhappily fostered by the very freedom of the prose poem, the *vers libre*, the unstructured form favoured by both groups. Or at the other extreme, in the opaque arabesques of Klingsohr's *Märchen* in *Heinrich von Ofterdingen* and in Mallarmé's *Un Coup de dés jamais n'abolira le hasard*, it may result in an imprisonment in an impenetrable labyrinth of metaphors.

Language itself tended to suffer the same fate, specially at the hands of the French Symbolists. Grammatical flexibility is the linguistic equivalent of the open door, as well as denoting a closing of the door on the grandiloquent rhetoric of French Neo-classicism that continued to haunt the French Romantic poets. This strand of iconoclasm in regard to language was largely absent from the *Frühromantik* because the Storm and Stress had so effectively carried out its liberating mission. But like the Symbolists, the *Frühromantiker* were attracted to the notion of a sound poetry, to *instrumentation verbale*, as it came to be known. Correctness of grammar, syntax and vocabulary were to be disregarded; what mattered were the inflections, the cadence, the vocal tone-scale that could carry and synthesize the poet's sensations. As in the case of the organization by symbols, so here too this new approach was fraught with possibilities and pitfalls. Its chief virtue is immediately evident in the euphonious flow characteristic of *Frühromantik* and Symbolist writing at its best. On the other hand, once the backbone of grammatical order is cast aside, the threat of dissolution becomes very real; harmonies of sound, no more than mosaics of symbols, may not be adequate to support and convey meaning. As an integral part of the opening-up process, the words and the symbols were to speak for themselves in direct address to the reader. The outcome, unfortunately, is often the opposite when the reader is barely able with ingenious effort to disentangle the contorted phraseology that faces him like a blank wall. Far from being re-created, the world here disintegrates in the insidious maze of esotericism.

That then is the ultimate closed door: non-communication. And here too the *Frühromantiker* and the French Symbolists are ensnared in the same singularly ironic situation: having set out to open up the cosmos through their powers of transcendental perception, they end up enclosed in a world of hermetic symbols impenetrable to the uninitiated. They appear, it is true, curiously unperturbed by the predicament. From the outset they had insisted that they were writing not for the masses but for an ivory-tower élite. Accordingly the poet had the right to demand an effort from his reader, August Wilhelm Schlegel maintained in a passage already quoted previously (see p. 140). Novalis, as we have just seen, went even further by advancing the idea that poetry could be 'ohne allen Sinn und Zusammenhang' ('devoid of all meaning and connection'). This is a subjective art in the profoundest sense of the term, i.e. an art prompted by its creator's need for self-expression and fashioned without heed for an audience. The reader becomes more like an eavesdropper on a soliloquy than the listener to a narration addressed to him, as had been his customary role. At times it seems as if obstacles were deliberately put into his way: 'il doit y avoir toujours énigme en poésie, et c'est le but de la littérature'[144] ('there must always be enigma in poetry, and that is the aim of literature'), Mallarmé staunchly asserted. Somehow the notion of incomprehensibility came to be allied to that of art's so-called 'purity', the implication being apparently that inaccessibility was a positive quality. The work of art was therefore conceived as a mystery couched in hieroglyphics which were a challenge to the subtlety of the reader's powers of decoding. Significantly Mallarmé adduced the image of the key needed to unlock its hermeticism.

But what of the reader not in possession of that key? Granted that the defect may lie in him, in a blindness to metaphysics, or an insufficiency of imagination, or even merely a lack of training in linguistic gymnastics. However, in the face of a large number of such readers the other possibility must also be considered, namely the presence of a flaw, or at least some resistance in the keyhole.

The charge of obscurity has so often been levelled at the *Frühromantiker* and the French Symbolists that it cannot be swept aside with impunity. Even among their adherents, in spite of their scorn for Philistines, it crops up occasionally as a moot point. Moréas, for example, in the preface to *Les Premières armes du symbolisme,* admonished his fellow Symbolists in 1889 to rid themselves of obscurity. Friedrich Schlegel's solution was more radical: anticipating modern advertising methods, he humorously suggested that a free slice of gingerbread be given to every purchaser of the *Athenäum,* which was frightening readers off by its abstractions (Ricarda Huch later wittily described it as a hedgehog of ideas). On the whole German critics, both contemporary and subsequent, were more inclined to leniency in their solemnly reverential tone towards the *Frühromantiker* than were their French counterparts, who scoffed without mercy at the Symbolists 'babblings', 'stammerings', 'des grimoires parfaitement inintelligibles, je ne dis pas à la foule, mais aux lettrés les plus perspicaces'[145] ('mumbo-jumbo totally unintelligible not just to the masses, but even to the most cultured and perspicacious').

Such hermeticism is one of the gravest threats to both the *Frühromantik* and to French Symbolism. It is the worm in the apple of élitist individualism, transcendental idealism and symbolic expression. For each of these facets in itself, and even more so in combination, leads away from the common and communal paths of experience and modes of communication. The aspiration to infinite suggestiveness may turn out to be a move towards the plane of silence; instead of revealing the mysteries of the universe, poetry itself becomes a mystery, an acrostic whose enigmatic elements do not fall into the charmed cohesive pattern. The danger has been spelled out clearly enough in relation to the *Frühromantik* as to French Symbolism by recent critics aware of the trends of modern writing already latent in the nineteenth century.

> Das romantische Kunstwerk als Träger einer ästhetischen Mitteilung, besser gesagt, als Aussage vom Unbekannten, distanziert sich schärfer von der gewohnten alltäglichen Verständigung und von der gegebenen Gestalt, als dem Durchschnittsleser billig erscheint.[146]

> (The romantic work of art as carrier of an aesthetic message, or rather, as enunciation of the unknown, detaches itself further from customary ordinary communication and from the usual form than is acceptable to the average reader.)

Gillian Rodger is even more specific in naming 'certain potential dangers' which she rightly describes as 'ominous': the danger that 'evocative atmospheric magic' may be transformed into 'obscurity', 'self-consciousness' degenerate into 'sterility', 'subjectivity' become 'esoteric', and 'the symbol, which in Romantic hands could at its best draw tangible and intangible close together in an invigorating relationship of near-identification', could come to act 'as an obstacle to contact with physical or spiritual reality'.[147] These phrases are wholly apt to French Symbolism in which the hazards inherent in the *Frühromantik* become fully manifest. The dimensions and implications of the problem have been brilliantly analysed by Bernard Weinberg in the appendix to his book *The Limits of Symbolism*. Under the title 'The Limits of Hermeticism, or Hermeticism and Intelligibility', Weinberg outlines the increasing tension between the traditional clarity and comprehensibility of poetry on the one hand, and on the other the growing tendency to cultivate obscurity and create works comparable to riddles without solution. Weinberg dates this development 'since Baudelaire';[148] the arguments are compelling, to my mind, for amending that to 'since the *Frühromantik*'.

The *Frühromantiker* and the French Symbolists were balanced on a dangerous tightrope. Theirs was a daring feat as they launched out beyond the *terra firma* of reality to explore new continents of experience and expression in the ocean of transcendentalism. They ventured much, and the rewards of that adventure could be dazzling, particularly in their opening up of great new territories that were to be mapped by those who came after them. But inevitably those who venture risk loss too; in paving the way for the art of the future, they forfeited some of the virtues of the past.

Thus the *Frühromantik* and French Symbolism are multi-faceted counterparts: in their historical position as a second wave of the tide of European Romanticism in their respective literatures; in their bold aspirations, in their conquests in substance and form, and also in the perils besetting them. Élitist though they appear, the *Frühromantik* and French Symbolism provoked a deeper and more telling revolution in the history of Western culture than the Storm and Stress and French Romanticism in spite of their popular appeal and rumbustious air. What had been initiated by the earlier generation was consummated by the later one. In these successive pairs of counterparts the transition was effected in Germany and in France from an orientation to the Classical to a recognizably modern aesthetics.

Notes and references

II *The emergence of the Romantic movements*

1. Dates given are those of publication. The date of composition may be earlier, as in the case of the *Rêveries*, on which Rousseau was engaged from the mid-1770s onwards.
2. Jean-Jacques Rousseau, *Rêveries du promeneur solitaire* (Paris: Garnier-Flammarion, 1964), 35.
3. Johann Gottfried Herder, *Werke*, ed. Theodor Matthias (Leipzig: Bibliographisches Institut, 1903), i, 287.
4. Herder, *Werke*, i, 290.
5. Rousseau, *Rêveries*, 40.
6. Rousseau, *Rêveries*, 104.
7. Johann Wolfgang Goethe, *Die Leiden des jungen Werthers* (Munich: Deutscher Taschenbuch Verlag, 1962), 43.
8. Goethe, *Werther*, 117.
9. Rousseau, *Rêveries*, 46.
10. Jean-Jacques Rousseau, *La Nouvelle Héloïse*, ed. Daniel Mornet (Paris: Hachette, 1925), iii, 14-15.
11. Rousseau, *La Nouvelle Héloïse*, iii, 183ff.
12. Mme de Staël, *De la Littérature*, ed. Paul Van Tieghem (Geneva: Droz, and Paris: Minard, 1950), 42.
13. Gotthold Ephraim Lessing, *Werke* (Stuttgart: Göschen, 1887), iv, 337.
14. Staël, *De la Littérature*, 359.
15. See also my article, 'Lessing and Mme de Staël *vis-à-vis* the

trans.

Literature of the Mediterranean', *Journal of European Studies*, 1, no. 2 (1971), 161–5.

16. Johann Christoph Gottsched, *Ausgewählte Werke*, ed. Joachim Birke and Brigitte Birke (Berlin: de Gruyter, 1973), iii, 34. I offer no English translation of this passage for fear of compounding Gottsched's sins.

17. Gottsched, *Ausgewählte Werke*, vi/1, 12.

18. Lessing, *Werke*, iii, 200.

19. Mme de Staël, *De L'Allemagne*, ed. Jean de Pange and Simone Balayé (Paris: Hachette, 1958–60), ii, 26.

20. Jean-François de La Harpe, *Lycée, ou Cours de littérature ancienne et moderne* (Paris: Didier, 1834), i, 421.

21. La Harpe, *Lycée*, i, 422.

22. La Harpe, *Lycée*, i, 435.

23. La Harpe, *Lycée*, i, iii.

24. Alfred de Musset, *Après une lecture*, stanza 10.

25. Staël, *De L'Allemagne*, ii, 8.

26. Pierre Moreau, *Le Romantisme* (Paris: del Duca, 1957), 64.

27. See F. G. Healey, *The Literary Culture of Napoleon* (Geneva: Droz, and Paris: Minard, 1959), appendix B, 156, for a list of the plays and the number of performances of each that Napoleon saw.

28. Benjamin Constant, *Wallstein*, ed. Jean-René Derré (Paris: Les Belles Lettres, 1965), 46.

29. Constant, *Wallstein*, 67.

30. For a detailed study of *Wallstein* see my article, 'Benjamin Constant's *Wallstein*', *Romanistisches Jahrbuch*, 15 (1964), 141–59.

31. Alfred de Musset, *Lettres de Dupuis et Cotonet* (Paris: Charpentier, 1887), 202.

32. Stendhal, *Racine et Shakespeare* (Paris: Garnier-Flammarion, 1970), 135.

33. See the illuminating essay by W. M. Simon, 'Historical and Social Background', in *The Romantic Period in Germany*, ed. S. S. Prawer (London: Weidenfeld & Nicolson, and New York: Schocken, 1970), 17–33.

34. Ralph Tymms, *German Romantic Literature* (London: Methuen, 1955), 190.

35. Novalis, *Werke* (Heidelberg: Schneider, 1953), 279.

36. Novalis, *Werke*, 303.

37. Sainte-Beuve, *Tableau historique et critique de la poésie française et du théâtre français au seizième siècle* (Paris: Charpentier, 1869), 3.

38. Sainte-Beuve, *Tableau historique*, 85.
39. Sainte-Beuve, *Tableau historique*, 61.
40. Sainte-Beuve, *Tableau historique*, 251-2.
41. Sainte-Beuve, *Tableau historique*, 283.
42. Sainte-Beuve, *Tableau historique*, 282.
43. Friedrich Schlegel, 'Über Goethes *Meister*', in *Kunstanschauung der Frühromantik*, Deutsche Literatur in Entwicklungsreihen, Romantik, no. 3 (Leipzig: Reclam, 1931), 150.
44. *The German Image of Goethe* (Oxford: Clarendon Press, 1961), 38.
45. *Kunstanschauung der Frühromantik*, 241.
46. *Weltanschauung der Frühromantik,* Deutsche Literatur in Entwicklungsreihen, Romantik, no. 5 (Leipzig: Reclam, 1932), 53.

III *The Storm and Stress and French Romanticism*

1. Johann Wolfgang Goethe, *Werke*, ed. Robert Plesch (Leipzig: Bibliographisches Institut, 1926), v, 90.
2. Goethe, *Werke*, v, 69.
3. Goethe, *Werke*, v, 68.
4. See section 46, 6 October 1767.
5. *The German Sturm und Drang* (Manchester: Manchester Univ. Press, 1953), 7.
6. *Romanticism and Revolt* (London: Thames & Hudson, and New York: Harcourt, Brace & World, 1967), 9.
7. Talmon, *Romanticism and Revolt*, 72.
8. Alfred de Musset, *La Confession d'un enfant du siècle* (Paris: Charpentier, 1884), 2.
9. Musset, *Confession*, 8.
10. Musset, *Confession*, 22.
11. Johann Georg Hamann, *Der Magus im Norden*, ed. Walther Ziesemer (Wiesbaden: Insel, 1950), 18.
12. *Le Globe*, 24 March 1825.
13. Victor Hugo, *Théâtre complet* (Paris: Gallimard, 1963), i, 444.
14. Hugo, *Théâtre complet*, i, 1147; italics are Hugo's.
15. Hugo, *Théâtre complet*, i, 1149; capitals are Hugo's.
16. Hugo, *Théâtre complet*, i, 434.
17. Hugo, *Théâtre complet*, i, 435.
18. *The German Sturm und Drang*, 236.

19. Pascal, *The German Sturm und Drang*, 190.

20. Victor Hugo, *Réponse à un acte d'accusation*, *Les Contemplations* (Paris: Hetzel, n.d.), 22.

21. Duvicquet, *Le Globe*, 6 December 1825.

22. See Fernand Baldensperger, *Goethe en France* (Paris: Hachette, 1904), 93–104, and Edmond Eggli, *Schiller et le romantisme français* (Paris: Gamber, 1927), i, 65–169.

23. *Histoire du romantisme* (Paris: Charpentier, 1874), 99–114.

24. *Histoire du romantisme*, 107–8.

25. *Histoire du romantisme*, 107.

26. *Histoire du romantisme*, 111.

27. François-René de Chateaubriand, *René* (Paris: Garnier, 1962), 205.

28. Goethe, *Werther*, 93.

29. Goethe, *Werther*, 94–5.

30. *Der Magus im Norden*, 33.

31. *Der Magus im Norden*, 58.

32. *Der Magus im Norden*, 61.

33. *Der Magus im Norden*, 11.

34. Goethe, *Werke*, v, 68.

35. *Briefe* (Hamburg: Christian Wegner Verlag, 1962), i, 190.

36. *Briefe*, i, 191–5.

37. Goethe, *Werke*, v, 177.

38. *Oeuvres complètes* (Paris: Charpentier, 1867), ix, 129.

39. *Oeuvres complètes* (Paris: Hetzel, 1881), xvii, 130.

40. *A Study of Goethe* (Oxford: Clarendon Press, 1947), 12.

41. See Lilian R. Furst, *Romanticism in Perspective* (London: Macmillan, 1969, and New York: Humanities Press, 1970), 97–110.

42. Chateaubriand, *René*, 245.

43. *Briefe*, i, 194.

44. *Briefe*, i, 194.

45. Jacob Michael Reinhold Lenz, *Gesammelte Schriften*, ed. Ernst Lewy (Berlin: Cassirer, 1909), iv, 86.

46. Lenz, *Gesammelte Schriften*, iv, 112.

47. Marcel Moraud, *Le Romantisme français en Angleterre* (Paris: Champion, 1933), 7.

48. *The German Sturm und Drang*, 304.

49. *A Handbook to Literature*, ed. W. F. Thrall and A. Hibbard (New York: Doubleday, 1936), 424–5.

50. 'Lettre-Préface' to William Reymond, *Corneille, Shakespeare et Goethe* (Berlin: Luederitz, 1864), xi.

51. *Oeuvres* (Paris: Gallimard, 1957), 259–73.

52. For a more detailed discussion of this topic see my article, 'Mme de Staël's *De L'Allemagne*: A Misleading Intermediary', *Orbis Litterarum*, 31 (1976), 43–58.

53. *Lettres philosophiques*, ed. Gustave Lanson (Paris: Cornély, 1909), ii, 79.

54. *Gesammelte Schriften*, iv, 268.

55. *Rousseau et la sensibilité littéraire à la fin du XVIIIième siècle* (Paris: Centre de documentation universitaire, 1961), 233.

56. *Oeuvres* (Paris: Gallimard, 1950), i, 344.

IV *German Romanticism and French Symbolism*

1. The term *Frühromantik* is used in preference to its English translation, Early German Romantics, because it has a readily understood acceptance in the history of German literature; it refers to the group of poets and thinkers who gathered first in Berlin and then in Jena around the turn of the century, i.e. the brothers Friedrich and August Wilhelm Schlegel, Novalis, Wackenroder, Tieck, Schelling, Schleiermacher, Baader, etc.

2. *Axel's Castle* (New York: Scribner, 1931), 2.

3. Gustave Flaubert, *Correspondance* (Paris: Conard, 1926–33), iv, 205.

4. *Oeuvres complètes* (Paris: Gallimard, 1945), 868.

5. *Kunstanschauung der Frühromantik*, 132.

6. 'Notes nouvelles sur Edgar Poe', *L'Art romantique* (Paris: Garnier, 1962), 636.

7. Friedrich Schleiermacher, *Reden über die Religion* (Berlin: Deutsche Bibliothek, n.d.), 94.

8. *Vorlesungen über schöne Kunst und Literatur*, ed. J. Minor (Heilbronn: Henninger, 1884), 91.

9. *Schriften*, ed. Paul Kluckhohn and Richard Samuel (Leipzig: Bibliographisches Institut, 1928), vi, 37.

10. *The Symbolist Aesthetic in France, 1885–1895* (Oxford: Blackwell, 1950), 148.

11. 'Die syntaktischen Eigenschaften der französischen Symbolisten', in *Aufsätze zur romanischen Syntax und Stilistik* (Halle: Niemeyer, 1918), 285.

12. Jules Huret, *Enquête sur l'évolution littéraire* (Paris: Charpentier, 1897), 67.

13. André Barre, *Le Symbolisme* (Paris: Jouve, 1912), 2.

14. *Entretiens politiques et littéraires* (September 1891), 96.

15. *Neophilologus*, 7 (1922), 244.

16. *Le Classicisme des romantiques*, 379.

17. *L'Influence du symbolisme français dans le renouveau poétique de l'Allemagne, 1892–1900* (Paris: Champion, 1933), 526.

18. *L'Âme romantique et le rêve* (Paris: Corti, 1937), 328.

19. *L'Âme romantique et le rêve*, 329.

20. 'The Genesis of Symbolist Theories in Germany', *Modern Language Review*, 41 (1946), 306.

21. 'The Metaphor of Hieroglyphics in German Romanticism', *Comparative Literature*, 7, no. 4 (1955), 312.

22. *Novalis und die französischen Symbolisten* (Stuttgart: Kohlhammer, 1963), 182.

23. Attributed to Régnier by Edouard Dujardin in *Mallarmé par un des siens* (Paris: Messein, 1936), 33.

24. Book II, section 3; *Sämtliche Werke*, ed. Rudolf Unger (Leipzig: Tempel, 1909), vi, 175.

25. *Sämtliche Werke*, vi, 191.

26. Thomas Carlyle, *Sartor Resartus*, ed. James Wood (London: Dent, 1902), 159-62.

27. See Kurt Jäckel, *Richard Wagner in der französischen Literatur* (Breslau: Priebatsch, 1931 and 1932); Grange Woolley, *Richard Wagner et le symbolisme français* (Paris: Presses universitaires de France, 1931); Isabelle Wyzewska, *La Revue Wagnérienne – Essai sur l'interprétation esthétique de Wagner en France* (Paris: Perrin, 1934); 'Wagner et la France', special issue of the *Revue Musicale* (1 October 1923). For a list of performances of Wagner's operas in France, translations of libretti, contemporary critical works and pictorial representations see the appendices (pp. 245–59) to Léon Guichard, *La Musique et les lettres en France au temps du Wagnérisme* (Paris: Presses universitaires de France, 1963). And for a careful re-assessment of Mallarmé's relationship to Wagner see Haskell M. Block, *Mallarmé and the Symbolist Drama* (Detroit: Wayne State Univ. Press, 1963), 52-82.

28. *Oeuvres complètes* (Paris: Gallimard, 1961), 1244.

29. *Oeuvres complètes*, 1237.

30. 'La Revue Wagnérienne', *Revue Musicale* (1 October 1923), 238.

31. *Revue Musicale* (1 October 1923), 240.

32. *Die Entartung* (Berlin: Duncker, 1893), i, 344.

33. 'Richard Wagner et Tannhäuser à Paris', *Oeuvres complètes*, 1213–14; the italics are Baudelaire's.

34. *Kunstanschauung der Frühromantik*, 92.

35. *Oeuvres complètes*, 1223ff.

36. *Oeuvres complètes*, 1211.

37. *Oeuvres complètes*, 1217.

38. *Oeuvres complètes*, 1220; the italics are Baudelaire's.

39. *Revue de Genève*, 2, no. 10 (25 July 1886), 257.

40. *La Littérature de tout à l'heure* (Paris: Perrin, 1889), facing 240.

41. *La Littérature de tout à l'heure*, 196.

42. *Traité du verbe* (Paris: Giraud, 1886), 23.

43. *The Symbolist Aesthetic in France*, 196.

44. *Mallarmé and the Symbolist Drama*, 59.

45. *Revue Wagnérienne*, 1, no. 8 (8 August 1885), 193.

46. *Oeuvres complètes*, 879.

47. *Servitude et grandeur littéraires* (Paris: Ollendorf, 1922), 225.

48. *The Symbolist Movement in Literature* (New York: Dutton, 1958), 9.

49. Stéphane Mallarmé, *Oeuvres complètes* (Paris: Gallimard, 1970), 869.

50. Arthur Rimbaud, *Oeuvres complètes* (Paris: Gallimard, 1954), 234.

51. *Oeuvres complètes*, 857.

52. Karl Wilhelm Ferdinand Solger, *Nachgelassene Schriften und Briefwechsel*, ed. Ludwig Tieck and Friedrich Raumer (Leipzig: Brockhaus, 1826), i, 268.

53. *Werke und Briefe*, ed. Alfred Kellerat (München: Winkler, 1962), 446.

54. *Le Symbolisme*, 5.

55. *Promenades littéraires*, 3rd ed. (Paris: Mercure de France, 1912), iv, 39.

56. *Les Origines du symbolisme* (Paris: Messein, 1936), 51–2.

57. *Romantiker als Poetologen* (Heidelberg: Lothar Stiehm, 1970), 94.

58. *The Symbolist Movement* (New York: Random House, 1967), 5.

59. *Les Origines du symbolisme*, 30.

60. *Schriften*, vi, 35.

61. *Kunstanschauung der Frühromantik*, 136.

62. *Oeuvres complètes*, 415.

63. 'Von der Sprache', in *Kritische Schriften*, ed. Edgar Lohner (Stuttgart: Kohlhammer, 1962), ii, 246.

64. *Le Décadent* (16 October 1886).

65. *Oeuvres complètes*, 257.

66. *Oeuvres complètes*, 407.

67. *Oeuvres complètes*, 879.

68. *Oeuvres complètes*, 202.

69. *Oeuvres complètes*, 203.

70. Wilhelm Heinrich Wackenroder, *Herzensergiessungen eines kunstliebenden Klosterburders, Kunstanschauung der Frühromantik*, 59.

71. *Vorlesungen über dramatische Kunst und Literatur* (Heidelberg: Mohr & Winter, 1817), iii, 15.

72. *Schriften*, x, 244.

73. *Oeuvres complètes*, 889.

74. *Oeuvres complètes*, 253.

75. *La Littérature de tout à l'heure*, 35.

76. See Brian Juden, *Traditions orphiques et tendances mystiques dans le romantisme français, 1830-1855* (Paris: Klincksieck, 1971).

77. *System des transzendentalen Idealismus* (Tübingen: Cotta, 1800), 5.

78. *Kritische Ausgabe*, ed. Ernst Behler (München: Schöningh, 1958), ii, 387.

79. *Kritische Ausgabe*, ii, 414.

80. *Schriften*, vi, 28.

81. *Schriften*, x, 443.

82. *Oeuvres complètes*, 1039.

83. *Manifeste du symbolisme, Le Figaro* (18 September 1886); reprinted in *La Doctrine symboliste*, ed. Guy Michaud (Paris: Nizet, 1947), 25.

84. *Thêatre* (Brussels: Lacomblez, 1908), i, x–xi.

85. Georges Vanor, *L'Art symboliste* (Paris: Vanier, 1889), 38.

86. *Oeuvres complètes*, 368.

87. Letter to Henri Cazalis (14 May 1867); reprinted in Henri Mondor, *Autres précisions sur Mallarmé* (Paris: Gallimard, 1961), 253.

88. *La Vogue* (18 April 1886); the italics are Mallarmé's.

89. *Oeuvres complètes*, 242.

90. *La Littérature de tout à l'heure*, 358.

91. *Oeuvres complètes*, 400.

92. *Kunstanschauung der Frühromantik*, 65.

93. 'Shakespeares Behandlung des Wunderbaren', *Vorbereitung*, Deutsche Literatur in Entwicklungsreihen, Romantik, no. 2 (Leipzig: Reclam, 1937), 121.

94. *Oeuvres complètes*, 870.

95. *Schriften*, vi, 33.
96. *Ideen*, no. 8, in *Weltanschauung der Frühromantik*, 160.
97. *Schriften*, vi, 100.
98. Jules Huret, *Enquête sur l'évolution littéraire*, 88.
99. *Schriften*, vi, 37.
100. *Oeuvres complètes*, 270.
101. *La Littérature de tout à l'heure*, 357.
102. Henri Mondor, *Autres précisions sur Mallarmé*, 357.
103. August Wilhelm Schlegel, *Vorlesungen über schöne Kunst und Literatur*, 91.
104. *Die Zeichensprache der Romantik* (Heidelberg: Lothar Stiehm, 1967), 27.
105. *Schriften*, ii, 571.
106. *Kunstanschauung der Frühromantik*, 59.
107. *Schriften*, i, 80.
108. *Weltanschauung der Frühromantik*, 41.
109. Baudelaire, *Oeuvres complètes*, 637.
110. *Oeuvres complètes*, 1044.
111. *Oeuvres complètes*, 705; the italics are Baudelaire's.
112. *Oeuvres complètes*, 705.
113. Ferdinand Brunetière, *Revue des deux mondes*, no. 104 (1 April 1891), 681.
114. *Oeuvres complètes*, 869; the italics are Mallarmé's.
115. *La Littérature de tout à l'heure*, 378; the italics are Morice's.
116. *Schriften*, x, 443.
117. See my article, 'Novalis' *Hymnen an die Nacht* and Nerval's *Aurélia*', *Comparative Literature*, 21, no. 1 (winter 1969), 31–46.
118. *The Symbolist Movement*, 6.
119. See E. L. Stahl, 'The Genesis of Symbolist Theories in Germany', *Modern Language Review*, 41 (1946), 306–17.
120. Albert Mockel, *Propos de littérature* (Paris: Mercure de France, 1894), 26.
121. *Traité du verbe*, 33.
122. *L'Art symboliste*, 38.
123. *L'Âme romantique et le rêve*, 400.
124. *Kritische Schriften*, i, 99.
125. In ordinary usage, denotes a fairy-tale. To the Romantics a short tale often involving the supernatural and always exploring areas beyond the limits of reality.
126. *Schriften*, x, 1013.

127. *Schriften*, ix, 238.

128. *Aufsätze zur romanischen Syntax und Stylistik*, 321.

129. *Gesammelte Briefe*, ed. Elizabeth Förster-Nietzsche and Curt Wachsmuth (Berlin: Schuster & Loeffler, 1904), iii, 293.

130. A. G. Lehmann, *The Symbolist Aesthetic*, 46.

131. Originally published as 'Structure intentionelle de l'image romantique', *Revue internationale de philosophie*, 51 (1960); reprinted in slightly revised English version in *Romanticism and Consciousness*, ed. Harold Bloom (New York: Norton, 1970), 65–77, and in *Wordsworth: Twentieth Century Views*, ed. Meyer H. Abrams (Englewood Cliffs, N.J.: Prentice-Hall, 1972), 133–44.

132. *Oeuvres complètes*, 232–3.

133. *Oeuvres complètes*, 242; the italics are Rimbaud's.

134. *Novalis und die französischen Symbolisten*, 48–9.

135. See my article, 'The Structure of Romantic Agony', *Comparative Literature Studies*, 10, no. 2 (June 1973), 125–38.

136. *Mélanges posthumes* (Paris: Mercure de France, 1903), 142.

137. 'Le Symbolisme', in *Le Chemin de velours* (Paris: Mercure de France, 1911), 220–1.

138. Henri Lemaitre, *La Poésie depuis Baudelaire* (Paris: Armand Colin, 1965), 40.

139. *Mallarmé and the Symbolist Drama*, 34.

140. *Mallarmé and the Symbolist Drama*, 131.

141. *Mallarmé and the Symbolist Drama*, 132.

142. *Schriften*, x, 286; the italics are Novalis's.

143. *Promenades littéraires*, iv, 6–7.

144. *Oeuvres complètes*, 869.

145. Jules Lemaitre, 'Paul Verlaine et les poètes symbolistes et décadents', *Revue blanche* (7 January 1888).

146. Marianne Thalmann, *Zeichensprache der Romantik*, 24.

147. 'The Lyric', in *The Romantic Period in Germany*, 167.

148. *The Limits of Symbolism* (Chicago: Chicago Univ. Press, 1966), 422.

Selected bibliography

To list all the major criticism on German and French Romanticism, the Storm and Stress, and Symbolism is obviously beyond the scope and intention of this book. This bibliography is therefore limited to works specifically devoted to Franco-German literary relationships or otherwise particularly significant to the topics under discussion.

General works

Atkins, Stuart, 'Mirage français – French literature in German eyes', *Yale French Studies*, 6 (1950), 35–44.

Carré, Jean-Marie, *Les Écrivains français et le mirage allemand* (Paris: Boivin, 1947).

Deutschland-Frankreich. Ludwigsburger Beiträge zum Problem der deutsch-französischen Beziehungen (Stuttgart: Deutsche Verlags-anstalt, 1954–66). 4 vols.

Dupouy, Auguste, *Les Littératures comparées de France et d'Allemagne* (Paris: Delaplane, 1913).

Fromm, Hans (ed.), *Bibliographie deutscher Übersetzungen aus dem Französischem 1700–1948* (Baden-Baden: Verlag für Kunst und Wissenschaft, 1950–3). 6 vols.

Krauss, Werner, *Perspektiven und Probleme – Zur französischen und deutschen Aufklärung und andere Aufsätze* (Berlin: Luchterhand, 1965).

Lévy, Paul, *La Langue allemande en France* (Lyons and Paris: IAC, 1950 and 1952). 2 vols.

Meissner, Fritz, *Geschichte des deutschen Kultureinflusses auf Frankreich bis 1870* (Leipzig: Renger, 1893).

Minder, Robert, *Kultur und Literatur in Deutschland und Frankreich* (Frankfurt: Insel, 1952).

Neubert, Fritz, *Studien zur vergleichenden Literaturgeschichte, im besonderen zum Verhältnis Deutschland-Frankreich* (Berlin: Duncker & Humblot, 1952).

Oppenheim, F. Horst, 'Der Einfluss der französischen Literatur auf die deutsche', in *Deutsche Philologie im Aufriss*, ed. Stammler, Wolfgang (Berlin: Schmidt, 1957), vol. III, 863–959.

Peyre, Henri, 'Franco–German Literary Relations: A Survey of Problems', *Comparative Literature*, 2 (Winter 1950), 1–15.

Reynaud, Louis, *L'Influence allemande en France au XVIIIe et au XIXe siècle* (Paris: Hachette, 1922).

Reynaud, Louis, *Histoire générale de l'influence française en Allemagne*, 3rd rev. ed. (Paris: Hachette, 1924).

Rossel, Virgile, *Histoire des relations littéraires entre la France et l'Allemagne* (Paris: Fischbacher, 1897).

Sieburg, Heinz-Otto, *Deutschland und Frankreich in der Geschichtsschreibung des 19. Jahrhunderts* (Wiesbaden: Steiner, 1954 and 1958). 2 vols.

Süpfle, Theodor, *Geschichte des deutschen Kultureinflusses auf Frankreich, mit besonderer Berücksichtigung der literarischen Einwirkung* (Gotha: Thienemann, 1886–90). 3 vols.

Van Abbé, Derek, 'Some Notes on Cultural Relations between France and Germany in the Nineteenth Century', *Modern Language Quarterly*, 8 (1947), 217–27.

Wais, Kurt, *An den Grenzen der Nationalliteraturen* (Berlin: de Gruyter, 1958).

Wellek, René, *A History of Modern Criticism* (New Haven, Conn.: Yale Univ. Press, 1955–65). 4 vols.

II *The emergence of the Romantic movements*

Bruford, Walter H., *Germany in the Eighteenth Century* (Cambridge: Cambridge Univ. Press, 1935; pb 1968).

Furst, Lilian R., 'Lessing and Mme de Staël *vis-à-vis* the Literature of the Mediterranean', *Journal of European Studies*, 1, no. 2 (1971), 161–5.

Hampson, Norman, *The First European Revolution, 1776–1815* (London: Thames & Hudson, 1969).

Healey, Frederick G., *The Literary Culture of Napoleon* (Geneva: Droz, and Paris: Minard, 1959).

Moreau, Pierre, *Le Classicisme des romantiques* (Paris: Plon, 1932).

Neubert, Fritz, *Die französische Klassik und Europa* (Stuttgart: Kohlhammer, 1941).

Simon, M. W., 'The Historical and Social Background', in *The Romantic Period in Germany*, ed. Prawer, Siegbert S. (London: Weidenfeld & Nicolson, and New York: Schocken, 1970), 17–33.

Talmon, Jacob L., *Romanticism and Revolt* (London: Thames & Hudson, and New York: Harcourt, Brace & World, 1967).

Van Tieghem, Paul, *Le Préromantisme. Études d'histoire littéraire européenne* (Paris: Rieder, 1924).

III *The Storm and Stress and French Romanticism*

Babbitt, Irving, *Rousseau and Romanticism* (Boston: Houghton Mifflin, 1919).

Bainville, Jacques, 'Rousseau et le romantisme français', *Mercure de France*, 66 (1907), 661–76.

Baldensperger, Fernand, *Goethe en France* (Paris: Hachette, 1904).

Baldensperger, Fernand, 'La *Lénore* de Bürger dans la littérature française', *Études d'histoire littéraire*, 1e série (Paris: Hachette, 1907), 147–75.

Baldensperger, Fernand, 'Esquisse d'une histoire de Shakespeare en France', *Études d'histoire littéraire*, 2e série (Paris: Hachette, 1910), 155–216.

Baldensperger, Fernand, 'Rousseau et le romantisme', *Athena*, 3 (1912), 317–35.

Benrubi, J., 'Schiller und Rousseau', *Deutsche Rundschau*, 157 (November 1913), 269–88.

Borgerhoff, J.-L., *Le Théâtre anglais à Paris sous la Restauration* (Paris: Hachette, 1913).

Bray, René, *Chronologie du romantisme* (Paris: Boivin, 1932).

Buck, Rudolf, *Rousseau und die deutsche Romantik* (Berlin: Junker & Dünnhaupt, 1939).

Cassirer, E., *Rousseau, Kant, Goethe* (Hamden, Conn.: Archon Books, 1961).

Dédéyan, Charles, *Rousseau et la sensibilité littéraire à la fin du XVIIIe siècle* (Paris: Centre de documentation universitaire, 1961).

Dédéyan, Charles, *Victor Hugo et l'Allemagne* (Paris: Minard, 1964).

Eggli, Edmond, *Schiller et le romantisme français* (Paris: Gamber, 1927).

Fouret, L. A., 'Romantisme français et romantisme allemand', *Mercure de France*, 194 (March 1927), 257–79.

Fuchs, Albert (ed.), *Goethe et l'esprit français* (Paris: Les Belles Lettres, 1958).

Furst, Lilian R., 'Benjamin Constant's *Wallstein*', *Romanistisches Jahrbuch*, 15 (1964), 141–59.

Furst, Lilian R., *Romanticism in Perspective*. A comparative study of aspects of the Romantic movements in England, France and Germany (London: Macmillan, 1969, and New York: Humanities Press, 1970).

Furst, Lilian R., 'Mme de Staël's *De L'Allemagne*: A Misleading Intermediary', *Orbis Litterarum*, 31 (1976), 43–58.

Gilman, Margaret, *Othello in French* (Paris: Champion, 1925).

Grivelet, M., 'La critique dramatique française devant Shakespeare', *Études anglaises*, 13, no. 2 (April–June 1960), 258–73.

Höffding, H., 'Rousseau et le XIXe siècle', *Annales Jean-Jacques Rousseau*, 8 (1912), 69–98.

Huesmann, H., *Shakespeare-Inszenierungen unter Goethe in Weimar* (Wien: Böhlaus, 1968).

Joachim-Dege, Maria, *Deutsche Shakespeare-Probleme* (Leipzig: Haessel, 1970).

Jusserand, J.-J., *Shakespeare in France* (London: Unwin, 1899).

Liepe, Wolfgang, 'Der junge Schiller und Rousseau', *Zeitschrift für deutsche Philologie*, 51 (1926), 299–328.

Monaco, Marion, *Shakespeare on the French Stage in the Eighteenth Century* (Paris: Didier, 1974).

Monchoux, André, *L'Allemagne devant les lettres françaises, 1814–1835* (Paris: Colin, 1953).

Nemer, Monique, 'Traduire Shakespeare', *Romantisme, 1–2* (1971), 94–101.

Pascal, Roy, *Shakespeare in Germany, 1740–1815* (Cambridge: Cambridge Univ. Press, 1937).

Pascal, Roy, *The German Sturm und Drang* (Manchester: Manchester Univ. Press, 1953).

Schmidt, Erich, *Richardson, Rousseau und Goethe* (Jena: Cotta, 1875).

Smith, Horace, 'Goethe and Rousseau', *Publications of the English Goethe Society*, 2–4 (1926), 30–55.

Tronchon, Henri, *La Fortune intellectuelle de Herder en France* (Paris: Rieder, 1920).

Trousson, Raymond, *Rousseau et sa fortune littéraire*. Collection 'Tels qu'en eux-mêmes' (Saint-Médard-en-Jalles: Ducros, 1971).

Voisine, Jacques, 'L'Influence de *La Nouvelle Héloïse* sur la génération de Werther', *Études germaniques*, 5 (1950), 120–33.

Wolff, Heinrich M., 'Der junge Herder und die Entwicklungsidee Rousseaus', *Publications of the Modern Language Association of America*, 57 (1942), 753–819.

Wyneken, F. A., 'Rousseaus Einfluss auf Klinger', *University of California Publications in Modern Philology*, 3, no. 1 (1912), 1–85.

IV *German Romanticism and French Symbolism*

Balakian, Anna, *The Symbolist Movement* (New York: Random House, 1967).

Beaufils, Marcel, *Wagner et le wagnérisme* (Paris: Aubier, 1947).

Béguin, Albert, *L'Âme romantique et le rêve* (Paris: Corti, 1939).

Block, Haskell M., *Mallarmé and the Symbolist Drama* (Detroit: Wayne State Univ. Press, 1963).

Boeck, Oliver, *Heines Nachwirkung und Heine-Parallelen in der französischen Dichtung* (Göppingen: Alfred Kümmerle, 1972).

Braak, S., 'Novalis et le symbolisme français', *Neophilologus*, 7 (1922), 243–58.

Cheval, R. J., 'Die deutsche Romantik in Frankreich', in *Romantik* (Tübingen and Stuttgart: Rainer Wunderlich, 1948), 253–70.

Coeuroy, André, *Wagner et l'esprit romantique* (Paris: Gallimard, 1965).

Dieckmann, Lieselotte, 'The Metaphor of Hieroglyphics in German Romanticism', *Comparative Literature*, 7, no. 4 (Fall 1955), 306–12.

Digeon, Claude, *La Crise allemande de la pensée française 1870–1914* (Paris: Presses universitaires de France, 1959).

Dubruck, Alfred, *Gérard de Nerval and the German Heritage* (The Hague: Mouton & Co., 1965).

Duthie, Enid L., *L'Influence du symbolisme français dans le renouveau poétique de l'Allemagne, 1892–1900* (Paris: Champion, 1933).

Furst, Lilian R., 'Novalis' *Hymnen an die Nacht* and Nerval's *Aurélia*', *Comparative Literature*, 21, no. 1 (Winter 1969), 31–46.

Furst, Lilian R., 'The Structure of Romantic Agony', *Comparative Literature Studies*, 10, no. 2 (June 1973), 125–38.

Guichard, Léon, *La Musique et les lettres en France au temps du wagnérisme* (Paris: Presses universitaires de France, 1963).

Jäckel, Kurt, *Richard Wagner in der französischen Literatur*. (Breslau: Priebatsch, 1931 and 1932). 2 vols.

Juden, Brian, *Traditions orphiques et tendances mystiques dans le romantisme français 1800-1850* (Paris: Klincksieck, 1971).

Koppen, Erwin, *Dekadenter Wagnerismus*. Studien zur europäischen Literatur des Fin de siècle (Berlin: de Gruyter, 1973).

Lehmann, Andrew George, *The Symbolist Aesthetic in France, 1885-1895* (Oxford: Blackwell, 1950).

Loos, Paul Arthur, *Richard Wagner – Vollendung und Tragik der deutschen Romantik* (Bern: Francke, 1952).

Man, Paul de, 'Structure intentionelle de l'Image romantique', *Revue internationale de philosophie*, 51 (1960), 68–84. Reprinted in *Romanticism and Consciousness*, ed. Bloom, Harold (New York: Norton, 1970), 65–77, and in *Wordsworth: Twentieth Century Views*, ed. Abrams, Meyer H. (Englewood Cliffs, N.J.: Prentice-Hall, 1972), 133–44.

Seillière, E., 'Le Mysticisme esthétique dans la cinquième génération romantique en Allemagne et en France', *Revue germanique*, 27 (1936), 259–67.

Sørensen, Bengt Algot, *Symbol und Symbolismus in den ästhetischen Theorien des 18. Jahrhunderts und der deutschen Romantik* (Frankfurt: Athenäum, 1972).

Spitzer, Leo, 'Die syntaktischen Errungenschaften der französischen Symbolisten', *Aufsätze zur romanischen Syntax und Stylistik* (Halle: Niemeyer, 1918), 281–339.

Stahl, Ernst L., 'The Genesis of Symbolist Theories in Germany', *Modern Language Review*, 41 (1946), 306–17.

Starr, Doris, *Über den Begriff des Symbols in der deutschen Klassik und Romantik, unter besonderer Berücksichtigung von F. Schlegel* (Reutlingen: Eugen Hutzler, 1964).

Symons, Arthur, *The Symbolist Movement in Literature* (London: Heinemann, 1899, and New York: Dutton, 1958).

Teichmann, Elizabeth, *La Fortune de E. T. A. Hoffmann en France* (Geneva: Droz, 1961).

Thalmann, Marianne, *Zeichensprache der Romantik* (Heidelberg: Lothar Stiehm, 1967).

Thalmann, Marianne, *Romantiker als Poetologen* (Heidelberg: Lothar Stiehm, 1970).

Thorel, Jean, 'Les Romantiques allemands et les symbolistes français', *Entretiens politiques et littéraires* (September 1891), 95–109.

Visan, Tancrède de, 'Le Romantisme allemand et le symbolisme français', *Mercure de France*, 88 (16 December 1910), 577–91.

Vordtriede, Werner, *Novalis und die französischen Symbolisten* (Stuttgart: Kohlhammer, 1963).

Wagner et la France. Special issue of *Revue musicale* (1 October 1923).

Weinberg, Bernard, *The Limits of Symbolism* (Chicago: Chicago Univ. Press, 1966).

Wellek, René, 'The Term and Concept of Symbolism in Literary History', *Discriminations* (New Haven, Conn.: Yale Univ. Press, 1970), 90–121.

Wilson, Edmund, *Axel's Castle. A Study in the Imaginative Literature 1870–1930* (New York: Scribner's, 1931).

Woolley, Grange, *Richard Wagner et le symbolisme français* (Paris: Presses universitaires de France, 1931).

Wyzewska, Isabelle, *La Revue Wagnérienne. Essai sur l'interprétation esthétique de Wagner en France* (Paris: Perrin, 1934).

Index